CHILDHOOD SHADOWS
The Hidden Story of the Black Dahlia Murder

CHILDHOOD SHADOWS
The Hidden Story of the Black Dahlia Murder

by

Mary Pacios

Copyright © 1999 by Mary Pacios

All rights reserved. No part of this book may be reproduced, stored in a retrieval system, or transmitted by any means, electronic, mechanical, photocopying, recording, or otherwise, without written permission from the author.

ISBN 1-58500-484-7

About the Book

ELECTRONIC DISTRIBUTION DATE: October 1999
PRINTED AND BOUND DISTRIBUTION DATE: November 1999

This is a unique and compelling account of the Black Dahlia murder—one of Hollywood's most infamous unsolved crimes. CHILDHOOD SHADOWS combines personal experience as a close friend of Elizabeth Short with in-depth research, bringing a unique perspective and opening up an intriguing new area of speculation about who the killer might be.

Author Pacios sets the stage by recreating the neighborhood she shared with Elizabeth "Bette" Short during the years of the Great Depression and World War II. The war ends, but instead of peace, the horrendous murder of the young and beautiful Elizabeth Short, sends shock waves through the nation. Years later, haunted by the unsolved murder of her childhood friend, Pacios sets out to discover the true circumstances surrounding her friend's brutal death. Because of her personal relationship with the victim, Pacios gains access to officials close to the investigation who discuss with her unpublicized details of the case and their own privately held theories about who murdered the Black Dahlia. A network of people send Pacios information and give her referrals. The research that Pacios expects to last only a few months turns into a strange ten-year odyssey, leading her to a well-known celebrity whose name as a suspect is likely to startle millions.

Appendices of public documents and an extensive annotated bibliography are included. Photographs.

For Bette

Elizabeth "Bette" Short
Born July 29, 1924 — Murdered January 15, 1947

Table of Contents

ACKNOWLEDGMENTS		xi
PREFACE		xiii
ONE:	Pennies From Heaven	1
TWO:	I'll Be Seeing You...	17
THREE:	The Unthinkable	29
FOUR:	Revisiting the Past	47
FIVE:	Cops and Reporters	67
SIX:	The Prime Suspects	89
SEVEN:	The Hollywood Connection	111
EIGHT:	The Saint and the Magician	125
NINE:	The Plot Thickens	147
TEN:	The Signature	173
AFTERWORD		199
APPENDICES		
Appendix A:	The Movie Set	201
Appendix B:	Photo Album	209
Appendix C:	The Inquest Report	233
Appendix D:	Profiles of The Major Suspects	245
Appendix E:	Annotated Bibliography	255

Acknowledgments

I wish to give special thanks to Janet Fitch, Lowell Fitch, Mike Hamilburg, Jeanne Jabbour, Ron Kenner, and John D. Nesbitt for their invaluable help in bringing this project to completion.

I wish also to thank the following people who have provided information and encouragement: Faye Adams, Rick Adams, Kenneth Alves, Mary T. Anderson, Ronna Anderson, John Babcock, Mary Bairey, Catherine Barrett, Lanny Baugniet, Jean Bekey, Yvonne Benedict, Joe Bento, Betty Bento, Juli Betwee, Dot Brady, Mike Bradford (Medford Historical Society), Charlotte B. Brown (UCLA Special Collections), Gary Bryson, Margaret Burk, Paul Burke, Dan Carbone, Gabriel Carey, Chuck Cheatham, Roxanne Ciparrone, Nate Cohen, Carolyn Cole (Los Angeles Public Library), Bruce Conner, Bob Danbacker (Los Angeles Coroner's Office), Mitch Douglas, Anna Dougherty, Michael Doyle, Andy Edmonds, Elvira (Los Angeles Coroner's Office), Matthew Evans, Lenore Feyleaves, Dr. Finkbeiner (Chief, Autopsy Services, UCSF Medical Center), Amanda Fitch, Ethan Fitch, Kate Fitch, Caeser Fittante (Medford Historical Society), Will Fowler, Rob Freeman, Det. Lt. Paul Freestone (LAPD), Sue Furderer, Det. Sgt. Dan Galindo (LAPD), Dr. Michael Gay, Ed Gelb, Sam Gill, John Gilmore, Goshen County Task Force on Family Violence and Sexual Assault, Thorne Gray, Carden Gray, Dan Graves, Rasa Gustaitis, Marge Hackett, Scott Harney, Larry Harnisch, Bruce Henstell, Dorothy Hernon, Ron Hernon, James Hewes, Charles Higham, Nieson Himmel, Jim Holmes, Natalie Holtzman, Roy Huggins, Clifford C. Humphrey, June Hunnefeld, Norm "Jake" Jacoby, Aram Jaranian, Ardys Jefferson, "Just Plain Bill" (Inspector, LASD), Det. Sgt. John St. John (LAPD), Emma Johnson, Mary Ann Kenner, Dr. Robert D. Keppel (chief criminal investigator for the Washington State Attorney General's Office), Candace Killian, George Kuchar, Mike Kuchar, Eleanor Kurz, Walter Lab, Martha Landy, Bob Laney, Shirley Launder, Julie Lee, Roselynn Lee (Los Angeles Public Library), Alice Logan, Dick

Lupoff, Katherine Mader (Deputy District Attorney, Los Angeles), Dennis Madruga, Chris Marano, Sally Marano, Robert G. Marshall (Urban Archives), Irene Masteller, Joseph McGonagle (City Clerk of Medford, MA.), Tom McDonald, Betty Medsger, Dina Mendros, Pia Mogollón, Larry Moncrief, Dr. John Money (Johns Hopkins University), Ray Morgan, Tony Mostrom, James Naremore, Steven Nickel, Ann Nakamura, Norine Nishimura, Octavio Olvera (UCLA Special Collections), Evelyn Otash, Fred Otash, Elmer "Skip" Pacios, Lucille Pacios, Robert K. Pacios, Richard Pacios, Sally Pacios, Stephen H. Pacios, Richard Pleuger, Frank Prescott, Margie Prescott, Gerry Ramlow, Karol Ramlow, Helen Reed, Ken Renfro, Eda Regan, Dr. Tom Reilly (Urban Archives), Mark Richardson, Joel Rodgers, Frank Roesch, Lionel Rolfe, Sonia Rummel, Shirley Saito, Joel Sarnoff, Ken Scarce (LAPD), Susan Schereschewsky, Neil Seldman, Dave Schleve (Criminal Justice Instuctor, Eastern Wyoming College), Mark Shostrum, Jan Siegel, Julia Simic, Jack Smith, David Smith-Gold, Joan Socola, Ralph J. Southworth, Eunice Staeffler, Michael Stoffen, Dace Taube (USC Special Collections), Brenda Taylor, Marilyn Taylor, William Taylor, Lorrie Tixner, Rilla Underwood, Tony Valdez, Dr. Joseph Valerini, (Medford Historical Society), Adel Von, Helena Walsh, Coy Watson, Delbert Watson, Sandra Watt, Richard Wolinsky, Kyle J. Wood, May Wuthrich, Michele Zipsy, Brad Zutaut, and all those who wish to remain anonymous.

Preface

Elizabeth Short—the mysterious "Black Dahlia"—Hollywood's most notorious victim. Crime anthologists have cited her as the classic example of a woman who "enticed" her assailant, a woman "who wanted to be killed," one whose lifestyle "made her ideal victim material." Fiction writers have classified her as a "whore."

But I knew the aspiring actress differently, simply as Bette, my next-door neighbor and friend—a warm, stunning young woman with a flawless complexion, the blackest of hair, and translucent blue-green eyes. I was only twelve years old when Bette was brutally murdered in January of 1947—one of the most infamous "unsolved" crimes of the twentieth century.

A few days after her murder, I began drawing pictures of Bette—first as Snow White, smiling, with a bird perched on each shoulder, then standing on a hill near a tree, much like the big elms that once stood in the Commons of our New England home town.

As I developed into a professional artist, Bette became my main subject—couched in mythological terms—Antigone, Eurydice, Medea. Finally in 1987, forty years after Bette's death, as one final gesture of catharsis I organized a touring exhibition called *In Memoriam*—work by artists based on the death of someone close. A triptych, *The Martyrdom of Elizabeth Short*, became my contribution to the art exhibit. But that was not enough.

For years, terrified of the darkness, I had walked around the edge of the long and painful shadow cast by my friend's murder. But there came a time when I seemed to have no choice, no recourse, except to go into the deepest and darkest part of that shadow and try to cast whatever light was humanly possible. In December of 1987, after waffling for months, I embarked on my ten-year search for answers.

—Mary Pacios

ONE
Pennies From Heaven

My mother said it was in 1939 that Bette Short befriended me and started taking me for walks and to the movies. She also said it was Bette's Mom, Mrs. Short, who saw the high school boy, Jackie, taking me into the field, and that it was Mrs. Short who yelled for my sister Margie to go and get me.

I had been at the bottom of the Court, close to Salem Street, drawing in the dirt with a stick. The dirt was softer there and didn't have a lot of stones like the dirt near our gray duplex.

Jackie, who lived across the street, asked me if I wanted to earn a nickel. He was holding a green tonic bottle. "I'll cash in this bottle and give you a nickel if you do something for me. Or I'll buy you an ice cream cone," he said.

I wanted the nickel. I was five years old, and I earned money running errands for my mother and my Aunt Dot—usually a penny, sometimes a two-cent bottle, but never a whole nickel.

Jackie took my hand. We crossed the street and walked towards the A & P Market at Washington Square. Jackie was tall and skinny with reddish blonde hair and freckles over his face and arms. He wore round thick glasses with metal rims.

The grocery store was dark and cool, almost deserted. I could hear the faint buzzing of flies trapped on the fly coils that hung from the ceiling and the whirring sound of the overhead fans. The clerk struck the cash register key, and with a ping the drawer opened. Jackie took the nickel from the clerk and put it in his pocket.

Outside, the bright sun hurt my eyes and stung my face. I kept skipping to the shady spots. Jackie took my hand again. We started back towards Medford Square, walking past his house, walking past the fried chicken place, and then stopping at the vacant field next door. "Here, cut across here," Jackie said.

The tall grass and weeds were light brown, almost whitish. They itched my bare legs. In the middle of the field Jackie stopped. He turned and faced me, holding his hand out, palm up, displaying the nickel. I looked at the nickel, new and shiny, and then up at Jackie.

"You can have this nickel if you pull down your panties," he said.

Then everything went black until the shouting—my sister Margie's voice. "What have you done? Mama's gonna kill you!" I was lying on the ground. Then I saw her head and shoulders through the tall grasses off to my left. I heard scuffling and rustling in front of me. I turned my head and saw Jackie running off, the soles of his sneakers looking like the large snowshoes I'd seen in books. I was on the ground, but I didn't know how I got there. I could only remember Jackie looming above me, and then a blackness. And now Margie, my eleven-year old sister, was yanking me up.

She pulled me along—out of the field, across the street, up the Court, and into the house to the little bedroom off the kitchen. It hurt me to walk, little jabs of pain between my legs, but I didn't cry. I wanted to. I felt afraid and hurt, but I couldn't cry. I crawled onto my bed and lay there, looking at the cracked and water-stained ceiling, searching for faces and the outlines of people. I waited for my parents to come home. I knew Margie would tell on me, tell what I had done; and I knew it was something awfully bad. And I didn't know what they would do to me.

I heard the screen door open and close—Margie's voice and my father's. I pretended to be asleep, thinking and wondering if God would forgive me for what I had done. I *knew* the pain I felt was my punishment.

My mother came home from work early. I heard more voices—Uncle Hector, Aunt Dot, and my big brother Bob. "I'll kill the sonofabitch!" Uncle Hector yelled.

I was lying in the now darkened room, wondering, "What sonofabitch?" I vowed that next year, when I received my First Holy Communion, I would confess my terrible sin.

"Mary, come here!"

I walked slowly from the bedroom into the kitchen. The big light in the ceiling wasn't on, only the small lamp on the kitchen table, faintly illuminating the figures sitting in chairs and standing around the room. My mother knelt in front of me, grabbing both my arms, holding them tightly. I saw the lines and tightness around her mouth and the redness in her eyes as if she had been crying. I looked down at the tiny pink flowers on her apron. Everyone started asking me questions, but I couldn't talk. I just kept nodding yes. I couldn't hear the words, just a droning, a rising and falling of sounds, and I kept nodding yes.

The boy's parents came over later that night with the priest. I could hear them from the bedroom. The voices were loud. I heard my mother's voice. "She don't need no doll!" Then I heard the priest. "We don't want to jeopardize the boy's future." And then I heard lower voices, mention of money and of doctor bills.

My mother scrubbed me extra clean the next day, rubbing hard against my legs, putting on the new underwear "to see the doctor." I waited outside while my parents stayed in the kitchen talking. Through the screen door I could see my father pacing back and forth. I looked down the Court and saw Jackie standing on his porch with his father and step-mother. A dark blue car pulled up. Jackie, carrying two large suitcases, ran down the stairs. He put the suitcases in the trunk and hurried into the back seat of the car. His parents stayed on the porch, waving goodbye as the car drove away.

I didn't feel scared in Dr. Goldman's clean-white office. I sat quietly on the stool in my new underwear while my parents talked with the doctor. My father was upset that I no longer was a virgin and wanted the doctor to issue a certificate of rape. Dr. Goldman said that was the least of the concerns.

I watched as the nurse put a sheet on a funny-looking metal table with brown leather cushions. Dr. Goldman spoke softly as he lifted me onto the table, reassuring me, asking where it hurt. I pointed between my legs. I winced when he touched me. He told my parents that I had an infection.

"And I should watch that," he said. "She needs to be seen weekly for a few months. But we're lucky. She should be okay."

A few days later, Bette Short, one of the big girls in the neighborhood, knocked on our back door. Bette went to high school with my brother Bob. All the neighbors liked Bette and thought she was someone special, someone who was "going places." They called Bette a "black Irish beauty" and remarked that Bette was "lace curtain, not shanty Irish." The neighbors would talk about how friendly she was, "only fifteen years old, and so poised, not a bit stuck-up."

Through the screen door I could see Bette's silhouette. I tried to hear what Bette and my mom were saying, but they were whispering. Then I heard Bette talking louder, and the words, *Gulliver's Travels*. I bolted past my mother, pushing the screen door open with both arms, almost bumping into Bette.

"Your mother says it's okay if I take you to the movies," Bette said, "to the Square Theatre." I remember looking up at Bette's face and thinking how beautiful she was—like Snow White.

In the darkened theater, small crescent lamps on the aisle seats cast an orange glow low to the floor. The usher led us down the center aisle, aiming his flashlight at the dark, floral-patterned rug. He halted and with a flourish brought the flashlight high, focusing the beam on two maroon velvet seats. Bette and I made our way through a row of people and eased into the seats, trying to keep them from squeaking. We would have been seated before the movie started, but when Bette bought the popcorn, the boy behind the candy counter spent too much time talking to her.

After the movie, Bette took my hand and we headed towards Liggett's soda fountain near the High School. I told Bette everyone was mad at me because I'd done something very bad.

"I don't think anyone's mad at you," she said and put her arm around my shoulder. "Your mother's worried about what happened to you. Don't ever think you're bad, Mary. Why, you know, if I ever have a little girl, I'd want her to be just like you!"

Going to the movies with Bette became a ritual. We saw *Mr. Hoppity Goes to Town* and all the Ginger Rogers and Fred Astaire movies. We saw *Gone with the Wind* twice. I'd sit quietly during the parts that I didn't understand, happy to be with Bette. When I broke my arm, Bette bought me a Scarlet O'Hara paper-doll book and helped me cut out the doll clothes.

In those children-should-be-seen-and-not-heard days, Bette always seemed interested in what a little kid had to say. She often included my cousin Ron in conversations. Bette would lean over the railing of her back porch while my Aunt Dot hung out the wash in the yard below. Bette and Aunt Dot would be yakking away, but Bette didn't ignore Ron, who played nearby. She'd ask him how he was and draw him into the conversation.

Bette made my Aunt Dot feel welcome in the neighborhood. Someone had called my aunt "shanty Irish" when she and my Uncle Hector moved into the salt box house to the rear of the Shorts'. Mrs. Sheehan used to live there before my aunt and uncle. She kept the grass so high that the younger neighborhood kids could sneak into the big yard and steal the apples and the rhubarb. When Mrs. Sheehan spotted the grass moving, she'd come running towards us, hunched over, dressed all in black, shaking her cane. "The witch! The witch! Run! Run!" we'd yell. "The old witch is coming!"

Bette told me that Mrs. Sheehan wasn't a witch, just a lonely old woman whose husband had died. "You shouldn't be mean to her," Bette said. "Mrs. Sheehan doesn't have any children, and she is very lonely. You should be nice to her, even if she looks strange or different."

Everyone—except Bette and my cousin Ron—seemed to shoo me away and call me "Pest." When I trudged over to Bette's building and rang her doorbell, her voice would crackle over the metal speaker telling me I could come up "for a little while"—even though the teen-aged Bette and her sisters weren't supposed to have visitors if their mother wasn't home.

Bette would lead me into the dining room, and we'd sit at the round oak table. She'd lay out a piece of paper for both of us. I'd draw with pencils, and Bette would write letters or do her high school homework. She'd carefully dip the pen into the Carter's ink bottle and wipe the point on the rim before forming words on the paper. Sometimes she'd let me use the pen, but I'd make a scratchy sound. She'd say, "No, like this," not harshly, but with a soft voice, showing me how to use a lighter touch.

On my first day of school, when the teacher asked if anyone could write, I proudly raised my hand and marched to the blackboard. In perfect script I wrote "Bette."

"Who is Bette?" the teacher asked.

"Bette's my neighbor, and she's my *friend*," I said.

In 1934, a few months before I was born, my family had moved to Fifield Court, a gray, run-down cul-de-sac of poverty starting at Salem Street and backing into the wrought-iron fence of the old graveyard. At one time my family had lived on Willis Avenue in a large house with fireplaces in all the rooms and brass knockers on the bedroom doors. That was when my father was prosperous and managed a chain of stores. But during the Great Depression he mostly sat around the house playing cards while my mother worked in a laundry, operating a mangle.

On Wednesday nights while my mother and my Aunt Dot were at the movies—induced by the free "Depression" glassware that went along with the ten-cent ticket price—my father would take me to the Veterans of Foreign Wars headquarters near Washington Square. He was proud to be a member of Post 1012. "You had to have fought on *foreign* soil," he'd say. "Can't be a member of the VFW if you didn't go overseas."

My father's cronies in the VFW sponsored Medford's local fife and drum corps. Mr. Fisher, the high school music teacher, taught the kids how to play the instruments. My brother Bob and sister Margie played fifes; my brother Richard, the bass drum. I was the gimmick—the mascot, a three-year-old drum majorette strutting out front, attracting the attention of the crowd.

The band's uniforms were simple—white ducks and white shirts with dark blue berets and neckties. Our mothers made the majorette costumes of white satin with gold braid and fancy epaulettes. And from a distance the homemade white oilcloth spats that covered our shoes almost looked like real boots.

My father was the drill master. In the good weather we'd practice a couple of nights a week in the Commons. Bette and her younger sister Muriel often joined the group of people watching as my father put the band through its paces. Sometimes Bette and her sister would stay after practice and have refreshments with the band. One of the band members, Kenny Schmidt, had a crush on Bette. Kenny's face would turn beet-red, and he'd stammer while the other band members ribbed him: "Hey Kenny, say hello to Bette! "Kenny, when you gonna take Bette to the movies?"

Bette and Muriel never missed a parade. Bette, especially, liked to tease me—laughing, calling my name, trying to make me look at her. But I'd keep marching straight ahead, sometimes peeking at her out of the corner of my eyes, catching a glimpse of her blue gingham dress, her favorite one with a crocheted collar.

Despite President Roosevelt's programs and the Democrats' promise of getting things going again, the Great Depression kept grinding on—ten long, poverty-filled years. The neighborhood children became familiar with talk of Mother's Aid, Soldier's Relief, and eviction—a life of hand-me-down clothes and carefully measured spoonfuls of food. When the dreaded landlord came to collect the rent, it would be the youngest child sent to the door to fib and say, "My parents aren't home."

My family, like many other proud Yankees, had learned to accept the government handouts—but didn't like it. Once or twice a week, early in the morning, I'd go with my sister Margie to the firehouse and wait in line for milk. We'd joke with her school chums, counting and making number games as the line grew longer and double backed. If we saw Bette and Muriel, we'd walk back home with them.

There were times when my mother would leave and be gone for a few months. Then she'd be back for a while. My parents were always bickering, unless there was company. Then they'd be very quiet and polite to each other. Most of their arguments were about money. I'd go outside, even in the bad weather, to escape the noise. Sometimes Bette would see me playing by myself, and she'd ask if I wanted to go for an ice cream cone, or she'd invite me into her apartment for a cup of hot cocoa.

All the neighborhood families had their stories of better times. Bette's family once lived in a large home on Magoun Avenue with beautiful parquet floors. But each time a landlord raised the rent, they had to move—finally landing in the railroad flat on the third floor at 115 Salem Street.

Bette was not with her family when they moved to Salem Street in 1937. She was sick with pleurisy and had to have a lung operation. One rib was removed, leaving an I-shaped scar that would show if she wore a two-piece bathing suit. Bette missed a lot of school and spent a few months in Maine with her grandmother.

The neighbors tried to make the best of life. Sometimes Mrs. Short was on Mother's Aid, but mostly she worked—first at the Mystic Bakery in Medford Square and later as a bookkeeper for Liberty Mutual in Boston.

On the way home from work, she'd buy groceries in the square. I'd see her every night at the same time, around six-thirty, carrying the shopping bags home.

On Sundays, when I walked up High Street to St. Joseph's Church, I'd see Mrs. Short with her five girls, heading towards the First Baptist Church on Oakland Street.

The neighbors thought Mrs. Short was a little stand-offish. They were curious about why Mrs. Short had no husband. The neighbors filled their gap with various stories about Mr. Short—why he wasn't there. "He went to the store for a loaf of bread and never came back." "He disappeared at a parade." "He was last seen at St. Joseph's Carnival." "He's dead."

Bette was six years old when her father disappeared in 1930 and left her mother, Phoebe, to deal with the problems: bankruptcy and the courts, keeping a roof over her family's head and food on the table. Cleo Short had tried to weather the stock market crash of 1929, but when he could no longer meet the payrolls, he up and left. His abandoned car was found on the Charlestown Bridge. Police assumed he had jumped into the water and drowned. A couple of years later, Cleo wrote to Phoebe. He was headed for California, he said, and would send for her and the children as soon as he raised enough money.

Phoebe Short hated Mother's Aid—nothing but relief. She was a true Yankee, born and raised in Maine. She'd never taken a dime in her life—always earned her own way. Mrs. Short sometimes lamented that maybe if she hadn't wanted to live near her Aunt Jo in Medford, things would have worked out differently. Cleo Short had a thriving car repair business in

Wolfboro, New Hampshire. He didn't want to move to Massachusetts, but Phoebe prevailed. Medford was a good place to raise children, insisted Phoebe. The city was peaceful, with libraries, churches, good schools, and the world-renowned Tufts University.

Bette's father started a new business, building miniature golf courses. While Cleo worked to get the business under way, the family scrimped and lived in the Hyde Park section of Boston. Bette was born there on July 29, 1924—her given name Elizabeth Short. By the time the family moved to Medford, Cleo's business had prospered. The miniature course he built at Howard Johnson Circle was considered one of the best around, a real money-maker, bringing in other jobs. Bette's mother was the bookkeeper and ran the office. They could afford new oak furniture, a new dark-blue Ford, and singing and violin lessons for their eldest daughter, Ginnie.

Medford was up and coming then, with almost 60,000 people, mostly working class. There weren't many cars, but it took only a thirty-minute trolley car or bus ride to go shopping in Boston, or go to work five miles away in nearby Charlestown and Chelsea. Medford kept smoke-belching factories out, allowing only two paper factories, neither of which had smoke stacks.

Neighborhoods were predominantly Irish and Catholic, with Italian neighborhoods in South Medford and Fulton Heights. A few Negro families were interspersed throughout the city, but most of the blacks lived in West Medford, across the tracks from the middle- and upper-class neighborhoods. The Hillside area, closest to Tufts University, was mixed; it had students, a few Portuguese families, people with Slavic-sounding names, and a sprinkling from all of Medford's ethnic groups.

Medford was proud of its historic past—the early settlers and the shipbuilding dating back to 1623. The city had a strong abolitionists movement. When the Commonwealth of Massachusetts outlawed slavery in 1787, Medford became a stop on the Underground Railroad. Runaway slaves on their way to Canada found refuge in the old slave quarters of the Royall House. Medford's George Stearns, a well-to-do merchant, became one of the "secret six" who helped fund John Brown's raid on Harper's Ferry.

During prohibition, people from Medford joked about the federal agents and their intermittent raids looking for bathtub gin and wine in South Medford. No one cooperated with the revenue agents. The city had a home-brew tradition dating back to the Puritans days when "Olde Medford Rum" was made for "medicinal use."

Early in her flying career, Amelia Earhart lived in Medford with her sister. The city was quick to adopt the aviatrix as its own "Lady Lindy." In 1928, Medford went wild with a celebration the likes of which wasn't seen again until the end of World War II. A cheering crowd of thousands greeted Earhart at Fulton Street Field and celebrated her trans-Atlantic flight.

A year later, in 1929, the bleak years of the Great Depression began. The movies and movie stars became *the* escape from the grinding poverty. I can remember summer days, sitting on the Shorts' big shady porch, listening to the big girls talk about Hollywood, and trying to imagine a life other than that of the hot dusty Court. We knew we were only pretending and playing games, except for Bette. For her it was *real*. And we believed that if anyone could get away and make something of herself, become a famous *movie star*, it was Bette Short. We really expected that one day we'd go to the movies, and it would be Bette's face we'd see on the silver screen.

Bette could sing, not opera like her sister Ginnie, but popular songs and the show tunes from musicals. "Another Deanna Durbin." That's what people said about Bette. "Another Deanna Durbin."

One afternoon we were using the Shorts' porch as a stage. We tried to ignore the dark sky and the breeze stirring the bushes. Splattering raindrops drove us inside to the Barretts' parlor, where we clustered around Helen's oak wheelchair. The thin, dark-haired teen-age girl, paralyzed by polio, clutched a pencil in her gnarled fingers. Rapidly she moved her hand back and forth across a piece of paper. We marveled as the likeness of Errol Flynn emerged.

I could hear Mr. Barrett's brogue and the laughter of another man coming from the kitchen, a Mr. Bleurre. The shower had stopped, and as we were about to leave, Helen grabbed my sister Eleanor's arm and begged, "Please, please stay, a little while longer. Don't go!" She was insistent and seemed frightened, an edge of panic in her voice.

My sister Eleanor and Dottie Short exchanged glances. "We'll stay." said Eleanor. The rest of you kids go home."

As we left, Bette pulled me aside. "Never, never go near that man," she said. Her face was close to mine. "He is *not* a nice man. Don't ever, ever be alone with him. And if he bothers you, you tell me or your sisters, Mary. I know you're too young to understand. But, promise me you'll do that?"

"I promise," I said.

"And you know the candy store, Pern's candy store?"

I nodded, yes.

"NEVER go in the back room. No matter what he promises you, you must *never* go in the back room!"

Summer nights during the Depression were livened up by the free band concerts—twice a week, June through August. I was allowed to stay up after dark. I didn't dance, but I enjoyed playing and watching the goings on. Around seven o'clock, the Model-T truck towing a shiny-black, wooden hay wagon would turn off Salem Street into the deserted City Hall parking lot. Mr. Barrett would be sitting at his usual place under the big tree on the grassy knoll of the Commons, smoking his after-supper pipe. He'd hike three-quarters around on his orange crate and watch as the driver maneuvered the vehicle into the center of the small parking lot. Two men in gray work clothes would jump out. They'd each grab an end of the side-stake, lift it up slightly, lower it down, then lean the stake against the wagon. A clacking sound would echo through the Commons as the two men scurried about on the flatbed, unfolding the slat-backed wooden chairs. From a corner of the wagon, they'd pick up black metal tubular bundles and with a few deft movements transform the bundles into music stands. Then they'd unfurl a banner, black with golden letters: "American Legion, Post 45."

Aggie Barrett was usually the first to arrive, pushing Helen in the wheelchair. Neighbors from the Court soon followed, carrying chairs and grouping together at the edge of the lawn near the curb, leaving the asphalt clear for dancing. People walked up Salem Street from both directions, some carrying blankets, and some pushing baby carriages. The jam-packed trolley cars stopped with a clang, their doors opening, spilling out people dressed in their Sunday-best clothes.

Bette and Muriel often joined my sister Margie and other high-schoolers clustered near the forsythia and lilac bushes that were close to Salem Street, while the men of the neighborhood sat together on the lawn arguing about sports.

"Best high school football team in the state?" My Uncle Hector asked, baiting my father. "Are you kidding, Elmer? Malden's better. They'll take Medford again this year."

"Bull shit! bull shit!" It was bum luck. Bum luck. Medford's got Bud Mahoney, and Chuck Edgerley..." (My father *always* took Uncle Hector's bait.)

"Elmer! Watch your language. There's kids all around." My Aunt Dot made tsking sounds and looked at the group of men as if she were scolding small children.

The musicians were the last to arrive, dressed in white shirts and black pants. Most of them walked to the Commons, carrying their instruments in worn, black leather cases. A few drove cars with two or three passengers. When the old Essex pulled up next to the wagon bandstand and unloaded drums, it was the signal the music was about to start. A few notes from random instruments would break through the shouts of children and chattering voices; then there'd be a burst of music, a polka!

> Roll out the barrel!
> We'll have a barrel of fun.
> Roll out the barrel!
> Let's keep the blues on the run.

The dance area filled with people—young, old, some girls dancing with other girls—everyone swirling around, bumping, colliding.

I remember Bette emerging from the crowd and walking

towards my father. But then someone tapped her shoulder, and Bette was off dancing. When the music stopped she was back again.

"Where is your son, Mr. Pacios?" she asked. "You *promised* me that you'd make him dance with me."

"Can't get Bob to one of these," my father said. "He's off running somewhere with Wesley Harris, the Negro boy. Track team. And they're gonna try out for varsity football this year."

"I'll dance with you, Bette," my brother Skippy piped up. "I'll dance with you, *please*?" Skippy was ten years old and loved to dance—waltzes, polkas, and the Lindy Hop. He was small and wiry like my father. Skippy's blond head barely came up to Bette's shoulder.

"But, you have to lead," Bette told him, and off they went. Some of the older high-school boys tried to cut in and became perturbed when Bette kept dancing with Skippy. She laughed, saying she had promised to teach him some new steps.

By the time summer ended, all the neighborhood kids were itching for school. A few weeks before classes began, we'd go to the Swan School for new shoes and new clothes. Women in the Ladies' Aid Society stitched night gowns out of the flour sacks—the pretty white cotton ones with small flowers. Some of the kids hated wearing the "welfare shoes" with the thick soles and thick shoe laces, but as our parents reminded us, they were better than no shoes at all.

School was just letting out the day the big hurricane came up from Long Island Sound—September 21, 1938. The school children were walking home, their bodies braced against the wind at a 45° angle. There was no radar to track the hurricane and give an advance warning. At first, people weren't aware it was a hurricane. For twelve hours, the city was battered with 120-mile winds. The big elm tree next to the Court blew down, blocking Salem Street. I remember listening to the howling during the night when the full force hit.

Early the next morning, the neighborhood kids were wandering all over the city streets. The sky was clear, a bright blue, and the streets seemed to sparkle. The autumn leaves of the fallen trees shimmered in the bright sunlight. My brother Skippy took me down Riverside Avenue. We stepped over fallen branches and tried to avoid the wet, slippery leaves. We walked up Oakland Street and then down Forest Street, where we joined Bette, Muriel, and some other kids. The group of us stared transfixed at the uprooted, criss-crossed trees lacing High Street.

People in the neighborhood were still jittery a month later, the night before Halloween, when they heard what seemed to be a warning of impending doom much, much worse than any hurricane. My family missed the hullabaloo. It was a Sunday night, and as usual, we were listening to the Edgar Bergen and Charlie McCarthy radio program. We stayed tuned to the same station all evening and didn't hear what many of our neighbors heard—the Mercury Theater's program, "The War of the Worlds." Mr. Barrett said for a while he actually thought Martians had landed in New Jersey and were headed our way—until he realized it was only a radio program. The next day all the neighbors were talking about Orson Welles.

Thanksgiving was an important holiday in Medford. No family went without a traditional Thanksgiving dinner—not even during the Depression. Three or four days before the holiday, a city truck loaded with baskets of food pulled up in front of needy homes. When people answered the knock on the door, they were greeted by two workmen, one holding a twenty-five pound turkey, and the other, a box filled with the fixings: fresh-pressed cider, a variety of vegetables, apples and mincemeat to make pies, fresh cranberries, and sometimes, olives.

Thanksgiving was the day of the *Big Game*. The traditional rivals, Medford and Malden, played the last football game of the season at the Medford High Football Field. The game started at ten in the morning; later, in the evening, Football Night was held at the Medford Theater.

The 1939 Medford team hadn't lost all season. They were sure to beat Malden. Although I was only five years old, I had been chosen to present the winning cup to Medford's Captain Zarella at the Football Night ceremonies.

There was a little snow on the ground Thanksgiving Day, just a dusting—early that year. Bette came to visit just as my father and brothers were leaving for the football game. The turkey had been in the oven since six o'clock that morning, sending the cooking smells throughout the house.

"Sure smells good in here," Bette said.

The boys and my father were wrapping scarves around their necks and chins and putting on earmuffs. They gulped a couple of sips of hot chocolate before my mother poured it into a thermos. She set two extra cups on the table and divided the remainder between Bette and me.

Bette had a cough and said she might not go to Football Night. She hoped I'd give her a peek at the outfit I was going to wear. I ran to my bedroom, my rag curls flopping and pulling against my head. I opened the closet door, climbed on a chair, and reached for two hangers. One had a small, navy blue pleated skirt, the other a child's bulky white sweater that my mother had knitted. Blue and gold letters spelled the acronym MHS on the front of the sweater. I held the hangers as high as my arms could go and ran back into the kitchen to show Bette.

"They're beautiful," Bette said. "Like a miniature cheerleader's. I've got to see them on you! She led me into the bedroom, lifted me up and stood me on the chair. Bette slipped my plaid skirt over my head. "I always let it drop on the floor," I said.

"If you do it this way, over your head, your skirt won't get wrinkled. You can hang it right up, and then your mother doesn't have to iron it," she said.

Bette slipped the navy skirt over my head, pulled the zipper up, and buttoned the waist band. When I started to put the white sweater over my blouse, she held out the sleeves, making it easier for me to slip my arms in. Then she stepped back. "Turn around," she said, "so I can see all of you." And as I turned, she kept laughing, telling me how cute I looked—just like a grown-up cheerleader.

By 1940, even if the promised "happy days" were not quite here, things were looking up. My father found a permanent job with the City of Medford—digging ditches for the Public Works Department. That Spring we moved to Salem Street at the end of the Court, into the big ten-room white house with the Ionic Greek columns. The house had been vacant for several years. My father made a deal with the owner, Mr. Griffin—for forty dollars a month rent and a couple of months rent-free, my father would fix and paint the house.

That same year, Bette Short turned sixteen and started traveling. Her asthma and lung problems had worsened, and she developed bronchitis. Mrs. Short thought Bette might be better off in a warmer climate, away from the coldness and the dampness. She arranged for Bette to stay with family friends in Miami Beach. Bette could spend the winter there earning money as a waitress, figured Mrs. Short, and come back in the spring.

Two or three times a week Bette's letters arrived, family letters addressed to Mrs. Short to be read aloud, and occasionally funny postcards for Muriel. Bette wrote that she liked Miami Beach but missed everyone, although she was glad to get away from the snow and ice. The family friends were nice, and she liked her room—small, with maple furniture just like she and Muriel had at home. Bette said she was feeling better— no colds or asthma attacks. Work was hectic at the delicatessen and the people sometimes fussy, but with a split shift Bette had time to go to the beach and soak up the sun. She was saving her money, and when the season ended in March she would be home to look for a summer job.

Sometimes when I came home from school, a postcard from Bette would be waiting for me on the dining room table. There were Saturdays when I'd rush through my dusting chores and I'd sit on my front steps waiting for the postman to make his morning rounds. And then after the movies I'd rush home and see if anything had come in the afternoon mail.

For the next couple of years, as soon as the leaves began to turn, Bette headed for Florida. She'd appear back in Medford just about the time the lilacs and lilies-of-the-valley were in bloom. I liked to sneak into the old cemetery and pick flowers for her. The small, bell-shaped lilies-of-the-valley grew wild near the black wrought-iron fence. I dreamed of growing up to be like Bette and getting away, of traveling and not being stuck forever in the dry, dusty Court.

TWO
I'll Be Seeing You...

My father said he wasn't sure if he heard right—a news flash about the Japanese bombing Pearl Harbor. He reached over and turned up the sound on the radio console. President Roosevelt's voice resonated through the parlor: "December 7, 1941, a date that will live in infamy."

Later that evening, I bundled up warm and walked to Ben Shuman's drugstore with my father to buy a newspaper. One word was blazoned across the headline: WAR!

Most of the grownups were pretty quiet for the next few days. But my father didn't seem troubled. "Going to war," he said, "is more like doing your duty." He had been a kid of seventeen, he said, when he was sent to France, fighting in the artillery, kicking the Krauts and the Kaiser. Now it would be his sons making the world safe for democracy—sending a message to the Axis: Tojo, Hitler, and Mussolini.

Everywhere I went, I heard talk about the "war effort" and about making sacrifices "for the duration." Posters with patriotic slogans sprang up, even in our schoolrooms: "Buy War Bonds," "Rosie the Riveter," "Put the Ax in the Axis," "Loose Lips Sink Ships," "Uncle Sam Wants You."

Over the next few months, everything seemed to change. When I ran errands for my mother, I had to make sure I took the ration book with me, or else Aram, the grocer, wouldn't sell me the meat or butter or most of the other food that we now could afford to buy. It seemed that everything was rationed or in short supply. When my sister Margie couldn't find nylons in the stores, she used a special leg make-up, and with her eyebrow pencil drew a line up the back of each leg.

Everyone in my family had a job, even my brother Skippy. It seemed I was the only one in the neighborhood who wasn't working. But I still felt as if I was doing my part for the war effort. I bought ten-cent war stamps, and with my school chums, I collected aluminum scrap that we tossed into the huge, wire-meshed collection bin that now stood on the Medford Commons.

My father took a leave of absence from the City to work at the Boston Navy Yard. Most of my brother Bob's friends were drafted as soon as they graduated from high school. Bob had a scholarship to Huntington Prep and a deferment. But after a year, at age nineteen, he enlisted in the army and joined his buddies. My brother Richard quit high school and enlisted in the navy. He was seventeen years old. My mother hung a small white flag with two blue stars in our front window, proudly announcing that she had *two* sons in the armed forces.

Mrs. Short had no sons, but she still hung a flag with one blue star in the window of her front door. At first, Bette's older and very slender sister Dottie had been rejected as "too thin" for the service. But Dottie would not take no for an answer. She went on a week-long binge of milkshakes, frappes, and double malts to bring her weight up. While my brother Bob went through basic training at Fort McClellan in Alabama, Dottie, stationed in Washington, DC, went through crash courses in cryptography.

On my brother's first week-end leave after basic training, he married his sweetheart, Sylvia Lothrop. Bob wore an army uniform; she wore a fitted light-blue suit and a corsage of white roses. They were married in her home, reciting their vows under a white, fluted-paper wedding bell. Bob and Sylvia danced to "I'll Be Seeing You." They were both nineteen years old.

More than ten million men were drafted during the four years of World War II; 200,000 never returned home. The women and girls in the neighborhood wrote daily letters to keep the servicemen's morale up. "Victory letters" arrived from the men overseas—three-inch-square envelopes with a reduced Photostat of the original handwritten letter inside. Heavy black lines of the censor deleted any hint of where the letter had originated.

USOs and night clubs catering to servicemen sprang up in Boston. My sister Margie and my mother argued about Margie's late nights. My mother said Margie was spending too much time in Boston and hanging around too many servicemen. "Be careful of those servicemen!" my mother warned.

"We only go out in groups," Margie said. "And besides, a

lot of the guys are only lonely kids who want someone to talk to, someone to have a little fun with before they ship out."

Bette had quit her job as usher at the Metropolitan Theater in Boston and started working at Child's restaurant. After work she'd stop by Liggett's Drugstore on Tremont Street, where my mother had taken a job as a cashier and my sister Margie worked the lunch counter. Bette would chat with Margie and spend hours dawdling over a cup of coffee. Sometimes they went shopping when Margie finished her shift. They dressed up in suits with the new fashionable hemline—to the middle of the knees. (Material was in short supply, and it was important not to appear *unpatriotic.*) Margie said that the servicemen howled and whistled when they walked by. She would giggle, but Bette would keep her stride, sometimes flashing a smile.

I noticed that Bette wore more make-up than Margie. According to Margie, Bette used the new pancake on her face, a light shade that made her pale skin seem even whiter and set off her blue-green eyes. Bette wore a bright red lipstick and, according to Margie, put a rinse in her dark brown hair, making it jet black.

One day a dog followed Bette home from Medford Square— a large, gray-brown police dog without a collar or tags. (No one dared call them German shepherds during the war.) Bette would take a few steps, then turn around and firmly say, "Go home!" But the animal gave her a hang-dog look and ambled behind her. As big as he was, to Bette he seemed as gentle as a baby and in desperate need of petting.

"Baby" stayed for a few months, following Bette around Medford, waiting outside the stores and at the trolley stop with her. He'd disappear for a few days and then be back, howling outside her bedroom window. Bette tracked down his owners, a family that lived two miles away in South Medford.

"Baby, you named him *Baby*?" his owners said in disbelief. "He is one *mean* dog!" They told Bette they called the dog *Tiger.*

With most people working or in the service, Medford became a ghost town. I spent a lot of time by myself. Sometimes Bette would spot me sitting on my front stoops.

"How about going for a walk and keeping me company?" she'd ask. Bette was usually all dressed up, but she didn't seem to mind if I was wearing old play clothes.

On one of our walks, we stopped at the gas station that had replaced the vacant field across Salem Street. The manager stopped what he was doing and came right over to Bette. I can remember standing there and shifting from one foot to the other as the two grownups exchanged a few words, laughing and planning to meet later that night.

Afterwards, Bette told me she wasn't going to Florida. "This year I'm going to California."

I figured that Bette was going there to be a movie star.

"Well, that's what I'm hoping," she said. "Not right away. It takes time. But if you want to break into the movies, it can't happen in Florida… or in Medford."

Bette's father sent her money for the train. Cleo was working in a shipyard at Mare Island Naval Station. He said there was plenty of work in California and Bette could stay with him in Vallejo. She could keep house for a while until she had a job. Bette's mom had misgivings. California was clear across the country—over two thousand miles away. But as long as Bette had someone to help her out, Mrs. Short thought it might be okay. She trusted her girls; she had tried to bring them up to have confidence and be resourceful. And Bette was right. If she was going to break into the movies, she had to go to California.

Bette still wrote home—optimistic letters, once or twice a week. Living with her father hadn't worked out, but she had found a job near Santa Barbara. Fingerprinted and with a photo I.D., she was now a civilian employee at Camp Cooke. In one of the letters she enclosed a clipping. Bette had won a beauty contest—she was the new "Camp Cutie."

A few months later Bette was back home. She talked of her plans and the contacts she was making—people who wanted to help her, who thought she had what it took to be a model, a stepping-stone to breaking into the movies.

I became excited when I saw Bette's shadow in the window, the signal that she was back. The shade was drawn, and I could see Bette walking back and forth. Margie and I sometimes caught Uncle Hector, Mr. Barrett, and our father watching Bette's shadow, especially when it looked like she was getting ready for bed. I'd hear them joking, and I'd become angry. But I didn't have the courage to say anything to them, and I never told Bette.

Sometimes late at night, my mother picked up broadcasts from Germany. Our console radio had short wave. Prisoners of war were supposed to give only their name, rank, and serial number, but some American and Canadian prisoners gave their home addresses and messages to loved ones. My sister Margie sat in front of the radio, writing everything down in shorthand. Bette, who also knew shorthand, occasionally joined Margie and helped transcribe the messages.

My mother mailed postcards with the transcribed messages from the prisoners: "On February 17, 1943, while listening to my short wave radio, I heard the following message from a soldier who said his name was..."

Most people replied to the postcards, some thanking her, a few angry because they had been informed by the War Department that the serviceman had been killed in action. It was rumored that soldiers sometimes exchanged dogtags for "good luck," and mistakes were made.

The grownups had expected the war to be over quickly, a year or two at the most before the boys were back home. But the roll call of men from Medford serving in the armed forces kept growing—a list memorialized with brass name plates inside a glass-and-marble case placed on the City Hall front lawn. The little white flag with gold fringe tacked to our front door still had two stars, but now one represented a purple heart.

In the winter of 1944, a few months before my tenth birthday, I was making my way home from school. Neighbors and people I barely knew kept stopping me and murmuring something about being sorry. Then they hastened away before I could ask them what they were sorry about.

The house was quiet when I walked in the door. No one was there. I spotted a telegram and a crushed-up envelope lying on the lace dining-room tablecloth. I picked up the telegram and read the pasted-on strips of words: "We regret to inform you that your son, Tech. Sgt. Robert K. Pacios, has been seriously wounded in action."

My mother later said that she was gripped by a strange feeling when she saw the Western Union Boy peddling up Salem Street. Her heart gave a lurch when he stopped in front of our house, checked the number on the granite wall and began to mount the steps. Before he had a chance to ring the bell, Mama opened the door and fished in her apron pocket for a dime. He shook his head when she tried to give him the tip. "I'm sorry," he said. Mama said she stood there holding the telegram and stared at the retreating back of the boy. Then she went inside to read the telegram from the War Department.

When she slipped on her hat and coat, Mama didn't even think to take off her apron and hang it up. She just had to get out... leave... now... right away. She walked to Medford Square, bought a ticket to the matinee, and sat huddled in the darkened theater, wrapping her coat tightly around her.

I couldn't answer when Bette asked what was wrong. I was standing on the sidewalk and kept looking up and down the street as if I was expecting someone but didn't know who. Bette took my hand and said, "Let's go for a walk down Washington Square." We went to the drugstore on the corner and sat at the soda fountain, drinking hot chocolate and sharing a banana split. Bette tried to get me to talk, pretending she wanted the ice cream on my side of the dish.

Ben Shuman, the druggist, motioned to Bette and pointed to the *Medford Mercury* on the newspaper stand just inside the door. I had seen the picture of my brother on the front page when we walked in and tried to ignore the headline: "Sgt. Pacios wounded in Belgium." Ben went behind the counter to the pharmacy in the rear and busied himself filling prescriptions. The clacking sound of the typewriter began to make everything seem almost normal.

I often heard Ben say that Bette was someone who was going places. "Always poised, even when she was a young kid," he told his customers. Ben called Bette "the sophisticated traveler." They chit-chatted whenever she went into the store. Sometimes they just shot the breeze. Sometimes they had long, involved conversations about the world situation. The clerk, Rusti, and later when he went in the service, Kenny, would fall all over themselves trying to help Bette with her purchases, becoming flustered when she bought her "female supplies."

My Aunt Dot thought it was a wonder we didn't have more car accidents when Bette walked down the street. "The way those guys crane their heads out the window!" she said to my mother. The neighborhood women always stopped what they were doing to watch Bette. They laughed about the way men looked at Bette and fell all over themselves. "Bette doesn't miss a step, even in platform shoes," my aunt said. "She carries herself straight and tall just like a model, swinging and swaying all the way up Salem Street."

My mother and Aunt Dot noticed that Bette didn't have a slew of clothes, but what she had looked very expensive. Bette told the two women that she bought her clothes wholesale where she modeled. Bette had stylish hats and coats (a couple were fur). She never wore much jewelry except sometimes a choker around her neck, and maybe a bracelet. Bette always wore gloves, and she seemed to prefer the clutch-style purses that folded over. "Always tasteful, never overdressed," my mother said.

I'd often see Bette in a black tailored suit. She'd wear a frilly pink blouse, white gloves, and a small pink hat with pink ostrich feathers. The feathers would float as Bette walked down the street.

My sister Margie's boyfriend, Frank, liked to tease Daddy about Bette. Frank was a tall, lanky, red-headed sailor from Alabama and Margie's new fiancé—her third during the war. "Hey, old man, quick, there she goes!" Frank would yell. He'd be looking out the front window, peeking through the Irish lace curtains. "Damn! She's prettier than any movie star," he'd say as my father ran from the kitchen almost tripping over a chair.

Daddy would push Frank aside, knocking him off balance, and grab the curtains. "That's Bette Short!" Daddy would say. "She's been to *Hollywood*!" Then the two men would stand at the parlor window, watching as Bette walked down Salem Street towards Medford Square.

In the good weather, my father sat on the wall in front of our house on Salem Street and waited for Bette to walk by. He'd talk to the people waiting for the trolley. Bette would stop and chat, tell him about her latest travels, what it was like trying to break into the movies. My mother thought my dad was sort of a substitute for Bette's missing father.

Most evenings after I finished my homework, I sat in the parlor with my father and listened to his favorite radio programs on the console—*The Jack Benny Show, Edgar Bergen and Charlie McCarthy, You Bet Your Life,* (with Groucho Marx), and *Duffy's Tavern.* When the Gabrielle Heater or Walter Winchell news program came on the air, I'd go to my bedroom and turn the dial of my small brown radio to my favorite programs—*The Quiz Kids, You Are There!, Quick As a Flash, I Love a Mystery,* and my all-time favorite, *The Shadow.* I'd lie quietly on my bed as Lamont Cranston's deep, menacing voice filled the room: "Who knows what evil lurks in the heart of man? The Shadow knows! Hahahahahahahaha!" I felt secure knowing that Lamont Cranston, in the guise of the Shadow, would catch the bad guys and bring them to justice—just as I knew our soldiers would catch Hitler and win the war.

Bette came back to Medford once or twice a year for visits. She'd work a month or two, just long enough for her train ticket back to Hollywood, or Florida, or Chicago, or wherever she was headed next. She took a job working as a hostess in a Belmont tea room for a couple of weeks, but she left that to work as a waitress at the Wursthaus in Harvard Square. She told my mother the tips were better and the owner was like a big Teddy bear, burly but soft-hearted and good to "his girls." Bette said she was often invited out after work, but usually felt too tired to go. Bette just wanted to catch the bus to Arlington Circle, then head for Medford Square, get a cup of coffee and see who was in the Medford Cafe, one of the favorite hangouts in Medford.

After a few months in Medford, Bette would be off again, driven south by the approaching winter. Bette wrote home once a week from Miami Beach. She had a job at a cafe owned by a former showgirl who called herself Princess Whitewing. In her letters, Bette said she was dating steadily, mostly double dates with lonely soldiers, "real gentlemen," or going out with groups of people to night clubs. For a while she seemed to be serious about an airman, Gordon Fickling.

But then in January, of 1945, Bette wrote to her mother: "I met someone New Year's Eve, a major, Matt Gordon. I'm so much in love, I'm sure it shows. He is so wonderful, not like other men. And he asked me to marry him."

Matt Gordon believed he had found the woman of his dreams. He wrote to his sister-in-law: "Beth is an educated and refined girl whom I plan to marry. I would like you to correspond with her and get to know her because when I return I plan to make Beth my bride."

Bette returned home to wait for Matt's return. The neighbors had never seen Bette so happy and radiant. She proudly wore Matt's pilot wings on her sweater. Whenever anyone mentioned her fiancé, Bette would beam.

My mother brought me along when she called on Bette to congratulate her. I stood quietly as Bette opened up her trunk and carefully lifted out the fine linens Matt had sent from the Philippines.

"This will serve as my hope chest for now," she said. Bette proudly showed us a gold Hamilton wristwatch with four small diamonds. "A pre-engagement gift," Bette said. "Matt is sending the engagement and wedding rings to his mother in Colorado."

The day the war ended, my brother Bob, his wife, Sylvia and son Bobby Jr., were visiting. Bob had been discharged a few months before. He was sitting in the front yard chewing the fat with some of our dad's cronies, vets from World War I. Bob tried to stay away from talk about his war experiences. I watched as my brother reluctantly rolled up his sleeve and showed the long jagged scar on his right arm. "Just lucky, I guess, to have almost all my movement back. But what about Wes? Anyone heard from Wesley Harris?"

"Wes was home on furlough a while back," my mother said. "I tried to give him advice. He was getting thrown off buses down South. Said he won't ride in back. Tried to tell him that maybe while he's there he shouldn't make a fuss. He should do as they do. Said he plans to go to medical school when he gets out...."

The loud deafening sound of the air raid siren drowned out her words. Little Bobby, started screaming and pulling at his ears. People looked at each other, shrugging their shoulders and shaking their heads, then looking up at the sky for airplanes. Some ran for cover.

"Oh, my God!" my mother screamed. "It's the signal! The war! The war's over!" Her words were almost soundless, overpowered by the steady wail of the siren. Bells started ringing and cars blared their horns. People poured into the streets, stopping the cars and the trolleys. In Medford Square most of the businesses closed. The ones that stayed open had people leaning out of windows, throwing scraps of paper and water balloons on the crowds below. Late into the night and next morning, the bedlam continued.

Ten days later, Margie saw Bette at the end of the court. They chatted a while about their plans. Margie was only eighteen and a long-distance supervisor with New England Bell. Bette was planning her upcoming marriage to Matt Gordon—a major in the Flying Tigers. "September, just a month away," Bette said. "We'll marry here—a small wedding—and then I'll go back with him to Colorado to meet his mother, on our way to California. But I'm still going to model and try to break into the movies."

When Margie left to go to work, she saw a Western Union messenger approaching on his bicycle. As Margie would tell it later, she felt her heart twinge. Then she chided herself. Oh, for heaven's sakes, she thought, the war is over. It can't be anything but good news. Margie watched to see where the messenger would go. He stopped in front of the Shorts' three-decker.

Bette tore open the telegram. "Oh, my God," she said to her sister Muriel. "It's not going to be. I can't believe it's not going to be." The telegram slipped from her hand and dropped to the floor. Muriel bent down and picked it up. "Matt killed in plane crash on way home from India," the telegram said. "My sympathy is with you. Pray it isn't so. Mrs. Matt Gordon Sr."

Bette spent the next few days reading Matt's love letters. She crossed out the words "and marry" in the clipping Mrs.

Gordon sent her. Bette left for Miami, the folded newspaper clipping about Matt's death close at hand, secure in her purse.

The war may have been over, but the return to normalcy wasn't quite as people had expected. Talk about beating the "Japs" and the "Krauts" gave way to grumbling about the returning GIs and the government's 52-20 Club—the $20 a week for 52 weeks paid to servicemen mustering out. Jobs were getting scarce again. The "gals" who had learned new skills, kept the home fires burning during the war, now lost their jobs to the returning GIs.

My mother and sisters were busy lowering their hemlines. The fashion language had changed. Dresses grew more modest with longer skirts. Women now wore "tea gowns" instead of "cocktail dresses." Night life for the American woman no longer was fashionable. Women were told, "Go back home where you belong."

Salem Street became quieter—the clang of the trolleys replaced with the hum of the "trackless trolleys," buses powered by the same overhead wires. There still weren't many cars, and the wartime housing shortage hadn't eased. The large homes made into boarding houses during the war kept their "boarders." A New York doctor just out of the service, Dr. Stan Landy, bought our big white house on Salem Street. With the strict rent control and housing laws he couldn't evict my family, even though all of my brothers and sisters were either married or in the service, and I was the only child left at home.

My parents allowed Dr. Landy to set up his practice in what had been the downstairs parlor, dining room, and bathroom. We kept the kitchen and the upstairs rooms. In the sixth grade now, I looked forward to my next year in junior high.

Doctor Landy gave me my first job. On Sundays while he and Mrs. Landy went out for a drive, I answered the telephone and wrote down messages. The doctor told me I could read any of the books on his shelves while I was waiting for the phone to ring. I went through all the anatomy books and anything remotely connected to the word "sex." I became familiar with hormonal deficiencies like cretinism and goiter and with advanced stages of venereal disease such as syphilis and gonorrhea. For a while my attitude towards boys suffered. I thought males were the cause of all of the diseases.

Bette stayed in Florida for a few months. When the tourist season ended, she returned home to Medford. Bette often told me that she thought I could become an actress. "Maybe I could help you get started—once I'm on my way and you've finished school," she said. It was the last time we spent time together. We had taken our usual route down Salem Street, stopping at the gas station so Bette could chat a few minutes with the manager. At Ruth's Dress Shoppe I sat in a chair and watched Bette's reflections in the mirrors as she turned this way and that. Lettie, the salesgirl, told Bette how wonderful she looked in the black dress with the pink roses. "You're lucky," Lettie said. "You don't have to wear falsies."

On the way back, we stopped at Liggett's soda fountain. I remember feeling very peaceful and contented as we made plans for the future. Bette told me she was going back to California. She said that she would send for me when I was older. "I'll put you up while you get settled," she said. I felt so proud that someone like Bette would be interested in me.

A few days later I saw Bette leave for South Station. Arthur's checker cab picked her up. I heard the car door slam, and I watched the taxi pull away from the curb.

Her letters home bubbled with optimism—talk of bit parts and modeling jobs. She wasn't waitressing anymore. She had made some contacts, and all her work was paying off. She was going to have a screen test—a well-known director was making the arrangements. "Keep your fingers crossed," she wrote. "This could be my lucky break."

THREE
The Unthinkable

January 15, 1947—a crisp and clear day in the Medford area—Remnants of the last snow storm formed an icy crust on the ground. I remember coming home late from school that day. My mother was sitting at the kitchen table, drinking coffee and reading the evening newspaper.

"How awful!" my mother said, "What is the world coming to? A young woman murdered, her body cut in half, left in a vacant lot. It happened in California, in Los Angeles." She looked up from the paper. "Isn't that where Bette Short is?" she asked.

I looked over my mother's shoulder at the newspaper, and I glanced at the small article. "No. Hollywood," I said, "Bette's in Hollywood."

Mr. Barrett was the first to find out. "He's the one who spread the news through the neighborhood," my mother said later. "Ran over without any coat on, right through the slush and snow. Coulda' caught his death 'a cold. When I answered the door, there was Mr. Barrett. 'Your girlfriend's dead, Mr. Pacios,' he yelled with that thick Irish brogue of his. 'Somebody killed your girlfriend!' Your father came running out wanting to know what the commotion was about. He couldn't believe it— Mr. Barrett standing there saying something about Bette Short being dead, being murdered in California."

Mr. Barrett always called Bette my father's girlfriend. Bette seemed to single out my father for special attention, talking and joking with him. Mr. Barrett would tease my father. "How's you girlfriend?" he'd ask. "What's your girlfriend doing these days?"

My mother said her first impulse was to call my brother Bob. She wanted to tell Bob personally, not have him read about Bette in the newspapers. Bob was studying at Boston University under the GI Bill and working part time in a diner.

"I heard about it," he told my mother. "But I can't believe it. You just don't expect something like this. Come back from the war, and you just want to get on with things. "A customer came in the diner just before I was ready to quit my shift and go over to BU. The guy was reading a newspaper with a photo of Bette on the front page. I got excited and said, 'Hey, I know that girl!' Then I caught the headline—MEDFORD GIRL SLAIN ON COAST. The guy gave me the paper and I read the story: Camp Cooke ID, movie career dreams, bit parts—and what the Los Angles police detective called, 'the most brutal example of a sex crime he had ever seen...' I didn't want to go to class afterwards, and ended up walking around."

My mother told Bob about the article she had read in the newspaper a couple of days before. "Never dreamed it was Bette Short," she said. "It's all over the neighborhood. Reporters are showing up. We'll tell Mary when she gets home. She's over at Eleanor's watching the children. Went right there from school, so probably doesn't know yet. Kids take these things hard sometimes, but not for long. Kids always bounce back."

I had left the bedroom door open a crack so I could hear if the girls woke up. I then tiptoed down the stairs into the living room and sat on the couch, mesmerized by the action of the old cowboys with the strange hats—Lilliputians on a four-inch television screen. The set was brand new, the first television in the town of Stoneham, Massachusetts.

And then, with the quiet of the house surrounding me, time seemed to slow down. A familiar face filled the small television screen. I remember thinking, what's Bette's face doing there? A staccato of words began to echo inside my head: "Special... announcement... body... found... Los... Angeles... two... days... ago... cut... in... half... tortured... identified... Elizabeth... Short... Medford." I stared at Bette's face, terrified, afraid to move. I wanted to cry, to laugh, but I couldn't move. Then the cowboys were back riding and shooting. Bette's face was gone.

I kept staring at the screen. Bette was dead, and I *knew* whoever killed her would want to kill me. Minutes, hours later, the front door opened. I ran towards my sister Eleanor and her husband.

"It's Bette! It's Bette! They've killed Bette!"

No one talked to me about the murder. I was only twelve

years old. I noticed that sometimes when I'd walk into a room, the conversation would stop and then someone would ask me something dumb like what was the color of the new linoleum? Was it blue or green? But I knew they weren't discussing the linoleum; they were talking about the color of Bette's eyes.

A few days after the murder, I was sitting at the dining room table and drawing a picture of Bette as Snow White. My father was reading the evening newspaper. I heard the paper drop. He sighed and I looked up. For an instant our eyes met. I can never forgot that moment—the deep sense of sadness and pain we shared. He quickly looked away, but I glimpsed the tears in his eyes.

Every day the newspapers had a different headline, each more sensational than the last:

VICTIM OF SADIST IN LOS ANGELES IDENTIFIED AS ELIZABETH SHORT • STRANGE LIFE STORY OF GIRL VICTIM OF WEREWOLF MURDER • HUNT BOYFRIENDS IN TORTURE KILLING • FATHER OF SLAIN MODEL WILL NOT AID IN KILLER SEARCH • BLACK DAHLIA'S LOVE LIFE TRACED IN SEARCH FOR HER FIENDISH MURDERER • POLICE GRILL RED-HAIRED BLACK DAHLIA SUSPECT • HUNT FOR KILLER OF BLACK DAHLIA BOGS DOWN

I read all the newspaper stories, skipping the parts that described what had been done to Bette—the torture she had endured. A suspect had been caught, the papers said. His name was Robert "Red" Manley. But then he was "exonerated." Manley, the papers said, was the last known person to see Bette alive. He told detectives he had driven "Beth" from San Diego to downtown Los Angeles the night of January 9, 1947, and left her at the Biltmore Hotel at 6:30 p.m. Beth asked him to drive her to the Biltmore hotel, Manley said, because she was meeting her sister there. "It was getting late and I was anxious to get home, so I didn't hang around," he said. He described the clothes "Beth" wore: a black tailored suit with a frilly white blouse, white gloves, a black purse, black stockings, and black suede shoes. She carried a camel's hair coat over her arm.

According to the newspapers, witnesses remembered seeing her in the lobby of the hotel. She was making telephone calls. But within an hour she was gone. Her mutilated body was found six days later in a vacant lot.

After a few days, the newspapers stopped calling Bette an aspiring actress. Movie studios denied she had ever worked as a bit player or extra. The description of the black tailored suit which Bette had worn when she was last seen alive was changed to "a tight skirt and a sheer blouse."

The papers which had called for the arrest of the "torture den killer" and the "werewolf who stalked innocent victims in the dark," developed a new slant—Bette had become the "Black Dahlia," an "adventuress" who "prowled Hollywood Boulevard." She was named the Black Dahlia by her Long Beach friends, the newspapers said, because of her jet-black hair, her black clothing, and her dark, mysterious ways.

Matt Gordon's mother distanced herself from Bette, telling reporters her son "had not really been engaged to Miss Short." Mrs. Gordon claimed the telegram about the flier's death had been sent "only as a courtesy." Gordon's sister-in-law, at first recalled that Matt had asked her to correspond with Beth, describing Beth as "refined... someone Matt was interested in." Later she said the relationship had not been serious.

Bette's family tried to get away from the hovering reporters stationed outside their apartment. I saw the family leave, heads bowed against the wind, ignoring the voices and questions yelled at them. Their pastor, Reverend Henderson, made arrangements for Mrs. Short to leave for California. He told her not to worry about the expense and not to worry about her three youngest daughters. Reverend Henderson would stay behind and help them. Mrs. Short's oldest daughter, Virginia West, lived in California and would be at the airport when the plane arrived.

The newspapers reported Mrs. Short's every move. Reporters boarded the airplane at her stopover in Chicago. At first Mrs. Short refused to talk to the newsmen, then relented. "Of course, I'll do anything to help catch the person who killed my daughter," she told them, "But why are you saying those things about my girl? My daughter was a good girl!"

I saw the newspaper photos of Mrs. Short sitting in the airplane. She was looking out the window. There were photos of her in a Los Angeles police station. She sat across the desk from Harry Hansen, the detective in charge of the case. Virginia sat on one side of Mrs. Short, and Adrian West, her son-in-law, sat on the other side. Detective Finis Brown, along with Chief of Detectives Jack Donahoe, and the autopsy surgeon, Dr. Frederick Newbarr, crowded against the walls.

Mrs. Short told Detective Harry Hansen that her daughter had no enemies. "None that I know of... People liked her..." Mrs. Short said. "She was brought up just like all my other daughters, no different, maybe a little... prettier. We called her Bette. She wrote all the time. In the Fall of '43 my daughter came back from California. Things did not work out with her father. For the next couple of years she worked in Florida during the winters. But then she decided to give it another try and break into the movies. The last time I saw her was the morning she left for California—April 6, 1946.

"I'd get letters from her once a week. Bette said she left Hollywood because of the movie strikes and was working at the naval hospital until they were over.

"When she came home I would wait up, and we would sit in the kitchen and talk about her dates—what they did, where they went. But she never mentioned anyone she was afraid of. I never worried about her the way I did the other girls. She was so sweet and *special*. And so good to her younger sisters, Muriel and Nonie."

Hansen told Mrs. Short he needed her to help with the investigation. "We have picked up Elizabeth's father," Hansen said. "And he isn't talking, not telling us much, other than she lived with him for a couple of months."

"He sent my daughter money to come to California," Mrs. Short volunteered. "He said he wanted to help her. That's what he told me. I never would have let her come out here if I didn't think there was someone to help her."

"Her father refuses to cooperate," Hansen said. "He won't

identify Elizabeth and we need someone who knew her, a next of kin to identify her."

Mrs. Short protested. "No, I can't," she said. "That's too much to ask!"

"You have her fingerprints. You know it is my sister. Why do you need us?" Virginia asked. "We want to remember her as she was."

"Are you sure this is necessary?" Adrian said. "Could I identify her?"

"Did you know Elizabeth very well?"

"I never met her. Only snapshots."

"That won't work," Hansen said. "I'm truly sorry, but it has to be done. *Visual* identification by a close relative is *essential*. There are no alternatives." He was insistent.

At first, Mrs. Short could not identify the battered body that was her daughter. Then she saw Bette's distinctive beauty mark.

"Yes," she said. "That is my daughter."

Detective Harry Hansen informed Mrs. Short the Coroner's Inquest was scheduled for 10:30 a.m. the next day, January 22nd. "Your testimony is needed," he said. "It's vital."

An oak table divided the claustrophobic witness room, separating the two groups of people waiting to testify. Mrs. Short, flanked by her daughter and son-in-law, studiously avoided eye contact with "Red" Manley, the last known person to have been with her daughter. He sat on the opposite side of the large table, clutching his wife's hand.

When the bailiff entered the room and called, "Mrs. Phoebe Mae Short," she jerked slightly and squeezed her daughter's hand. Mrs. Short stood up and walked through the doors held open for her. Looking straight ahead, she walked across the hall and past the rows of spectators. She raised her right hand, murmured the appropriate response and took one step up to the witness stand. Coroner Ben Brown began his questions.

"Please state your name," he said.

Clutching her gloves in one hand, Mrs. Short leaned towards the judge. With the other hand she gripped the microphone. Softly, almost in a whisper, she said, "Mrs. Phoebe Mae Short."

"Where do you reside?"

"115 Salem Street, Medford, Massachusetts."

"Have you viewed the body of a deceased person in the mortuary here?"

Mrs. Short hesitated. "I have," she said.

"Was that someone you knew in life?"

"It was."

"What was her name?"

"Elizabeth Short."

"Did she have a middle name?"

"No middle name."

"Was she related to you?"

"My daughter."

The coroner cleared his throat and leaned towards Mrs. Short. "Do you know where she died?" he asked.

The spectators strained to hear the soft-spoken woman. Mrs. Short hesitated and gazed about the packed court room. People were standing in the back and overflowing into the hallway. She half-rose from the witness chair and exclaimed, "She was murdered here in Los Angeles!"

The newspapers reported that Mrs. Short seemed stunned by her own outburst and sank back into the chair. She looked down at the gloves in her hands and then resumed answering the questions with a detached air until excused.

Shielded by her daughter and shaking her head at the reporters' questions, Mrs. Short left the inquest room. Outside, on the steps of the Hall of Justice, Adrian West pulled a folded piece of paper from his pocket and read a prepared statement thanking the police and reporters for their efforts to apprehend the killer.

Only four other witnesses were called to testify during the forty-five-minute proceedings.

Jesse W. Haskins gave his occupation as "Detective Lieutenant, Police Department, Los Angeles, University Division."

"Mr. Haskins," the coroner asked, "were you called to the scene of the finding of the deceased person, Elizabeth Short, over whom we are holding this inquest?"

"I was."

"When did you receive this call?"

"Approximately 11:05 the morning of the 15th of January."

"And what time did you arrive at the scene?"

"At 11:18."

In answer to questions, Haskins described the location of the body and the murder scene at 39th and Norton. He described a tire track he found at the murder scene, with "what appeared to be a possible bloody heel mark" pressed into the grooves.

Robert Manley next testified, giving his address as 8010 Mountain View in South Gate. "I had known Elizabeth Short for about a month," he said.

"When did you see her, meet her the last time?" the coroner asked.

"I saw Miss Short January 9th, which was the last time."

"Where was that?"

"I left Miss Short at the Biltmore Hotel at 6:30 p.m. January 9, 1947."

"And you haven't seen or heard from her since?"

"No, sir."

Harry Hansen gave the briefest testimony, answering just six questions. "As of now, we have no definite information as to who perpetrated it," he said.

"And are you following all clues you receive?" the coroner asked.

"Every effort to locate the criminal is being made."

The last witness, the autopsy surgeon, Dr. Newbarr, carried a black binder to the witness stand. He settled into the chair, resting the voluminous open binder on his lap, preparing to answer questions in depth. After the first detailed responses, Coroner Brown interrupted Newbarr's testimony. "Doctor, I don't believe it will be necessary for you to read all this," he said. "It is rather long. The essential findings with regard to the cause of death have already been expressed."

The Coroner's Jury returned their verdict: "Death by hemorrhage and shock due to concussion of the brain and lacerations of the face; and from the testimony introduced we find said person or persons unknown at this time to this jury, and at some location unknown to this jury; and we find this to be a homicide and recommend that every effort be made to apprehend the perpetrator or perpetrators responsible therefore."

Mrs. Short met one more time with Detective Harry Hansen. She wanted some of Bette's photos and personal belongings.

"The linens, that's all I can let go," Hansen said, "The stuff from the Philippines that you said came from her fiancé, that's okay. But everything else is booked in as evidence. And we need to check and double check it. That can't be released until the case is closed."

The newspapers announced the date and time of Bette's funeral in Oakland, California. But no onlookers or curiosity seekers went to the service. No friends made the trek to Mountain View Cemetery to pay their last respects. The three family members sat huddled near the edge of the hillside gravesite. They were outnumbered by the police and reporters standing in the distance, watching for someone "suspicious" to show up.

People in Medford Square who didn't even know Bette said that Bette had brought it on herself, that Bette had worn too much make-up, dated too many men and gotten what she deserved. I heard all the gossip, and I heard someone call Bette a *whore*. But I didn't care what people said. I could only think about how nice Bette had been to me, and how, even though I was a kid, she'd listen to me and talk to me in a serious way.

A few days after her murder, I went to my room and sat on the edge of my bed. I stared at the blue-flowered wallpaper, not knowing what to do. I thought of Bette with her pale, pale skin. I reached over to my bureau, picked up a large powder puff, and dusted white bath powder all over my face. I sat there until dark staring back into the mirror, staring at the blue eyes peering through the white mask. But I couldn't shed a tear.

The reporters wouldn't go away. I saw them hovering in front of the Shorts' apartment and spilling over into my aunt's yard, where they watched the rear of the Shorts' building. My aunt didn't shoo the reporters away. "Won't do any good, anyhow," she said. "They don't listen to you."

The neighbors clammed up. When the reporters tried to talk

to my mother, she told them, "In a nutshell, I know nothing. Bette kept to herself."

Muriel made daily visits to my Aunt Dot. As they sat at the kitchen table and drank hot coffee, Muriel would begin to relax and talk about Bette—not about the murder, but about how good Bette had been to her and to her other sister, Nonie. Muriel would talk about the times Bette took them to the movies and bought little presents. But then after a few months Muriel seemed to want to forget, my aunt said, and Muriel never mentioned Bette again.

I began walking home from school on the other side of the street, avoiding the hovering reporters. I'd wander around the Medford streets, scuffing my feet through the slush, not caring if I was cold or wet, not going home until it was dark and only a couple of stragglers were left. I couldn't talk to anyone. I couldn't even tell Bette's family I was sorry.

A few days after the inquest, I began to feel terribly sick and could hardly swallow. I still went to school, because there I could think about other things. I remember starting to feel much worse after my art class.

My mother found me delirious on the living room couch, still with my coat on. She said she knew I was really sick when I started singing Christmas carols in a croaky voice.

"Pneumonia," Dr. Landy told her. He treated me with penicillin, a new miracle drug still difficult to obtain. "First civilian I've used it on," Dr. Landy said. He had to treat me at home because Dr. Landy was Jewish and in 1947 Jewish doctors were refused privileges at Medford's Lawrence Memorial Hospital.

A few months later, when my parents moved to a rooming house a couple of blocks away, I stayed behind with the doctor and his wife in the big white house. I wasn't completely well. Sometimes I'd have dreams or fantasies about Bette, usually when I was dozing off or starting to wake up. I'd see her in a distance, coming out of the Biltmore Hotel, walking through ornate bronze and glass doors. I'd be off to the side, calling her name. "Bette! Bette! Don't go!" I'd yell, "Come with me! Over *here*! Over *here*! Sometimes she'd turn as if she heard something, hesitate, then start walking away. Sometimes she'd smile and walk towards me.

I joined my parents in the rooming house after Memorial Day. In a corner of their spacious room, behind a Chinese screen, they'd set up a cot for me. A small dining table placed in front of the bay window helped to give the room a homey appearance.

"We don't expect to stay too long," my parents said. They had bought a house in West Medford, using my brother Skip's allotment checks as down payment. But the post-war housing shortage was still severe—it might be another full year before the renters could be evicted and we could move in.

The fighting of my parents woke me up one night. I pretended to be asleep and pulled the blanket tight against my chin. I could hear the scuffling as my father tried to grab my mother's suitcase. He called the police. I heard the policeman tell my father, "If she wants to leave, she can. I can't make her stay."

The next day Goldie, the landlady, gave an ultimatum. She ran a respectable rooming house and couldn't have scenes "like that" with police banging on the door and waking everyone up. We were asked to leave.

My father and I moved to West Medford and lived with my Uncle Phil's family. Every night my father and I went for a walk. He would tell me how heartbroken and lonely he was since my mother left. He'd talk about all the terrible things she'd done, recalling events going back to the 1920s. We'd stop at a diner. I'd dig into a mocha cake and drink Pepsi as he talked. I seemed to crave sweets all the time, and it showed. I was becoming very fat.

I started going for walks by myself, and I stopped attending church. The art museum become my new haven. I'd spend Saturdays and Sundays wandering around, finding consolation in the great works of art.

One day as I passed a newsstand, a headline caught my eye: "Four Teens Killed in Auto Wreck." The young people were from another city. I didn't know them. But something uncontrollable welled up inside me, and I began to cry heavy, convulsive sobs. I hurried away, not wanting people to see my tears.

For months I cried—I'd think of Bette, and I'd cry. I'd barely make it through a day at school. I avoided my classmates. I'd stay in my room crying for hours—every day. I wrote a poem for Bette. I drew pictures of Bette standing on a hill beside a tree, much like the one in the Commons. The wind was blowing her hair.

I slimmed down, and as soon as I turned sixteen, I started wearing black—a black sheath dress, black lacy underwear, black garter belt and black stockings with seams down the back. I compared myself to Bette: I do not wear powder... unlike Bette; I wear high heels and black stockings... like Bette; my forehead is not high... unlike Bette; my eyes are blue... like Bette; I am a brunette... like Bette; I am "boy crazy"... like Bette; I buy my clothes at Ruth's... like Bette; I go for walks, alone... like Bette; I do not drink... like Bette; I do not smoke... like Bette; I do not swear... like Bette; I am a *nice* person... like *Bette*, and I am going to be an *actress... like Bette.*

I didn't talk to anyone about her. I went to art school, received a master's degree, married twice, raised four children, but never once did I mention Bette, not even to my husbands. She had become a separate part of me, something disconnected and stored in a black space deep inside of me. Sometimes I'd think about my last time with her. And I'd play it over and over in my head like a scene from a movie, but in slow motion.

I'm looking through the lace curtains watching Bette walk up the front stairs. She knocks on the door. My mother answers, and I run past her, onto the porch. Bette takes my hand and we walk down the steps, across the street, stopping at the gas station. She's talking to someone and I shift from foot to foot. We continue on our way. It's spring and the light is dancing off the buildings.

We stop at Ruth's Dress Shoppe, where Bette tries on different dresses. I sit and watch Bette's reflections in the three-way mirror. We leave the dress shop and go into the ice cream parlor. It is dark and cool inside. Bette is laughing and raising a spoon to her lips. She is talking, but I cannot hear the words. Her face comes closer, and she is talking and smiling, but there is no sound.

When I moved to California with my second husband, Cliff Humphrey, I almost expected to find Bette waiting for me. I could imagine her standing in front of the palm trees, or I could see her reflection in the store windows. In Hollywood I paid homage to Bette's presence, walking the "walk of the stars," reading the names: Errol Flynn, Clark Gable, Jane Withers, Rita Hayworth, Deanna Durbin....

I had long since forgotten the address where Bette lived; it could have been any one of the apartments I passed. I didn't want to see or think of where her body had been left. That was not part of the pilgrimage.

I became a professional artist, but I harbored a deep need to work for social change. I worked as a county social worker for a while. In the late 1960s, I became committed to causes—first, against the Viet Nam War and then for protection of the environment. While living in various parts of California, I worked with my husband, Cliff Humphrey, on ecological issues and pursued my career as an artist—until a series of isolated events sent me down an unexpected path.

One evening, while I was relaxing and watching a television newscast with Cliff, a teaser came on the screen—an advertisement for a true-crime TV movie that was to be aired later that week. At the mention of a body cut-in-half, a sense of unreality seemed to descend on me. I abruptly turned the television set off. My husband asked me what was wrong.

"I knew her," I said.

"Knew who?" he asked.

"The woman they're talking about. That's about the Black Dahlia."

I asked my husband if he remembered anything about the murder—he had grown up in the Los Angeles area.

"Vaguely," Cliff replied. He thought it happened a few days

after his tenth birthday. "She had been cut in half. That's what I recall. A scary murder for a kid. But you never said anything about *knowing* her. How did you *know* her?" he asked.

"From my hometown. She lived next door. She was nice to me when I was a kid," I said. I began to feel confused, as if some long-forgotten thoughts were trying to break through to my consciousness.

The next few nights there were more announcements. I caught the name of the movie: *Who Is the Black Dahlia?* starring Lucy Arnaz. My anxiety increased. I'd jump when the phone rang. I developed strange fears. I didn't want to be alone at night. I wouldn't use the restroom in the library because it was in the basement and down a long corridor. I felt as if I could not bear to see the movie, and yet, I felt *compelled* to watch it.

I was only dimly aware of Cliff's presence as I viewed the made-for-TV film. Most of the movie seemed irrelevant; too many facts were changed. The lead actress didn't project the beauty and magnetism of Bette. I was able to stay removed—until the long shot of a 1940s car driving up to the vacant lot. There were sounds of the car door opening and the engine idling. The exhaust was rising in the air as a shadowy figure moved about in the lot behind the car. Then the car door slammed again, and the car drove off.

Bette's ordeal was over.

I started painting with a vengeance: the head of the Blessed Virgin weeping tears of blood; three women, also weeping; a woman holding a flower; a woman in a cave; a woman staring straight ahead with a challenging, almost vengeful look. I gave mythological titles to the paintings: *Antigone*, *Medea*, *Iphigenia*. I painted another series with deep cadmium red and brilliant yellow eyes, "reminiscent of Munch," an art critic said.

A couple of years later, on a 4th of July weekend, my husband's cousin, Jeanne Bekey, came to visit. Cliff was working, our son was off with his friends, and I was left to entertain the company. Jeanne told me she liked to visit old cemeteries and sometimes made rubbings of the gravestones. "There's an old cemetery near here, Mountain View," I said. "I've never been there. But a friend who died, who was murdered years ago, is buried there. And I've always wanted to put flowers on her grave."

We stopped in the cemetery office and were given an oversize leather-bound volume from 1947. Written in a beautiful script was the name: Elizabeth Short, plot number 798.

The lawn on the hillside was cut, but most of the flat stones were overgrown with crabgrass. We started at the top, each taking a row on the hillside, brushing aside the growth. On the fourth row I came to a pink stone and the words: "DAUGHTER, Elizabeth Short, 1924-1947." I felt a sense of poignancy as I pushed the grass aside; a feeling that at last, forty years later, I was facing the fact that Bette is *dead*, and that she had been *murdered*.

A few weeks later I made a print unlike anything I had done before—*Urban Landscape*—Bette lying in the vacant field. I called an artist friend, Jan Siegel, and told him I needed to show him my latest piece.

As I sat in my darkened studio waiting for Jan, I thought about Bette, how sometimes when I crossed the railroad tracks, or heard a train, I'd feel her presence.

Jan told me he remembered the murder. He had grown up in Southern California, halfway between Los Angeles and San Diego. "I was a kid, but I remember hearing about the woman cut in half, the Black Dahlia. She sounded so notorious."

"The murder was never solved," I said.

"Your print is very strong," Jan said. "Very powerful."

Jan called me a few weeks later. "Mary," he said, "there's a new book out by Kenneth Anger, *Hollywood Babylon II*, and there's a few pages devoted to your friend's murder. There's photos of her body, and Mary, it's uncanny," he said. "They're like your print, but from a different angle. It's as if you were there, off to the side, and the photographer was standing straight on."

Jan asked me if I wanted to read the book. I said no. "I don't think I ever saw photos of her in the field," I told him. "I'm sure photos like that wouldn't have been printed in the 1947 newspapers."

Around Christmas time, my husband and I went to a party. I

became a little tipsy from the eggnog and wandered into another room. I spotted the Kenneth Anger book on the coffee table. I hesitated, opened the book slowly, and turned to the page of the photos. My vision seemed to blur and then become intensely sharp, as if looking through a tunnel. People's voices sounded far away, in the background with a hollow sound. I told Cliff I had to leave. He was feeling sociable and wanted to stay. "Right now! I have to leave!" I said, a note of hysteria creeping into my voice. Cliff said he'd get our coats.

I couldn't talk for a couple of days. It was as if my mouth was sealed shut, or I had lost the ability to speak. I didn't answer the telephone. I sat for hours in my studio.

I wrote to Kenneth Anger, asking if the photos had been published before, if I possibly could have seen them as a child. I included a photo of my *Urban Landscape* print. He wrote back: "This is the first time they have been published. I think you have a psychic link with Elizabeth Short."

A few months later, the gallery that handled my work, Lawson's, displayed a group show. A particular piece by the artist Bob Laney caught my eye. On a wooden bier, a black waxen figure of a woman lay covered by rose petals—only her face showing. A horrific gargoyle head with a long neck emerged from the petals near her feet and faced her. That night I dreamt the rose petals were crying tears of blood.

I spoke to Peggy Gotthold, the manager of the gallery, about my strange dream. "You didn't know?" she asked. "That was Bob's homage to his sister. She was murdered in Santa Cruz. They were very close, and he had a hard time when she was killed. She was a student at the University in Santa Cruz."

I couldn't get Bette out of my mind. I felt compelled to do something. I talked to Bob Laney, and we came up with the idea of a show called *In Memoriam*—works done in memory of someone close to the artist. In all, fifteen artists took part in the exhibit. They each wrote a statement about their work. When public venues turned the exhibit down as "inappropriate," Don Lawson said he'd show the work in his gallery.

I turned my print into a triptych, *The Martyrdom of Elizabeth Short*. The first panel, *The Red Ribbon*, represents

Bette alive, holding a red ribbon that symbolizes her fate; the second panel, *Urban Landscape*, depicts Bette's cast-off body; the last panel, *The Blue Flame*, has two figures; a blue flame, symbolizing the truth, jumps from the hand of the figure in the foreground.

Jan Siegel called me the week before the scheduled opening of the exhibit and said he had something for me. He gave me a book by James Ellroy, a work of fiction titled *The Black Dahlia*. I opened the book gingerly, and there, on the first page, the word "whore" jumped out at me. I slammed the book shut, and a deep, deep anger welled up inside me. I sat for a few minutes. Then opened the book again and started to read the staccato of words. Real names and places were mixed up with the author's fictionalized account.

I wrote a letter to Ellroy. "I'm not offended," I said, "because your book has nothing to do with Bette Short, nothing to do with the real person who was known as the Black Dahlia."

He called me one night, around midnight. My husband and I were sitting in the kitchen having a late night snack. Ellroy said that I was the first person he talked to who actually *knew* the Black Dahlia. He asked me if Bette's mother, Phoebe, was still alive. He would like to talk to her. "It's *Mrs.* Short," I said. "We called her *Mrs.* Short. And she would not talk to *you*. Not after what you wrote about her daughter and the family."

Ellroy said he was going to call me back, but never did. I wrote him a couple of letters. He didn't answer.

Then my friend, Jan Siegel, sent me a clipping from People magazine—an article about the Black Dahlia murder. Bette was described as "the perfect murder victim... the woman no one would miss." I thought of how deeply I *missed* Bette. I thought of Ellroy's book and his description of Bette as a "whore." I was filled with a blinding rage. After all these years, after so much had transpired and changed, why?

A strange energy began to propel me—a deep need to find answers, to tell the true and complete story. But the burning question was not *why* Bette had been murdered, not even *who* killed her, but why Bette must be described as someone of no account, someone who got what she deserved—a *WHORE*.

FOUR
Revisiting the Past

I was timid at first, and fearful. I didn't have the foggiest notion of how to interview people, or what questions to ask. Calling strangers and probing seemed against my nature. After weeks of hesitation, I decided to start with people I knew, and in December of 1987, I called my brother Bob.

The tenderness in his voice surprised me. "Yes," he said, "I'll talk to you about Bette Short. And I can put you in touch with some of her boyfriends."

In forty years we had never discussed Bette or her murder. If someone broached the subject at family gatherings, my mother would say, "Why do you want to talk about her? Best to let sleeping dogs lie!" But this time when I called my mother, she talked nonstop about the old neighborhood and about Bette— what Bette wore, how she walked, how friendly Bette was to all the neighbors. At one point, towards the end of her monologue, my mother paused and heaved a sigh. "I liked Bette. I couldn't help it," she said, as if Bette was someone she wasn't supposed to like.

My mother suggested that I take a trip back east in the spring time when my sister Margie would be visiting from Missouri. My mother lived in the same New England city as my brother Bob. My eldest sister, Eleanor, lived a few miles away. "Maybe if we're all together," suggested my mother, "we can help each other remember better. It was all so long ago."

In May of 1988, I embarked on my first trip back east in fifteen years. I went by train to Boston, caught a bus to Maine, stayed a few days, and then visited my hometown—Medford, Massachusetts. My Aunt Dot and Uncle Hector still lived there. For my return trip home, I planned a stop-over in Los Angeles. I had tracked down a few of the original reporters who covered the case, and they'd agreed to an interview.

I traveled by coach on the first leg of my trip. In Chicago I switched trains and changed to a sleeping car. The three-day train ride became a symbolic journey back in time. I thought about Bette and her travels back and forth across the country. I felt as if I was retracing her steps. I made notes of questions to ask during the interviews. My memories of Bette were through a child's eyes. I wondered how other people recalled her.

From Boston's South Station I took a cab to the Greyhound Bus Depot. (The old railroad station had yet to be transformed into Boston's transportation hub.) My two sisters, Eleanor and Margie, greeted me at the station when the bus pulled into Lewiston.

Our mother had a pot of strong coffee and homemade apple pie waiting for us. When my brother Bob arrived, we served ourselves and gathered in the living room. The afternoon sun flooded my mother's small apartment, and the sounds of distant children floated in from the outside. Bob made himself comfortable in a dark blue overstuffed chair in the corner. My mother sat opposite in a blue-patterned chintz armchair and rested her feet on a matching footstool. Margie and Eleanor sat side by side on the couch. I chose the maple rocking chair.

For a while we discussed the old neighborhood. Bob drew a map of the houses on Fifield Court and Salem Street, and the stores in Washington Square. We recalled the poverty of the Depression years.

"If you had a job, any job, you were considered rich," Bob said.

We talked about the difficulties of the war years. After a few moments of awkward silence, I broached the subject of Bette Short.

"Forget about the murder," I said. "Think about Bette alive—what you remember about her, the first time you met her, the last time you saw her."

My family needed no other prompting. Everyone seemed eager to talk, as if compelled to express thoughts and emotions harbored during years of silence. I placed a tape recorder with a microphone on the coffee table and pressed the "Record" button. My mother looked directly at me and began to speak.

"Bette liked your father, you know—and you," she said. "You and Bette looked so cute together. Both of you had dark hair and bright blue eyes. And you weren't like other kids. She could take you to the movies and you'd watch, not jump around, or be asking for candy or tonic. She'd always tell me how good you behaved. Sometimes she'd come over for a cup of coffee, usually when Bob was around. She and your father used to tease Bob awful. He'd blush so." My mother leaned over, glanced at Bob, and whispered, "I think Bette was sweet on Bob."

As my mother spoke, I could visualize the old black stove in the buff-colored kitchen of our house on Fifield Court. Shadow figures slowly emerged into the light—my father egging Bette on, Bob with his open books and face turning crimson as he tried to study. I could see myself in the little bedroom off the kitchen. I was supposed to be asleep, but I was listening and watching.

Bob's laughter jarred me back to the present, reminding me that the year was 1988 and that I was in Lewiston, Maine.

"If you were shy, Bette loved to tease you—kiddingly, not mean," he said. "I'd get so embarrassed by the two of them when they ganged up on me, I'd have to leave the room! I'd tell them I had to study. I was uncomfortable around girls. I guess, in a sense, I was *afraid* of Bette. We were the same age, but she seemed so *sophisticated*. Maybe we were fifteen or sixteen then. Dad tried to get me to take her to the Senior Prom. But I didn't dance." Bob was silent for a moment. "He kidded me about someday marrying Bette."

I turned towards my sisters. "What about you, Margie?" I asked. "What comes to mind when you think of Bette?"

"Bette was prettier without her makeup on," Margie said. "That's what I think. I remember one day going up to her apartment on the top floor, and she answered the door, standing there in a light blue chenille bathrobe, with a towel wrapped around her hair. She had just washed her hair. And she looked so pretty. Her high cheek bones and creamy skin. I always thought she had cat's eyes. You know, the kind that change colors. Sometimes they'd be blue, and other times they looked greenish. It depended on what colors she was wearing.

"I used to pal around with Muriel sometimes. We were the same age, in classes together. Bette and Muriel were the two Shorts I knew. I remember Muriel being very popular and having a lot of friends. Do you remember the song, 'Personality?' That described Bette and Muriel to a 'T.' They had *personality*." A note of sadness crept into Margie's voice.

"I always felt bad for Mrs. Short," Margie said. She glanced away, towards the window. "Mrs. Short was a hard-working woman, just trying to bring up her girls! What happened to Bette, it's a mother's worst nightmare." Margie let out a sigh, then continued. "The sisters did fight. But I don't think Bette and Muriel fought, or Nonie. Sometimes, when the windows were open you might hear the older girls, especially if their mother wasn't home.

"I remember the newspapers made a big deal about the condition of Bette's teeth, that she had cavities."

"Everyone had bad teeth. Who had the money for dentists during the Depression?" my mother asked. "And during the war where were the dentists? They were all in the service. That's where they were. Even if your face was puffed up, you'd have to wait days to find one. By then it would be too late. I'm lucky I still have most of my teeth."

"I can remember going to the Forsyth in Boston to have my teeth cleaned," Eleanor said. "We'd have a holiday. Be bussed over in groups. But I never really saw a dentist or had a tooth filled until much later, after the war."

I changed the subject and asked Margie if she remembered the last time she saw Bette.

"The last time I saw Bette? That would be in 1945," Margie said. "The war was still on, and I was working at the soda fountain in Liggett's on Tremont Street in Boston. I wore a beige-and-green uniform with an apron and a little doohickey on my head. I thought I looked horrible. But Bette would tell me the colors looked good on me. She'd come in and sit at the counter. Have a cold drink. She didn't try to pick up anyone, but just would be friendly to people around her. I can't remember much of what we talked about, just remember it was always interesting to talk to her. The manager didn't like her. I think it was because she wouldn't give him a tumble.

"I saw her a couple of times after that, when her boyfriend was killed. I'm pretty sure the war was over, because Frank and I eloped soon after.

"Bette had a walk like none I've ever seen—standing very straight and tall, walking very fast, taking short quick steps, even in platform shoes. You couldn't help but notice her, the way she walked."

Everyone in the room laughed. We all knew that walk!

"An *un-be-liev-able* walk!" Bob said. "Her body moved *smoothly*, didn't bounce. I felt she could have had a full glass of water on her head and wouldn't have spilled a drop." I remember her as being tall and slender, with dark hair, pale, very pale skin, and blue eyes. Quite something... and with that walk! How the wolves did howl when Bette walked by!"

"Sometimes," Margie continued, "when I'd see her walk down Salem Street [in Medford] I'd see her sort of *casually* look around. I'm sure she was looking to see if anyone was watching her. Bette liked to be *noticed*. And the way her hips moved, it wasn't just a wiggle. *Different*. You could never forget that walk."

Margie heaved another sigh, and for a few moments no one spoke. There seemed to be a heaviness permeating the room—a futile desire to bring Bette back to life, or wishful thinking that *it* had never happened.

Bob broke the silence. "I can never remember Bette roughhousing," he said. "But she wasn't quiet—not a shrinking violet. She was always friendly, never at a loss for words. And it wasn't just that she was so pretty. There are lots of pretty girls. There was something *different*. She was someone you liked to *watch*, the kind of girl that boys might *sneak* looks at, but would get tongue-tied if she spoke to you."

"You can take your Marilyn Monroe!" my mother exclaimed. "She's *nothing* compared to the way Bette walked down the street!"

Margie began to speak again. "Sometimes Bette would meet me and we'd go shopping together in Boston. The day I bought my peacoat was very embarrassing. The sales lady asked me if I wanted to wear it home, and I told her, yes. She put the sales slip with my old coat and wrapped them inside a box. On the way out we were stopped by the store detective, and brought to a small room. I unwrapped the box and showed him the sales slip.

He apologized and said everything was okay. I had been a little nervous, but Bette wasn't flustered. Just took it in stride!

"One night we were sitting on the stoops and talking about her trips, and her plans. She could hardly wait to turn twenty-one—a few more months. She hated the work permits that women under twenty-one had to carry.

"Bette's boyfriends treated her with respect, like a lady. If I had a date with a guy who had a car, he'd honk the horn and I'd come running out. But not Bette! I remember watching as her dates went all the way up the three flights of stairs, and when they came out, they opened the car door for her, helped her in and out. She was treated like a lady."

"Well," my mother said with a touch of huffiness in her voice, "I always thought Bette was *look*, but *don't touch*!"

My mother paused, and Eleanor began to speak. "Bette always seemed on *stage*," my sister Eleanor said. "I was a pal of Dot Short's. We were two years older than Bette, and graduated from Medford High in 1940. Dottie was a cut-up, a character—used to get me in trouble in school, call my name and then when I'd turn around the teacher would catch me.

"Dottie, Bette, and I were going to be movie stars. We were entranced with movie stars, star struck. Every Friday, as soon as the song sheets came out, we'd pool our money, get the latest sheets, and spend hours singing. We each had a favorite movie star that we identified with. Dottie was Judy Canova, and I was Jane Withers. Bette imitated Deanna Durbin—walked like her, talked like her, and in my eyes, sang like her.

"I remember Mrs. Short as being very strict with her girls. She worked and wasn't home during the day. The girls couldn't have friends in the house when she wasn't there. Or we couldn't come over around meal time. The house was always very neat and clean. The girls all had chores, helped out. Bette and Dottie were in demand as baby-sitters. The rates were twenty-five cents before midnight and an extra ten cents if you stayed after midnight.

"Last time I saw Bette was in 1941, just before the war, at Griffin's across Salem Street from our house. Do you remember it? A small square icecream parlor, it later became a fried chicken place. When you walked in, the stools and counter were to the right. I remember Bette sitting at the stool wearing a leopard fur coat and hat. Dressed to the *minute*. Sophisticated. I was very impressed! She was so striking! And I thought, 'Dottie's kid sister has sure *grown up*! I felt like a country bumpkin. Bette had just come back from a trip. She was very *up*. Looked like she could have been a movie star."

"I thought she might be going with Mr. Griffin," my mother said. "Bette was in the restaurant across the street all the time. I think she had a father complex. I never saw her with a man, except once on the trolley, coming home from work. She was with an older man."

"I don't remember Bette having boy friends when we all hung out," Eleanor said. "Ginnie, the oldest daughter, dated a lot. We used to envy her because she was old enough to go on dates, and could wear make up. That would have been around 1937-38. Don't recall Bette sneaking out on dates. That was *unthinkable*. She didn't seem interested in boys, just in being a movie star."

Bob said he couldn't remember the first time he saw Bette. "Always seemed to know her from first grade at Washington School on," he said. "She was in my classes until high school. But if you asked me what I remember most about when we were kids, it would be the day the airship, the *Hindenburg*, went over Roberts Junior High School—early May 1937. Something you can never forget! The ship had made good time crossing the Atlantic and was a few hours early. The newsreel cameras weren't set up in New Jersey to catch its arrival, so the captain veered off course and went sight-seeing up the New England coast. Word spread about the ship coming and the teachers went crazy. All hell broke lose! Kids were running back and forth across the hall to the classrooms on the other side, afraid they'd miss something. We were supposed to use fire-drill procedures and watch from the schoolyard. Hardly anyone made it outside.

"The shadow first, that's what we saw—a huge shadow moving on the ground, darkening the school, blocking the light almost like an eclipse. Kids were crowding around the windows. The airship was moving pretty fast, faster than what we expected. I remember looking around the room and catching a glimpse of Bette—one of the other boys helping her onto a chair so she could get a better look.

"Throughout 1937, '38, '39, '40, '41, maybe even '42, Bette was coming over our house, especially when the fife and drum corps practiced. I remember her being sick off and on, so she never became a majorette.

"She dropped out of school, but she was in town when I graduated and signed my yearbook. I brought it with me so you can take a look." Bob rummaged through his briefcase and took out a dark blue book with white lettering on the cover: Medford High School Yearbook—1942. He opened the book and flipped through a couple of pages. "It's funny," he said, "the day she came over to sign it, we couldn't find a pen, and she signed in pencil. Everyone else signed in ink." He handed me the open book. For a couple of minutes I stared at her penciled signature. Then I passed the book around.

"What about the last time you saw her, Bob?" I asked.

"The last time I saw Bette was in Spring of 1944. I was home on leave, and Bette was walking down the street towards Medford Square. She was wearing a fur coat. Dad wanted me to go out and say hello to her, but I was married then, and didn't think it was a good idea." He paused. "I've always regretted that I didn't go and say something to Bette Short."

Before Bob went home, he gave me some names and phone numbers—old boyfriends of Bette. "Over the years, when we'd get together," Bob said, "Her name would come up, and we'd talk about her. After all this time, it's still hard to accept what happened to her."

Bette's former boyfriends all agreed to an interview. "I'm not wearing rose-colored glasses," I told each of them. "Please, don't hold back."

As I sat drinking coffee with Ralph Southworth in a beachside cafe, he said that Bette was his first love. "When we both went to Roberts Junior High School. I always thought it was funny that Bette wouldn't let me come to her house," he said. "We'd always meet somewhere and once in a while go to a movie, but mostly talk, and sometimes hold hands, and occasionally kiss—once or twice."

Ralph was an orphan at the time, living with a foster family in Fulton Heights. He said he always felt like an outsider. Ralph played the harmonica, and sometimes Bette would sing along. "She liked to hear me play the latest songs," Ralph smiled. "I always thought of Bette as a porcelain China doll—fragile. Bette was moody. Sometimes she'd be shy, other times she'd be talkative."

Ralph remembered taking Bette to the Medford Theater to see movies—always a musical. "She liked to take a roundabout route down Ashland Street with its big oaks and elms."

"Do you think maybe you took the roundabout route because Bette wasn't supposed to be dating?" I asked.

Ralph laughed. "Come to think of it, could be. I always thought it was strange. We were fourteen or fifteen then. We'd go to the United Farmers Ice Cream Parlor after a movie and share a banana split. And as dainty and as ladylike as she seemed, she'd plunge right into the ice-cream. She was a very sweet girl. No matter what the papers said, I never could think of her as the *Black Dahlia*."

I visited Joe Sabia in his large two-story home. He waited for me in a cluttered, upstairs office. "Everything at my fingertips," Joe said and then laughed. He sat in a plush office chair that rolled around on its casters. Joe Sabia was disabled. "When I was in my early thirties, I was told I'd never get out of a wheelchair," he said. "So, I never got in one."

Joe told me that he and Bette Short weren't really boyfriend and girlfriend. "I knew Bette in 1944. Maybe it was in late summer or early autumn," he said. "I remember the weather was mild. And I remember her wearing a light blue two-piece dress or suit that reflected the color of her eyes. And a black or dark-colored raincoat, which in those days was an all-purpose coat. She'd come into the Medford Cafe. It would be late at night, around midnight. I was a student at Leland Powers School of Radio, my last year. I was 4F. Sometimes I'd be alone. Sometimes I'd be with some pool-playing buddies, usually Stewie, Snuffy and Warren. The pool hall, which was downstairs in the same building as the Medford Cafe, closed at midnight, and we'd go upstairs to the Cafe to get something to eat.

"You didn't enter the Medford Cafe off the street. There was an alcove or windbreaker entryway. When you went in, you'd take a check from a machine on the right, pull it out, and with a little ring of a bell the next check would appear. The cafe was dark, high ceilings, with globes hanging from chains. The walls were dark and paneled with booths across two of the walls, and lots of dark-wood tables and chairs in the center. It was a large square room, and the front wall had windows across it. The Cafe served all kinds of meals and great cheeseburgers—the best. Sugar was rationed, so Al, the counterman, would put the sugar and cream in your coffee. My friends liked to sit at a table in the middle of the room. Bette liked the booths out of the spotlight. She seemed like a private person, embarrassed by the guys' off-color remarks.

"Sometimes Bette would join us, and we'd move to a booth, but then she'd leave if the conversation got rough or vulgar. Usually she could handle things, had a way of freezing you with a look. She disliked Warren and Stewie's innuendoes. Warren was a professional wolf. He figured every woman put out, just a matter of the amount of time and effort needed. He'd say that Bette was built like a brick shit house, and that every brick lays. Stuff like that. Stewie wanted to be like Warren, imitated him, but somehow never could score, while Snuffy envied them because he didn't dare try. I was the quiet one, serious, in radio school, wanting to be an announcer. Most of the time Bette would ignore the other guys and talk to me. Sometimes we'd have a booth by ourselves."

Joe said he enjoyed sitting alone with Bette, drinking coffee and talking about who was in the service or home on leave. "We'd discuss how school was going for me," Joe said, "my plans to be a radio announcer, and about Bette's trips and dreams of being a movie star. We'd talk about what we were going to do after the war. Sometimes I couldn't hide my embarrassment about being 4F. Bette would try to make me feel better, telling me that she was sure I was doing my part for the war effort, and that people in radio were needed.

"Bette didn't laugh a lot, more like quiet smiles. She had a soft voice, low, refined, not tough—a shadow figure. I remember her flawless white, white alabaster skin and black, black hair. She had lipstick-shaped full lips, no rouge. She wasn't brazen, not a hussy. If it's true what they say, that she was a prostitute, she'd be a high-class one. I felt that she was afraid to come out of her shell, that the world intimidated her. She would never admit that anything troubled her. 'It's nothing, nothing important,' she'd say. I can't see her picking up just any guy casually. But then, everyone is naive at twenty-two." Joe stopped talking, and for a few moments we sat in silence.

"When I think of Bette," he said, "I think of her as a victim of our time. She wanted to be somebody famous. She had stars in her eyes, dreams rather than plans. Nature gave her a great endowment. She didn't wear seductive clothes, didn't need to. She was meticulous, neat. I think of her as beautiful, but a very private person with a sadness about her—a void, something missing. She seemed older than her years, more mature. Somehow I felt she didn't know how to cope with the changes after the war.

"I could never equate Bette with the *Black Dahlia*. I sometimes think about the nights that I watched her walk up Salem Street, watching until I no longer heard the clicking of her heels on the pavement and she disappeared from sight. Maybe it was her walk—maybe that was her downfall."

Jeff Tyler, a tall, distinguished man with thinning gray hair asked that I not use his real name. He was a well-respected legislator, a statesman. I interviewed him in my brother's study. "Not sure how my wife or my constituents would take it," he said, "even though it all happened years ago. I was the manager of a store in Medford then—in the nineteen forties, 1944 to 1948, to be exact. I lived in a rooming house on Ashland Street in Medford, a big rambling, Victorian house. I had a deferment. I raised a lot of money on war bond drives for the war effort. With a quota of selling seven-thousand dollars in War Bonds, I led a drive that sold close to three-million dollars' worth.

"I met Bette when I moved to Medford in 1944. Saw her whenever she came back for a visit. I was shocked by her murder, and felt so sorry for her. Bette was condemned for things she never should have been. She was *sexy*, and people condemned her for the way she flaunted herself.

"I felt that Bette had been through a tough life, and I wanted to help her. Somewhere she was looking for something. She was smart enough, but I always felt she was not utilizing her full capabilities. I tried to tell her.

"She never talked about her family, and she never took me home. We'd always meet at places. She seemed to want companionship. If I tried to talk serious, she'd say, 'Let's just live for today... forget our problems... just enjoy the time together. Often we'd go out for a cheeseburger and just sit and talk. I had a good reputation at the time. I told her I wanted to wash the make-up off her face, wanted her to be her natural self, but I never firmly said to her, 'Be yourself!'"

"She had a white fur coat, and I always figured she had a sugar daddy in Florida. Bette was out to have a good time, but sex wasn't involved. She was very trusting. Sometimes we'd give each other massages—nude. It was really innocent. I'd sneak her into my room. Of course that wasn't allowed in the rooming house. It was sort of daring. I was basically very shy, but she had a way of drawing you out, and making you feel relaxed. Bette had a beautiful body. I think she took a lot of pride in it. I remember she had a large brown birthmark the size of a quarter on her shoulder. Bette never mentioned boyfriends. She was a loner. And seemed to be floating, wandering with no direction. I was questioned by the FBI. They said my name was in her address book."

On the drive down to Medford with my cousin Ron, we talked about growing up next door to each other and the directions our lives had taken. I had moved away when I was eighteen. He stayed in Medford, married, and only recently moved to New Hampshire.

When we reached Medford, we drove by the old neighborhood. I was startled when I saw the freeway overpass. A small office building stood in place of the big white house where

I once lived.

Ron parked the car. The city hall was still there, and, amazingly, the old forsythia and lilac bushes at the edge of the Commons. "The expressway came through in the fifties," Ron explained, as we started to walk around. "Fifield Court and all the houses on Salem Street clear up to Washington Square are gone. Your old house was the only building that was not torn down right away. It stood there for quite a while, but vacant. No one wanted to live next to the expressway. So, finally it was razed."

"What about the Revolutionary War Cemetery that was at the end of the Court?" I asked.

"That was relocated to Oak Grove. Taking out the old cemetery was very controversial." Ron pointed to the expressway. "Under the overpass, that's where I figure the Short's three-decker used to be."

My Aunt Dot had lunch waiting—tuna fish sandwiches on white bread and strong, hot coffee. "Your Uncle Hector's having lunch with some friends, so it's just us three," my aunt said. While we ate lunch, the three of us chit-chatted. We talked about the weather and about the past—the bad years during the Depression and how times have changed. "We never ate Spam, not in *my* house, not even during the Depression," my aunt said with a note of pride in her voice.

As soon as there was a lull in the conversation, I began to talk about Bette. Aunt Dot cut me off. "I know you're writing a book," she said. "Ron told me all about it. But I can't help. I can't say anything bad about Bette. My Aunt shook her head. "I can't say anything bad about Bette."

"Aunt Dot, I don't want you to say anything bad about her. Why do you think I want you to say something *bad* about Bette?" I asked.

"That's what it's about. Everyone trying to dig up dirt. You say something, and they twist your words around. I never believed what the newspapers said about her! They said so many conflicting things." My Aunt Dot was becoming agitated. "Maybe Bette was different in California, but I can't believe she changed that much!"

During our exchange, my cousin Ron didn't say a word. He just sat at the table, sipping his coffee.

"Look, I want to write the *truth* about Bette, from the viewpoint of people who *knew* her and remember her. Everything written about her, it's by people who didn't know her."

"It was hard, really hard when Bette was murdered," my aunt said. She took a Kleenex from her apron pocket and wiped the tears that were forming in her eyes. "Your father and Hector really liked Bette. Your Uncle Hector won't talk about her, and he doesn't like me talking to you about her. Bette's murder really hurt him. She liked to tease Hector. Called him Horace.

"There was nothing quite like watching Bette chase Hector's chickens when they got loose. She'd spot them from her kitchen window and come running down her backstairs so that Butch [the dog] wouldn't get them. There'd be Bette running around the yard. She was slim, but busty, and she'd jiggle up and down when she chased the chickens. They'd be squawking and running every-which-way. There'd be feathers everywhere! The chickens would flap their wings, stirring up whirlwinds. I'd laugh like crazy watching her as she herded the chickens back into the coop. Then she'd try to cover up the hole they got out of with a piece of cardboard while the chickens poked their heads out, trying to make another run for it.

"And then there was the time when one of the chickens pecked Butch on the nose. So you had the dog howling, the chickens squawking, and me unable to help Bette because I was laughing so hard.

"When Hector came home from work and started puttering in the victory garden, Bette would lean over the railing of her back porch and start teasing him. 'Horace! I had to round up your chickens again! You better do something about your chickens, Horace!' He'd yell back at her, 'My name ain't Horace!'

"Bette would laugh and shake her finger at him. Bette was such a *good* person—nice... and funny... not a bit stuck up. She always stopped and chatted, made you feel at ease. She talked a lot to your father. I don't know what they talked about. Just that they'd talk a long time when he was sitting on the wall. I bet he didn't swear in front of Bette!"

"And *that* walk, Bette's walk!" My aunt grinned—a wide smile. "She just looked so *graceful*, but eye-catching, something to *look at*. The truck drivers and men would stare when she walked down the street. She *always* dressed to the nines.

"Bette and Muriel used to visit me, came over a lot. Bette was very good to Muriel, and the other sister, Nonie. Nonie was the shy one, and a little chubby growing up. Sometimes, when the windows were open, I could hear the oldest girls, Ginnie and Dottie, fighting with Bette and Muriel, but that happens with sisters.

"The reporters were all over my back yard. They'd try to talk to me, but I'd just run in the house, and I kept the kids away from them. Muriel couldn't go out alone, not even to the store. She needed someone to keep the reporters away.

"Afterwards, right after Bette died, Muriel would come over and talk about Bette, all the things she did for her, bought her little presents, was nice to her. But a few months later she seemed to want to forget. And never mentioned Bette again. The mother came back from California after the funeral and stayed for a few months. She left again after Muriel and Nonie married. The two girls and their husbands stayed in the apartment for a while. But the reporters wouldn't leave them alone. For a few years, every anniversary of the murder they'd show up. I saw them chase Muriel up the stairs when she was pregnant..."

The sound of the front door opening jarred my aunt, and she stopped talking. I saw my Uncle Hector standing in the entryway.

"Uncle Hector," I said, "It's great to see you!"

"What you up to, Pest?" he asked.

Uncle Hector knew I didn't like to be called by that name. He had given me the nickname when I was very young. My uncle had said I was a little kid who asked too many questions.

"Goodness, look what time it is!" my aunt exclaimed. "I'll make a fresh pot of coffee. I have brownies for dessert. Why don't you have dessert with us, Hector, if you're not too full." My uncle sat down and joined us at the table. For a while, the four of us made small talk, until Ron stood up and said we had to go, that he still had a few places to take me.

Outside, Ron said I looked as if I had just run ten laps around the track in one-hundred-degree heat.

"It's been an intense afternoon with your mother," I said. Ron offered to take me out for a lobster dinner. "To rejuvenate you," he said.

"I can't believe I'm doing this," I told Ron, as we waited for our lobsters to be served. "Every time I make a phone call or meet with someone, I get a terrible bout of anxiety. My stomach does flip-flops. And so far, it's mostly been relatives, or people I know! In a few days I'll be in Los Angeles talking to some old-time reporters, and maybe the police. Someone who lives in Pasadena, a young writer by the name of Mark Shostrum, gave me the phone number of the woman who discovered Bette's body. That's going to be a hard call to make."

"We need to make a toast for good luck," Ron said. He ordered a bottle of white wine. The waiter half-filled our glasses. "Here's an old Irish saying to help you along the way, " Ron said. He raised his glass. "As you go about your travels, may the road rise up to greet you, and may the wind be always at your back." We clicked our glasses together and drank the wine.

On subsequent trips back to Medford I found more people to interview: Helen Reed, Anna Dougherty, and Faye Adams (who were friends of Bette) and Aram Jaranian, our old grocer. The City Clerk of Medford, Joseph McGonagle, introduced me to Medford's former police chief, Charles V. Donovan, who remembered having late-night chats with Bette.

"I wasn't chief then," Donovan said. "I made captain in 1955 and became chief in 1961. In the 1940s I was a lieutenant. I remember seeing Bette Short in the Medford Cafe, around 1945, 1946. Bette worked in Cambridge, would come in the cafe late, around 1:10 a.m. She'd leave around 1:30 p.m. She'd always walk home alone. We'd kibitz. Bette was stunning, like a model. She wasn't shy. I used to wonder why she picked me to talk to. I was married at the time. Then I figured maybe I was protection against some of the guys who were ogling her.

"The Medford police cooperated with the Los Angeles

police at the time, but there wasn't much we could tell them. Nice family—none of the girls ever in trouble."

I met with Aram Jaranian in his large family home. He was in his late seventies. The black hair I remembered so well had turned snowy white. My family hadn't been Aram's customers for forty years, but he still remembered everyone's first names and the major events in our lives. "How's your mother?" Aram asked. "Emma, isn't it? And your father, Elmer? And your brother, Bob? Did he recover okay from his wounds?"

Aram told me he remembered Bette Short quite well. "A very nice, a very pretty girl," he said. "Such a shame. I remember seeing her taking you to Ben Shuman's for ice-cream cones. She seemed to be very good to you. Sometimes she'd stop and chat—when I was out front sweeping the sidewalk. Her mother shopped across the street at the A & P, so I didn't know her mother too well."

Bette had been Helen Reed's babysitter. "She took care of me and my two brothers," Helen said. "We loved her as a babysitter! Bette liked children. She entertained us, told us stories. She'd act out the different parts with hand motions and different voices for the characters. She never raised her voice, but would say, 'Don't do that. Your *mother* would not *approve.*'"

Helen described Bette as pretty, very neat, and stylish—not a hair out of place. "Bette was well brought up and acted like a lady," Helen remarked. "She seemed proud of her looks, and she was very polite. You'd think she was upper-middle class. I think it was her father who wanted her to get into the movies, sent her money to go to California. Bette Short was gone and came back changed—went Hollywood. She looked, dressed, and acted like a movie star, as if she had already made it! We thought that maybe she had. People in cars would look at her when she walked down the street. She had a sultry walk. It was like Bette was saying, 'I am here. I am a star! I think Medford was too quiet for her. She wanted excitement."

Anna Dougherty knew Bette Short casually. "Never friends, just to say hello, from around 1938 to 1946." Anna said. "I'd see her in classes—Bette a porcelain China doll with beautiful eyes.

I think of them as blue, but sometimes they would change color, depending on what she wore, and look green. She'd be here for a few months and then disappear. 'Porky' O'Neil from Washington Square took Betty to a prom. When he went in the service, Bette wrote to him. Her family was haunted by reporters. A lovely, lovely family. Just terrible. In those days your children were your whole world."

Faye Adams, the last home-town person I interviewed, said she only knew Bette by sight. "Bette was a friend of my cousin," Faye said. "They were school chums for years, good friends. Bette used to be over my aunt's house all the time. And then my cousin and Bette had a falling out. Bette told my cousin something, around 1942 or 1943. I don't know what it was. But it shocked my cousin. And she didn't want anything more to do with Bette. My cousin would never say what it was. Just said she didn't want to talk about it. I mentioned you to my cousin. I told her you were writing a book, but she won't talk to anyone."

I puzzled over Bette's secret, unable to imagine what could be so terrible. Her boyfriends had implied that Bette seemed troubled about something. People described Bette as a "private person, not one to confide." No wonder, I thought, considering the strong reaction Bette received when she confided a secret to a close friend.

I had been prepared to devote a few months to research—looking through old records and conducting interviews. But what I thought would last a few months turned into a strange ten-year odyssey.

I read old newspaper stories and put together a chronology that grew to eighty pages. Reading the old newspaper accounts jogged more than just my memory; I learned to live with constant anxiety. Sometimes it seemed as if I was caught in a time warp. I could almost feel the mugginess of the East Coast summers and the bitter cold of the winters.

From a variety of sources, I constructed a computerized list of more than 400 names—friends, neighbors, former boyfriends, and the police and reporters who covered the case. I tracked many of the people down. During some of the interviews I felt as if I was taking part in a ritual—almost a dance. I was the *one* being quizzed until the person felt confident I was, indeed, a friend from Bette's home town who wanted to tell the true story and "set the record straight."

At times my lack of interview skills worked to my advantage. When the conversations reached an awkward moment and I couldn't think of anything to ask, people would start talking, almost non-stop, as if they couldn't bear the silence. Information that I didn't even dream existed would tumble out.

I consulted with experts in the fields of police science and forensics, with doctors specializing in sexual aberrations and the pathology of sexual psychopaths. A network of people sent me information and gave me referrals. I gained access to officials close to the investigation who discussed with me unpublicized details of the case and their own privately held theories about who murdered the woman known as the Black Dahlia.

At university libraries I searched through little-known special collections. In the basements of the Los Angeles city and county buildings I went through dusty archival records, not sure what I was looking for.

My quest took me across the country many times—from California to Massachusetts with stopovers in Arizona, Illinois, Indiana, Missouri, New Mexico, Oklahoma, and Tennessee. In the third year of my research, the quest led to my divorce.

I was warned by former policemen and ex-reporters to be careful. While I waited at a bus stop on my way home from one "fact-finding" mission, my purse was slashed. During one of my trips to Los Angeles the house where I stayed was burglarized. Another time, I was held up at gun point—in broad daylight. My artwork was vandalized and torn off my walls. These were coincidences, most likely, but they made me pay attention to the warnings and become more alert to my surroundings.

FIVE
Cops and Reporters

The first reporters to reach the murder scene said they expected to find a drunk, possibly dead. With luck, they thought, it would be a has-been actor good for a human interest story describing how liquor ruined a once-great star. But none of the reporters were prepared for, and some never fully recovered from, the atrocity that greeted them on that clear, beautiful California day of January 15, 1947, when they responded to the police radio call of a "390 Down."

The newspapers reported two witnesses. An unidentified neighbor claimed he saw a medium-sized "hawk-nosed" man near the site on January 14th, the evening before the murder. The witness said the man was driving a light-colored older sedan.

Robert Meyer, a neighbor who lived at 3900 S. Bronson Avenue (one block over), told reporters that shortly after six, on the morning of January 15th, he opened his back door to let his dog into the yard. The man said he noticed frost on the ground and black smoke trailing across the sky. "From the smudge pots, I figured," he said. "Lit during the night to protect the orange groves."

The night had been cold, unusually cold, almost freezing. The sound of a car in the still morning air drew the man's attention—an older dark Ford. The man glanced towards the large vacant field a couple of blocks away on S. Norton Avenue. The car had parked in the driveway leading into the weeds, the engine idling, the headlights off.

The police logged an anonymous call at 10:40—a woman describing someone in a vacant lot on S. Norton Avenue between 39th and Coliseum. "A person needs attending to," the caller said, and abruptly hung up without giving her name. A few days later she called again and identified herself as Betty Bersinger.

"I didn't know the police were looking for me," Mrs. Bersinger told me when I interviewed her forty years later. She was leading a very private life and was still married to the same man.

"I made the call and then became very busy with my family. My daughter was sick with a cold. And I didn't have much time to think about what I saw," Mrs. Bersinger said. "I was on my way to the cobbler's, pushing my little girl in a Taylor Tot—remember them, light weight strollers, different from the baby carriages?

"It was the whiteness that caught my eye, the waxy whiteness. I turned the stroller around almost instinctively, to block my little girl's view. It was near the curb, and separated from the top. I thought a mannequin must have fallen from the truck," she said.

The head was turned slightly towards her, but Mrs. Bersinger couldn't see the features. Everything was blurry; she could just make out shiny dark reddish hair against a waxen figure. "I really thought it was a mannequin."

"But you knew you had to call the police?" I asked.

Mrs. Bersinger was silent for a moment. "Yes," she said. "Yes, I did. I knew I had to call the police. But I didn't run. I remember crossing the street, and not looking back. I just kept walking. When I reached the nearest house, I knocked on the screen door and asked the woman if I could use the phone..."

After making the call and thanking the woman, Mrs. Bersinger continued on her way. "But I went down another street." On the way back from Leimert Village she avoided Norton Avenue, taking Crenshaw Boulevard instead. "From a distance I could see a commotion, over a dozen cars and people milling about. I thought—Well, it's being taken care of."

A few minutes after eleven, Police Officers Frank Perkins and Will Fitzgerald in Radio Patrol Car 71 responded to the routine dispatch out of University Station... "Code 390... man down... 39th and Norton."

Agness Underwood, the aggressive police beat reporter for the *Los Angeles Herald Express,* was one of the first at the scene. The paper ran a photo of Aggie standing near her car and talking to the two policemen.

Aggie said Fitzgerald thought the woman was about thirty-five. "No," Aggie told him, "she's much younger, not much out of her teens." Aggie had noted the smoothness of the victim's skin and the firm thighs—a young woman, for sure.

"Looks like she must've been pretty, but hard to tell," Fitzgerald said to Aggie.

Perkins immediately made a call over the police radio to the watch commander at University Station, Lieutenant Freestone. "A bad one," Perkins told Freestone, describing the gouges and the mutilations. "The body's severed through the middle, and she's been cut from ear to ear." Like a "hideous clown's grin," reported the newspapers. The body had been left in plain view at the edge of the vacant lot, a stone's throw from where Ringling Bros. and Barnum & Bailey had set up their circus tents a few years back, in 1939 and 1941.

Freestone told Perkins to keep everyone out of the area. "I'll send Haskins right away, and the coroner. Keep everyone away. I'll put through to Central. Then I'll be on my way."

Lieutenant Jess Haskins carefully noted how the body was *arranged*. "Not dumped," he said, "laid out, like the perpetrator wanted it to be noticed." Haskins scribbled descriptions of the small wounds and the knife marks at the bridge of her upturned nose and in her pubic area, made, it seemed, after she was dead. There appeared to be rope burns on her wrist and ankles. He could see no blood, except a few watery drops splattered on the sidewalk and then on a cement bag that lay nearby. And the body looked clean, as if it had been washed. The sunlight gave the hair a reddish tinge, as if freshly shampooed or dyed.

Haskins told Aggie Underwood that he thought it would be his case. They speculated that the killer was someone who had medical knowledge or who was familiar with human anatomy, possibly a mortician.

By the time Watch Commander Freestone arrived on the scene, the trickle of cars had turned into a steady stream. The crime scene was becoming another circus. The five Los Angeles dailies had sent their people. Police from other divisions cruised by and offered their help. The inevitable onlookers appeared, some just driving by. Others parked down the street, standing on their car tops, straining to get a better look.

Reporters and detectives surrounded the uncovered body, standing, kneeling, peering closer—posing as if they were assisting Ray Pinker, the police chemist, search for clues. Newspapers reported a bloody heel print and a tire track in the driveway near the body. But no plaster casts were made by police, and despite all the press photographers, no photographs were taken of the tire track and the heel print. Microscopic fibers were found on the body and sent to the FBI Laboratory in Washington, DC for analysis.

"If the murder was never solved," Gerry Ramlow, a *Daily News* reporter told me later, "it was because of the reporters."

We were sitting in his cabin at Bear Lake in the San Bernardino Mountains outside of Los Angeles, the first of many visits. Gerry was retired—a short, wiry man, a chain smoker living with his wife, Karol, in "San Berdoo" near other retired newspaper and law enforcement people. Gerry had converted a summer residence to year-round.

"Jack Donahoe, the new Chief of Homicide, had just transferred from Robbery. He'd been buried for years in Administration. He knew next to nothing about homicides," Ramlow said. "For the first few days, before Donahoe could bring the investigation under control, reporters roamed freely, sat at desks, and answered the phones. Sometimes information was passed on to the police; sometimes a tip was pocketed and the reporter rushed out to get the scoop.

"They were all over, trampling evidence, withholding information. Hearst spent a lot of money on the investigation. The reporters of Hearst's two dailies, the *Los Angeles Herald Express* and the *Los Angeles Examiner*, were very aggressive and had huge expense accounts, while we had only our ingenuity and gas money.

"Not many people know that Hearst helped out the *Daily News*," Ramlow said. "Put $50,000 a year into it so it wouldn't fold. That was a lot of moola back then. We figured it was to keep the competition going.... Keep his reporters on their toes. The same with Harry Chandler loaning Hearst over a million dollars. But on this one, the Black Dahlia, Hearst wasn't helping *anyone*. He wanted to be the one to catch the guy."

"When I read the old newspapers," I said, "I was surprised that the Hearst papers seemed more sympathetic to Bette than the others. I would have expected his papers to be the most sensational."

"I think Hearst expected that with all the money he was pouring into it, they were going to catch the guy," replied Ramlow. "Imagine how many papers that story would have sold!"

I asked Gerry why this murder received so much attention over the years. There were a number of unsolved murders of women in Los Angeles around that time, but the crimes did not achieve the notoriety and the media coverage of the Black Dahlia murder. "What was so different about this one?" I asked. "Was it the name, The Black Dahlia?"

"No!" Ramlow said without hesitation. "More than that. It was the *way* the body was put on *display* for the whole world to see. I'll show you." Gerry went over to his file case and took out a folder of glossy eight-by-ten photos, all of dead women. "Are you okay with this?" he asked.

I nodded yes. I was prepared. Before starting my first research, I had tried to desensitize myself to the photographs of Bette's body by looking at the photos in Kenneth Anger's book. At first I could glance at them for only a second before slamming the book shut. But gradually I became accustomed to the scene and could study the photographs for a few minutes, almost dispassionately.

"See," Gerry Ramlow pointed out, "this photo of Jeanne French."

I looked at the glossy photo of a woman's body in a vacant lot.

"See all the blood. This is a copy-cat killing a few days after the Black Dahlia. The killer wrote "BD" in lipstick on the body. But look at all the blood. You know it's not the same guy. Not the same M.O. And this one, Roseanne Montgomery, see how the body is left there, and the blood."

Gerry showed me ten photographs of ten different women. "Now look at these," he said, and placed on the coffee table three photographs of Bette's body taken from different angles.

The photos were different from the ones in Kenneth Anger's book, and larger. They reminded me of a tableau by the artist Kienholz, or like a stage set, the body carefully placed for maximum impact.

"It was a *classic* sex crime except for how the body was dealt with *afterwards*. See how *clean* the body is. The body had been drained of its blood, washed, and placed there, not just thrown out of the car and dumped. Not just *discarded*. You take one look and *know* she was murdered elsewhere, but not *dumped*," Gerry said, "and *very* clean..."

He pointed to the breasts. "See these mutilations. Done after she was dead." Then he pointed to the lower section of the body—the legs spread wide apart, the left leg bent at the knee. "She'd been cut in half just above the navel," he said. "And the way the legs are. The killer did that. Why? It was like to humiliate her—*after* she was dead. Like the killer lording over everyone and saying, see... see what *I've* done to *her*. There's never been anything like it."

Other reporters showed me the same photos, offering them as "proof" that they had been first at the scene with *their* photographer. It seemed very important to claim to be "first."

Gerry pointed out the wedge-shaped gouge in her leg. "People said there was a rose tattoo there. Did you ever see one?" he asked.

"No," I said, "but I remember a vaccination on her leg."

I asked Gerry about the gashes on Bette's face—did he know of other murders in which the victim was cut from ear to ear?

"Usually involves a low-level crook, someone who talked too much," he said and looked at me as if he had just realized something.

Gerry went to his files and took out other photos—reporters horsing around. One photo showed two big guys holding Gerry horizontal, a cigarette dangling in his mouth while a guy in a hat took aim with a pistol. Another photo showed a group of reporters sitting around a table littered with glasses and beer bottles; crime reporter Aggie Underwood was sitting in the middle of the pack.

"Everyone loved Aggie," he said. "When Jack Smith lost his job with the *Daily News*, Aggie gave him one. She was City Editor then. Looking out the window, she happened to see Jack walking down the street. She yelled to him, 'Where you going?' He just shrugged his shoulders. So she yelled back at him, 'Come on up here,' and hired him on the spot. And during the newspaper strike against Hearst, she helped some of her people on the Q.T."

The reporters I interviewed from that era—Will Fowler, Gerry Ramlow, Chuck Cheatham, Nieson Himmel, Norm Jacoby—all said much the same thing: the 1940s were "exciting, right out of *Front Page*." They weren't only journalists, the reporters said, but investigators working long irregular hours, ferreting out information, tracking down leads and calling in their scoops to the rewrite man sitting at the desk.

The rewrite man had the task of searching for the new angle, the dramatic headline, and piecing together a coherent story as minute-by-minute updates were phoned in by a variety of reporters. Jack Smith, who later became an award-winning columnist for the *Los Angeles Times,* was Gerry Ramlow's rewrite man at the *Daily News*. Jim Murray, who became famous as a Pulitzer Prize-winning sportswriter, handled Will Fowler's rewrite for the *Examiner*.

Pranks were common among the reporters—a missing battery in a rival's car, a wrong address. According to Ramlow, the only one who pulled the real *dirty* tricks was Sid Hughes. Hughes went around impersonating Harry Hansen, the detective in charge of the Black Dahlia investigation. "Harry got pissed off," Ramlow said.

Police and reporters often worked together; playing a game of one-up-manship, "a game of cops and reporters." Freedom of information depended on good relations with an inside source and a gentleman's agreement of what could and could not be printed. Sometimes police would recruit a reporter to help elicit a suspect's confession. There was little concern about a fair trial.

Gerry told me that he was called in on more than one occasion while a suspect was told by the police interrogator: "Talk to Gerry, here. He's with the press. He'll tell your side of the story."

The suspect would be cajoled into opening up while his lawyer sat quietly by and the press photographer clicked away with a Speed Graphic. For the police it was an easy conviction, for the reporter an exclusive headline story. Inadmissible evidence was not much of a legal concern in the 1940s.

"We weren't out-and-out callous. Reporting crime, you see some stuff that maybe no one should ever get to see," Ramlow said. "So if you didn't fool around and joke, you never could've stood it. And rule number one was you don't take it home with you. You're a goner if you do. Maybe that's why we all drank so much.

"Bevo Means was with the *Herald Express*. He was someone everyone liked. A big drinker and a real ladies' man. But never got nasty like Sid Hughes."

I asked Ramlow if the Black Dahlia name had been made up by one of the hard-drinking reporters.

"No, that's for real," he said. "Chuck Cheatham in Long Beach. He's the one who came up with that info."

Gerry gave me Chuck's phone number. "Chuck must be close to eighty now. I was one of the young hot-shots, just out of the army, frisky," Gerry said. "Cheatham was with the *Long Beach Independent*, old guard, been around a long time, liked to shoot the breeze."

Chuck Cheatham was thin and frail, a little taller than Gerry, but hunched over from osteoporosis. He lived alone in a small apartment. "Not as sharp as I used to be," he said. "Hard to remember everything. We were making twenty dollars a week then. It was a lot of money. I liked 'The Hat.' 'Harry the Hat,' that's what we called Hansen. He wasn't on the take... not The Hat. Some people say they were all on the take, the police. They all had their circles of people they protected. But not Harry. Straight as they come. His partner Finis Brown, that's another story. Harry was well-liked by some, and hated by others.

"Harry had been in vaudeville. He was usually called upon to be master of ceremonies at police events. A real ham—and sharp. Couldn't put one over The Hat."

Sergeant Harry Hansen, the senior homicide detective,

supervised most of the murder investigations in Los Angeles then. He worked out of Central, and when Donahoe, the new captain, called and told Harry to "drop everything," Hansen high-tailed it over to 39th and Norton with his partner Finis Brown. Hansen thought the murder would be solved quickly, in a few months at best. But the case plagued him for over twenty years until his retirement in 1968.

"In a murder, for reporters, the general rule was all the tomatoes were beautiful. That's what we'd write," Cheatham said. "But this one, the Dahlia, this tomato really *was* some looker... and white. A reporter's dream girl. If she was Filipina or a nigger, forget it. Wouldn't make the papers.

"Long Beach was quiet then, no protected prostitution. Ramlow knows the prostitution angle. He broke the Brenda Allen scandal. That was after the Dahlia, maybe a couple of years later. Involved a lieutenant in Vice. Gave Parker the ammunition he needed. Parker became the new Chief of Police. Getting rid of 'Cowboy' Horrall. He [Horrall] was chief of police at LAPD during the Dahlia case.

"In Long Beach the Dahlia hung out at the drug store on the corner of First, and at the Lafayette Hotel. High class, the Dahlia was high class. Ed Boynton was the detective who told us about the name. Bevo Means was with me."

It was a slow news day and the two reporters were looking for an angle. "We were making the rounds, went to her old address at 56 Linden Street; then over to the Long Beach Police Station. Boynton said he might have something for us," Cheatham said.

"Boynton told us people at the drugstore said she was something of a mystery woman and that the guy working the counter said her friends gave her a nickname. 'They called her the Black Dahlia, because of her jet-black hair,' Boynton said. It was a takeoff of the Blue Dahlia, the Alan Ladd film that had been playing in the movie house around the corner. You couldn't have made that one up!

"I raced Bevo to a phone and called the story in. But the *Herald Express* ran a special edition. Our paper didn't get out until later in the day." Chuck paused and shrugged his shoulders.

"Over the years I wondered about her. She had a lot of guys drooling after her, the Dahlia did. I figured she didn't fit in, wasn't jaded enough... was a tease. Didn't play by LA rules. And she got some guy mad."

Reporter Will Fowler said it was his phone call that sent the *Los Angeles Examiner's* city room into high gear. "I told the City Editor, Jim Richardson, she was a good-looking gal, from what you could tell," Fowler said. "Looked like a butcher knife to me, and maybe a razor; another Jack the Ripper situation. But clean. The guy had medical knowledge."

William Randolph Fowler (named after William Randolph Hearst), is an imposing man—over six feet tall, heavy set, erudite. He has written a number of books, most notably *The Second Handshake*, the biography of Will's famous father, Gene Fowler. Will grew up surrounded by Hollywood legends—John Barrymore, Ben Hecht, John Dekker, and fighter Jack Dempsey. Will's godfather was W.C. Fields.

Will showed me photos from the murder scene, similar to the ones Ramlow had.

"I was a cub reporter, and this was my first big one," Fowler said. "Bill Gammon, the Assistant City Editor, pushed for a *second* extra edition. Jim Murray, the sportswriter, was on rewrite then. Murray banged out the stories as fast as they poured in.

"Jim Richardson rushed every *Examiner* reporter and photographer to 39th and Norton and called the night shift in early. Sid Hughes followed the coroner's black truck—we called it the *Black Mariah*—to the morgue.

"Hughes stayed with the coroner. Tommy Devlin was working on the Mocambo heist. Arrests were about to be made. Devlin was told to drop whatever the hell he was doing and get back to the city room, pronto!"

Fowler went to his file cabinet and retrieved an old newspaper. "This was *our* story—front page for thirty-five days!" Fowler told me. "We were one step ahead of the police all the way. The *Examiner's* January 15th extra edition with its red headlines blazing 'FIEND TORTURES, KILLS GIRL,' sold more copies than the bombing of Pearl Harbor!

"Everyone was calling in their chips—*Daily News, Hollywood Reporter, LA Times,* and of course the two dailies of 'Old Man,' Hearst. We were priming and pumping police sources, long-eared stoolies, and anyone else who might give a lead.

"At the *Examiner,* it was Woolard, our Assistant Managing Editor, who got the idea for using the sound photo to identify her. And that put us *way ahead* of the other papers.

"When Woolard was told the prints had been sent to the FBI by airmail special delivery, he called Donahoe and blasted him. 'For Christ's sake,' Woolard told Donahoe, 'They're snowed in back there with two feet of snow. You got a murder like this and you're waiting a week to find out who she is? Your killer could be in Timbuktu by the weekend! Those prints might not even make it to Chicago.'

"Woolard suggested sound photo. Told Donahoe we could send her prints over the wire. It had never been done before. It wouldn't take any more time than sending a newsphoto or anything on the wire, something like a fax machine works today.

"International News Photowire opened at four in the morning. Woolard promised Donahoe that the prints would be the first thing on the wire. Said they'd go right to the Hearst Bureau in Washington. Ray Richards, who managed the news bureau, used to be an *Examiner* reporter here in Los Angeles. Woolard set it up for Richards to be standing by, take the prints right off the wire, and hand them to the Feds.

"Woolard knew that if the FBI got a name on the prints, we'd get a jump on every paper in the country.

"The first transmission over the telephone wires failed—too blurry. Russ Lapp, a photographer at the news bureau, came up with the idea of blowing each fingerprint up and sending them over the wire, one by one, as eight-by-tens.

"Bingo! In less than an hour the FBI had searched a million prints and came up with a match—from Camp Cooke, California, and a photo ID."

Elizabeth "Bette" Short had been fingerprinted when she applied for a job on January 30, 1943. The FBI also had one arrest on file—for breaking juvenile laws on September 23,

1943. Mrs. Phoebe Short, 115 Salem Street, Medford, Massachusetts, was listed as next of kin.

When the *Los Angeles Examiner* scooped the other dailies, irate reporters from the *Los Angeles Times* and the wire services called the FBI and blasted the Bureau for favored treatment of the *Examiner*. The Bureau denied favoritism and immediately referred all calls back to the Los Angeles Police Department. But internal FBI memos indicate that the angry accusations were not unfounded—the Bureau considered the two Los Angeles Hearst papers, the *Examiner* and the *Herald Express*, as "friendly" and the Chandler *Los Angeles Times* as "unfriendly."

"*The Examiner* held the identification from the other papers just long enough for Wayne Sutton to make a call to Mrs. Short," Fowler said. "I'm damn glad I wasn't Sutton. 'Tell her anything,' Richardson told Sutton. 'Just don't tell her that her daughter's *dead* until you get the information you want.' Imagine having to make that call? Pump the mother and then tell her that her daughter's been *murdered*."

Richardson sent Tommy Devlin down to Pacific Beach and Will Fowler up the coast to check out Santa Barbara and Camp Cooke. "Way ahead of the pack," Fowler said. "I expected a by-line on this story. I was operating on an adrenaline high. Didn't sleep for days. None of us did."

Fowler said he hadn't expected to have such a gut reaction to a photo that looked like a mug shot. He hadn't expected she'd be so beautiful and photogenic—high cheek bones, full lips, and eyes so translucent he knew they were blue even in the black-and-white photograph. Fowler's gaze stayed riveted to the eyes in the photo—eyes that stared straight ahead with an intensity and seemed to demand a vengeance for what had been done to her.

"I remember her," Officer Mary H. Unkefer, a Santa Barbara policewoman, told Fowler when he showed her the photograph. "Someone you wouldn't forget. She stayed with me a couple of days, then at a neighborhood house for about a week. I was worried about her. So I arranged for temporary custody. She was very soft spoken and polite, very refined. She had the blackest hair I ever saw. Not your typical bar fly. I don't think she had hardly anything at all [to drink] the night she was picked up. She was just spotted at a table that was getting a little rowdy, and the place, the El Paseo Restaurant, wasn't too careful about checking IDs. Nothing serious, but she looked a little young. She was worried about what her mother would think. I brought her to Greyhound and put her on a bus to Boston. I told her she should wait a little while and come back when she was older. The neighborhood house gave her ten dollars for spending money—you know, food, cokes. A five- or six-day trip. I know she made it home because she wrote to me—several times."

Fowler's next stop was Camp Cooke.

"She only worked a couple of weeks for me before she took off, not long after being chosen *Camp Cutie*," Ralph Aylesworth, the manager of the post exchange, told Fowler.

Aylesworth was a short, energetic man, and slim, with thinning hair pushed back neatly. "She said she came out here for her health, but that she was okay now and needed to work so she could stay in California."

Aylesworth slid open the bottom drawer of his desk, pulled out a photograph, and gave it to Fowler. Bette was standing in the middle of the photo, a few inches taller than the men on each side. Her hair was braided and pinned up. She was smiling, squinting into the sun, and wearing a light-colored two-piece cotton dress.

Aylesworth said he didn't remember the soldier's name. "I'm the one on the left," he said. Aylesworth thought the dress was light blue. "She was nice," he added. "Real nice and polite."

Aylesworth told Fowler he didn't expect her to leave. She had talked about breaking into movies. Aylesworth thought she had the equipment but seemed a little young, and he worried about her when she left. "She wasn't hard or tough," he said.

Aylesworth picked up a yellowed clipping from the desk and handed it to Fowler:

> Business in the PX seems to be on the upswing these days, and it might have to do with our new "Camp Cutie" Miss Elizabeth "Bette" Short who can be seen brightening the cash register at the PX...

"Inez Keeling is the one who hired Beth," Aylesworth said. "Inez was the manager of the PX before me. She lives on Edgeware Road. Inez might know something."

Inez Keeling told Fowler that she was won over by Beth's "childlike charm and beauty."

"Beth told me she was out here for her health, that doctors back East were afraid she was becoming a victim of tuberculosis," Mrs. Keeling said. "Beth asked me to give her a chance. She was one of the loveliest girls I had ever met. She didn't smoke, or drink. Even after I left the post, she'd come by to see me. Then she suddenly dropped out of my life and I never saw her again. That was in 1943."

Paul Veglia, a nineteen year old from Casmalia, near Camp Cooke, remembered Beth. "It would've been in the summer of 1943," he said. "Every morning, all during the month of August I saw her. She was living in the old bunkhouse on the ranch, Rancho Santo Antonio, with another girl, just a few miles out of Casmalia. She would wear almost the same outfit every day, a white blouse and black slacks, sometimes jodhpurs, and the spectator shoes. I remembered her shoes, the white parts meticulously clean and white, and the black parts shining except where the dust had scuffed around the edges.

"I almost knew the time just by seeing her appear in the distance, seven-thirty in the morning. She'd be carrying letters to mail. I arranged it so I'd be working near the roadway when she passed by. I was fifteen at the time, could barely manage a 'Good morning.' She was always friendly and would give me a big smile. I couldn't take my eyes off her keister when she walked by. I think she knew I was watching her."

"We kept ahead of everyone for the first few days, until Sid Hughes pissed off Harry Hansen," Fowler boasted. "We found her trunk. Bob Irwin, another *Examiner* reporter, tracked it down at the Railway Express office. He had to part with a few bucks, but it was right there at Railway Express, shipped out from Chicago. Had been there for a while."

According to Fowler, Richardson struck a deal with Donahoe—the *Examiner* would get an exclusive, and the police would get the trunk *after* the reporters checked it over.

Captain Roy Geise and Detective Sam Flowers were sent to pick up the trunk and bring it to Central; *nothing* was to be touched until Geise and Flowers arrived. Under their watchful eyes, reporters pawed through the contents. There were photo albums and loose photos (Fowler said he was able to snatch one), packages of neatly bundled letters tied with pink ribbon. The dates covered a number of years—1942 through 1946. Some of the letters appeared to be ones she had written and never sent; others with cancellation stamps had been returned to her. Seventeen of the returned letters were written on the same day to the same person, Major Matt Gordon.

Flowers obliged the photographers and tipped up one of the black photo albums, holding the pages open for a clear shot of the smiling couple in the night club photo. Campaign ribbons and wings decorated the uniform of the man, an air force major. The woman wore a simple pastel dress, her face framed by a mass of dark curly hair; a black velvet choker and white rose corsage were her only adornments. The airman clasped her right hand, and she rested her left hand lightly on his arm. Mounted on the back of the page was a telegram informing Bette of Matt Gordon's death.

Many of the snapshots and nightclub photos found their way into the newspapers, but the more professional photographs were never released.

Geise held up a black print dress with pink flowers, silky to the touch, then more clothes—blouses, mostly light colors. In the bottom of the trunk were small leatherette autograph books, the ice-cream colored pages filled with limericks and well wishes: "To Medford's own Deanna Durbin, Always be faithful, Always be true, and the Lord himself will be good to you...."

"Within a few days... *eight* people confessed to the murder," Gerry Ramlow told me. "They were coming out of the woodwork, including a dyke from Barstow, and a couple who couldn't even speak English, only Spanish." Bilingual police officer, Danny Galindo, was brought in to translate during the Spanish-speaking interrogations. (He later made detective grade and brought the infamous serial killer, the "skidrow slasher," to justice.)

Dr. Paul de River, the police psychiatrist, took part in the interrogations. He predicted the confessors would keep coming. "And the police will keep talking to them," he said. "The type of mind which conceived the Elizabeth Short murder will some day have to boast about it."

Dr. de River theorized that the culprit hated women and sought "above all the physical and moral pain, and the disgraceful humiliation and maltreatment of his victim."

"The murderer," de River said, "was led on by the thought of what was happening in the mind of the victim. He enjoyed the *play*—his object [the victim]... was a psychosexual component of the dramatis personae in which *he* was the *star performer*"

On February 2, 1947, eighteen days after the murder, Assemblyman Don Field, at the urging of District Attorney Simpson, introduced legislation to create a Sex Case Registry. The legislation quickly passed, and California became the first state in the nation to require the registration of convicted sex offenders.

Two weeks later, the FBI was tipped off by the *Examiner* that a nervous Mayor Bowron planned to ask the Bureau to officially join in the investigation. Bowron hoped to stifle accusations of police incompetency and to alleviate the mounting pressure on Police Chief Horrall. Even the unions had joined the foray. The CIO's newspaper, *The Labor Herald*, called for police to stop strike-breaking activities and concentrate on solving the Black Dahlia murder.

Bowron's move was nothing more than a publicity gimmick cooked up with the *Examiner*. The mayor and the editorial staff of the newspaper knew that Director J. Edgar Hoover had given his approval for only limited FBI involvement. Top level agents had advised Hoover against entering the case. They theorized that if the Bureau investigated and didn't solve the murder it would have no impact on either the Bureau or the LAPD, but if the Bureau *solved* the case, "it would destroy all public confidence in the police department." The FBI maintained the official position that they lacked jurisdiction.

To create the impression that the FBI had acceded to Bowron's request and was actively conducting an investigation, the *Examiner* went ahead with a planned story and placed comments about the FBI's laboratory at the end of the feature.

The FBI did help behind the scenes—running background checks and interviewing a number of "unknown subjects" or "unsubs," as they were called—the designation given to suspects when the identity of the killer is unknown. The investigation of one unsub, a World War II vet whose photo was found in Bette's trunk, revealed he had spent time in a mental institution after his wife killed their two year old daughter and committed suicide. At first thought to be a hot lead, the unsub was quickly cleared. He was not in California at the time of Bette's murder.

The FBI tracked the whereabouts of another unsub who, it was believed, was Bette Short's husband. Postcards from Bette and the man were turned over to the Los Angeles police by a Medford resident. The postcards, dated September 21, 1946, said that Bette and the unsub were married and living happily in Hollywood. FBI agents from the Pittsburgh office interviewed the unsub who claimed that the postcards were a joke instigated by Bette, and that they had never married.

As the leads ran out, detectives asked the FBI to obtain Elizabeth Short's employment records from the Social Security Administration. Despite repeated attempts, in which the FBI cited the precedent set during World War II, (records were released if "subversive" activities were suspected), the Social Security Administration remained non-cooperative. They were adamant. Elizabeth Short's records could not be released unless the murder was "war related."

While the behind-the-scenes communications were going on between the Social Security Administration, the FBI, and the *Examiner,* Hearst's other newspaper, the *Herald Express,* ran sidebar stories to maintain public interest. Mystery writer Leslie Charteris, creator of "The Saint," dismissed the theory that death occurred "unintentionally" during an "amateur sadistic orgy." He noted that there is "no evidence that Elizabeth Short was ever associated with an organized vice racket, or that she was what you might call a party girl."

He also dismissed the idea of a homosexual connection. "The girl's record does not show any excursion into such fields," he said. "The fact... [that] all the male associates who have been questioned insist that in spite of appearances, she never delivered what they were after, has, I think, an important bearing on the case."

Charteris saw the killer as a lone wolf, alcoholic, from thirty-five to fifty-years old, not a sadist, but someone who, in a rage over his impotence, slashed at the victim's face. "Someone probably underweight or overweight, meticulous... a white collar worker probably married with a family."

Alice La Vere, a consulting psychologist, wrote a feature-length article for the *Herald Express*. She theorized that the killer was a maladjusted veteran with repressed sexual impulses, someone with a dominant woman in his past—a woman whose power over him he resented.

La Vere speculated that there was something "abnormal" in the backgrounds of the perpetrator *and* the victim. "Some gnawing feeling of inadequacy was eating at the mind of this girl," wrote La Vere. "She needed constant proof to herself that she was important to someone and demonstrated this need by the number of suitors and admirers with which she surrounded herself."

La Vere thought the killer wanted to "show the world." She believed that he vented "his vengeance, anger, and rage in one destroying act.

As a counterpoint to La Vere's analytical sidebar, sob sister Caroline Walker pulled heart strings writing about the "children of the night"—tragic young girls growing up too fast, wearing too much makeup, dressed with a "fictitious smartness" who were following down the "Dahlia's path" to a predictable and violent end.

As predicted by Dr. Paul de River, the number of people confessing to the Black Dahlia murder continued to grow. The FBI ran immediate background checks on each confessee. Judge Louis Kaufman, angry because the bogus confessions were wasting valuable police time, began handing down sentences to the would-be killers—sixty days in jail for interfering with a police investigation. The judge called the people "Confessing Willies."

"Word was," Ramlow said, "that Hansen had some trick question up his sleeve, something about the condition of the body that got rid of the confessing creeps real quick." Within a month, Hansen had eliminated fifty-nine suspects.

"We all came up with the same information," Ramlow said. "The Dahlia would be broke, and then she'd have money. That's what some of her roommates said, but 'secretive, never one to confide.' Most gals can't keep a secret, blab all over the place, but this one, the Dahlia, never said what she was doing, or where she was going. One minute with you, hey, the next gone. That's what the word was on her. Secretive, very secretive."

As tips poured in and reporters fanned out, the *Examiner* maintained its early news lead. Tommy Devlin, with the information passed on to him by Wayne Sutton, beat everyone, police included, to Elizabeth Short's last known address, the home of Elvera French at Camino Padera in Pacific Beach.

Tommy Devlin said that Mrs. French expressed no surprise when he appeared at their modest pre-fab housing project. "My daughter Dorothy and I thought the description fit Beth," Elvera said. "We knew someone would show up sooner or later, but we thought it would be the police."

Mrs. French told Devlin that Beth had left on January 8th with a red-haired man about twenty-five years old. "He was driving a light-colored coupe with a Huntington Beach sticker," she said. "The day before she left, he had sent Beth a telegram telling her to wait and signed it, 'Red.' "

Elvera and Dorothy described Beth's traveling outfit: a black collarless tailored suit, white frilly blouse, white gloves, black suede shoes, and black stockings with seams. "When Beth walked towards the car," Elvira said, "she carried a pinkish beige camel's hair coat over her arm and clutched a black purse in her hand. Beth called the red-headed man, Bob. They seemed happy when they left, laughing and joking as they loaded her two suitcases and hat box in the trunk of the car." Faith Forest, a neighbor, confirmed the departure account.

Beth had worked only a few days during the four weeks she

lived with the Frenches, but in mid-December, a former boyfriend, Gordon Fickling, wired her one hundred dollars (approximately one thousand dollars in today's money). "To help tide her over," noted the mother, Mrs. Elvera French. "The money should have helped Beth for a little while. He wrote her a very nice letter, very concerned. He told Beth that she had to be more practical, that times had changed."

Elvera's daughter Dorothy said she met Beth at the Aztec Theater in downtown San Diego. Dorothy, working as a cashier, felt sorry for the dark-haired young woman sitting forlornly in the theater. Times had been rough since the end of the war eighteen months before.

Many women lost their jobs to the returning soldiers. A severe housing shortage, strikes, and the phasing out of price and wage control pinched everyone's pocketbooks. People charged with "keeping the home fires burning" during the war now found themselves out on the streets, homeless. More fortunate individuals living in rent-controlled apartments or rooms often shared their meager resources, bringing a stranger home, sometimes even a family, and letting them stay until they could get back on their feet.

The Frenches portrayed Elizabeth Short as somewhat mysterious and reluctant to talk about her past. They said she was "polite but secretive." Sometimes Beth seemed depressed and moody, which the Frenches attributed to her lack of success at finding work. Beth told them she decided to try her luck in San Diego when jobs became scarce in Los Angeles because of the big movie strikes.

Beth often talked about her husband, Major Matt Gordon, who had been killed in a plane crash in India a few days after the war ended. She had plans to break into the movies and mentioned that a Hollywood celebrity promised to help her. They said Beth also mentioned someone named "George."

Responding to Devlin's questions, the Frenches described Beth as fearful of a suitor. There was a puzzling incident one night. Two men and a woman were knocking on the door. Beth wouldn't answer, but she peeked out the curtain. "Beth seemed relieved when the trio finally departed," Elvera said.

"We had to ask her to leave. Our place is very crowded with my teenage son Cory and daughter Dorothy, and I'm a widow," explained Elvera French. She showed Devlin an expensive black velour hat with a veil. "Beth worked as a hat model. When she left, she gave me this Leo Joseph hat that I admired. I think it was her way of thanking me for letting her stay."

After leaving the Frenches, Devlin canvassed the motels along the Pacific Coast Highway between San Diego and Los Angeles. Devlin told Will Fowler he could not believe the registration book he found at one of the motels. Devlin said it was the damnedest thing.

"She signed her own name, Elizabeth Short," Devlin said. "There it was in black and white: Robert Manley of Huntington Beach and Eliz. Short of Chicago. No one ever used their real names when they stayed at a motel. Usually the man would sign Mr. and Mrs. Jones."

Red had been identified as Robert Manley, a salesman who lived on Mountain View Street in South Gate. Manley was on a business trip in San Francisco with his boss, Harry Palmer. They were due back Sunday night.

Gerry Ramlow was tipped off about the impending arrest. "We waited at Harry Palmer's house," Ramlow said, "like an ambush. It was four days after the murder. The two detectives, Sam Flowers and Jasper Wass, were out of sight behind the porch stairs with four back-up policemen. Two policemen were against the fence, two on each side of the garage. Me and my photographer hid in the bushes along with someone from the *Examiner*. When Flowers saw the headlights, he motioned us to lay low."

The headlights from the car streamed across the front of the house and came to rest—two round spotlights flooding the garage door. A tall man opened the driver's side and walked towards the garage. The police yelled for him to freeze. Blinded by the lights, Harry Palmer couldn't see who was pushing him against the garage door.

"We got a shot of Manley getting out of the car with his hands up. He was moving very slowly," Ramlow said. "Wass patted him down. We got a shot of that, too. 'I know what this is about,' Manley said. 'Listen, I knew Beth Short. I turned sick inside when I read the papers in San Francisco last Friday.'

"That pissed Wass off. He thought for sure Manley was their man.

"Can you imagine the spot Manley was in? Jeezus, Manley was married. He had a beautiful wife and a four-month-old son. Said he was afraid of the publicity. 'My wife. What'll she say?' Kept repeating that. Flowers told him he should have thought about that when he went after a little poontang."

While the police officers kept reporters and photographers busy inside the garage checking out Manley's car, Flowers and Wass crept away with their prisoner. They put their car in gear and rolled it halfway down the hill before turning the engine on. Flowers and Wass radioed ahead and were told to avoid the horde of reporters waiting at Central and to bring Manley directly to the eastside Hollenbeck Station. Everything was set up at Hollenbeck—lie detector, relay teams, the whole works. Donahoe was waiting there. Hansen and his partner Finis Brown were on their way.

SIX
The Prime Suspects

The handsome couple faced each other in profile— Robert Manley and his wife, Harriet. The pretty woman had an upturned nose like Beth Short, and full lips that were poised for a kiss. A flowered kerchief tied in back covered her honey-colored hair. Harriet was looking up, meeting her husband's gaze. Her hands gently touched his cheeks, an expression of faith minutes before Robert "Red" Manley, Suspect Number One, was booked. The tender moment was caught by a Hearst photographer and sent over the wire, making front page news across the country and a full-page spread in *LIFE* magazine.

Captain Donahoe led the relay teams questioning Manley throughout the night, hoping to wring a confession before turning Manley over to the reporters. The detectives *knew* they had their man. The FBI's search through army records turned up information that Manley had been discharged as "mentally unfit for service."

Ray Pinker administered the polygraph test. "The results," he said, "were inconclusive." The exhausted Manley kept falling asleep. Another polygraph was slated for later in the day.

Manley told of a few uneventful dates, dining and dancing, and admitted kissing "Miss Short," describing her as "rather cold."

"Miss Short talked endlessly about 'Matt' someone, her dead husband," Manley said. "I confided to Miss Short the problems I was having adjusting to married life."

Manley admitted staying at the motel on January 8th en route to Los Angeles, but "Nothing happened," he said. "She was sick with chills and sat up all night in a chair."

Manley ignored the squadron of reporters hurling questions at him when he was escorted back to his cell by Finis Brown and a guard. If a reporter approached his cell, Manley closed his eyes, pretending to be asleep. Manley definitely was *not* talking to the press.

Agness Underwood joined the newsboys across from his cell

and flashed Manley a friendly smile. Sid Hughes told Aggie to forget it. "We've all tried to talk to him," he said.

Aggie quipped something about it needing a woman's touch and walked over to the cell. She told Manley he looked like he had been on "one helluva drunk" the night before, and she offered him a cigarette. Manley said he sure could use a drag. Aggie gave him a whole pack.

"Look, I don't think you did it," Aggie said. "And I'd like to tell your side of the story."

The guard and the other reporters hung back while Aggie talked. They could see Manley hesitating, as if he might open up to Aggie.

"Hey, if you can trust anyone, you can trust this little lady," the guard said. "She'll do right by you."

"You a vet?" Aggie asked.

"Musician," Manley said. He took a puff on the cigarette, slowly blowing the smoke out. "I was in the Army Band."

Manley told Aggie that "Miss Short" had made a telephone call from Sheldon's Cafe on the Pacific Coast Highway before they left Pacific Beach. He was sure the call was to Los Angeles. After the call, Beth seemed anxious to get rid of him, telling Manley she had to meet her sister. He mentioned the Biltmore Hotel and she said, yes, that was where she had to go.

Manley said he paid to have double taps put on Beth's shoes when he stopped to make his business calls. They arrived in Los Angeles around five o'clock, he said, and he brought "Miss Short" to the Greyhound Bus Depot on 7th Street. He helped put Beth's hatbox and suitcases in a locker.

He was reluctant to leave her alone in that part of town, he said, so he drove to the exclusive Biltmore Hotel on Olive Street. Beth asked him if he would do one last favor, inquire at the desk to see if her sister, Virginia West, had registered at the hotel. It was now past six o'clock on the evening of January 9th, and Robert Manley was eager to go home. The desk clerk told Manley that no one by that name had checked in.

When Manley said goodbye, Beth touched him lightly on his arm and thanked him with a smile. He remembered vividly gazing at the pretty girl with jet-black hair. Manley could recall in detail the black tailored suit, black stockings, and black suede shoes she was wearing, and the light-colored coat she carried over her arm. With her soft alabaster skin and aquamarine eyes, she made a stunning figure, difficult to forget.

As he left, he glanced back, he said, but Beth had turned away and was talking to the clerk at the cigar stand. The newspapers reported that hotel employees saw her walking back and forth across the marble floor to the telephone booths. They estimated she stayed in the lobby for about an hour.

"I had nothing to do with it," Manley kept repeating to Aggie. "I felt sick when I found out." Manley insisted that he was playing cards with his wife and a couple of friends, Mr. and Mrs. Don Holmes, the night of the murder. The friends substantiated his alibi.

Aggie knew she had front page on this interview—"Red Tells Own Story of Romance with Dahlia; Suspect Squirms as Science Tests Alibi."

Finis Brown and Ray Pinker administered Manley's second polygraph test. They were given the autopsy report and were now "inclined to believe Manley's story."

Aggie's photographer, Perry Fowler, caught the trio on film. Perry crouched down, angling his Speed Graphix and dramatizing the ominous shadows on Manley's face. Pinker and Brown stayed in the background. Manley looked as if he was sitting in the electric chair—a wide band was strapped across his chest, while wires connected to his arm led to a box-like contraption on a sturdy mahogany table.

Red Manley never recovered from the ordeal. He had a number of breakdowns, always around the anniversary of the murder and his interrogation. In March of 1954, his wife Harriet committed him to Patton State Hospital for the fourth time. He was not violent, she said, "But hears voices and scribbles nonsense. He cries and feels guilty."

For years, Harry Hansen remained suspicious of Manley. During one of his confinements, Manley agreed to take truth serum. An official police source told reporters that the results indicated Manley "knows nothing of the crime."

In the 1970s, Ed Gelb, the renowned polygraph expert,

found Manley living alone in a trailer. Gelb, working as a private investigator, had been hired by a movie studio to track down people connected to the Black Dahlia case and obtain signed releases.

Gelb said he didn't know much about the case at that time and didn't know Manley had been a prime suspect. "Manley was just another name I was checking out," Gelb said. "I told Manley he would be portrayed favorably in the TV movie that was starring Lucy Arnaz. Manley was very cooperative. We sat for a while and drank a lot of beer. We started to B.S."

Gelb wasn't sure what set Manley off. "It could have been when I asked Manley how he was connected to the case," Gelb said. "Manley suddenly grabbed an ax and chased me out of the trailer, saying he was going to kill me. He never did sign the release form. A few days later, Manley checked himself back into a psychiatric hospital."

Elizabeth Short's father, Cleo, became a suspect briefly, until his alibi checked out. He was interrogated twice. The police couldn't figure out why he hadn't come forward once his daughter had been identified as the victim. Cleo was found a few days after the murder by Ken Scarce, a policeman who happened to reside in the same Los Angeles apartment building. "My landlady tipped me off about Cleo Short," Ken Scarce told me. "One of her tenants, someone she described as 'secretive,' had a photo of the girl she saw in all the papers. The landlady let me in with a key, and sure enough, there was the photo, the one with the curl over her forehead. We were waiting for him when he got home. He said he had a right to the photo of his daughter. I didn't know what to make of it."

Cleo Short told reporters he wanted nothing to do with the investigation. "I broke off with the mother and the family several years ago. In 1943 I told her to go her way, I'd go mine." Cleo said his daughter was more interested in going out dancing with servicemen than doing the dishes and keeping house.

Ken Scarce went on to become a police lieutenant and LAPD's resident polygraph expert, refining the technique to discern "half truths." The major benefit of the polygraph, Scarce said, is to narrow down the investigation, clear the innocent quickly, and point out people who should be checked out further. "The polygraph is useless with schizophrenics and someone who has been grilled," said Scarce.

He explained: "If you hammer away at a suspect saying, 'You did it... You did it...,' when he takes the test he may be responding not to what he *actually* did, but to what he was *told* he did. Scarce, who hates the use of the word "lie detector," said the polygraph was new to LAPD in 1947. "Because of the intense questioning Manley underwent," Scarce said, "Manley's polygraph tests were useless."

After Manley was exonerated, the reporters had a hard time coming up with new angles. "You could only interview the ex-roommates so many times," Will Fowler said. "By this time, no one except the crackpots wanted to admit they knew the Dahlia."

A middle-aged ex-con and self-proclaimed artist, Arthur James Jr. alias Charles B. Smith, claimed to have made some sketches of the Black Dahlia and painted her in oils. They met, he told reporters, at the City of Paris cocktail lounge in August of 1944. In November of the same year, James was arrested in Tucson, Arizona, for passing bad checks and violating the Mann Act. The fifty-six-year-old James had brought Geraldine Ann Gillig, age nineteen, across the California state border for "immoral purposes." At the time he was arrested, James told police he was "the son of one of the twelve richest men in the world." One of the bogus checks he signed was for $50,000. According to Tucson police, James also claimed to have been everything "from a switchman for the Southern Pacific to an FBI agent."

When Bette Short left California in September of 1943, she did not return until April of 1946. Arthur James' "Dahlia" story was just another of his fantasies.

"The Best Suspect Yet," a bellhop named Leslie Dillon, became more than just an embarrassment to police officials. Upon his release, Dillon filed a $100,000 lawsuit against the City of Los Angeles for false arrest. Dillon came to the attention of the police when he wrote a letter to Dr. Paul de River, expressing an interest and more than a passing knowledge in "sexual sadism." Lured from Florida under the guise of "helping" de River write a book, Leslie was held "incommunicado" in San Francisco and subjected to a relentless third degree. Dillon's friend, a bit actor and writer named Jeff Connors who claimed to have known the "Dahlia," was also arrested, questioned, and finally released.

Bette's friendships became open to interpretation, with comments about her "bizarre behavior" sprinkled throughout the news stories. A simple statement, "She readily made friends with men and women," had sexual overtones that implied "deviant" and "sinister" behavior.

"Elizabeth Short wasn't a bad gal," the prize-winning *Los Angeles Times* columnist Jack Smith told me over the telephone. "I sure have seen a helluva lot worse."

I asked Jack about his work as a rewrite man on the *Daily News*.

"Well," Jack Smith said, "in those days, we tended to infer... We had deadlines to meet."

"What about her boyfriends?" I asked. "Was she sleeping around?"

"None that we found. But look how Manley was raked over the coals."

"Lesbian?" I queried.

"No, nothing."

I asked Jack Smith if it would be possible for me to look through his old files. "If I had them," he said, "but a few years ago I took them out back and burned them."

"Burned them? Why?"

"For my wife," he said. "She wanted me to stop thinking about it. So out of respect for my wife, I burned them."

Gerry Ramlow agreed that there was nothing to the lesbian angle. "After Manley was let loose," he said, "Aggie thought a woman might be involved. If she wasn't sleeping with guys, we figured she must have been doing something. Bevo was acting like he knew something we didn't know, like directly from the horse's mouth, a horse named Harry. Bevo was saying something about 'lesbian pathology,' whatever the hell that meant. That's what sent Hughes chasing the dykes.

"Sid Hughes wouldn't give up on the lesbian angle. He

checked it out pretty thoroughly. Over at the Duchess', a dyke bar down on Olive, they knew her in there. Some of the dykes made passes at the Dahlia, but she wasn't interested. She was friendly to everyone, but would 'politely' fend them off. That's what Sid was saying, *politely*."

"Hughes hit every bar on Main Street and the Boulevard, and we were on his tail. That gal sure got around. 'Adept at fending off passes'—that's what one of the guys said. Could've made dough as a B-girl, but didn't. She liked coming and going as she pleased, making the rounds. And no complaints about her decorating the place. Guys would buy drinks, and she'd talk to them, nursing the drink, be friendly. Then just when the guy thought he had something going, she'd up and leave."

"Someone told me that some of the guys even complained to the police," I said.

"Yeah, could be," Ramlow said. "Figure that one. Sid thought either some lesbian was jealous or the Dahlia gave some guy a real bad time. Sid said she was one f---ing tease and that's what did her in. He thought she might have been asking for it. He said she probably was giving guys head, because she sure as hell wasn't putting out as we know it."

Will Fowler said much the same thing. "The Dahlia liked to turn men on and leave them high and dry. "Call it what you will," he said, "she was a cock-tease and asking for trouble."

Detective Harry Hansen in a newspaper interview years later said, "The killing seems to be based on an unbelievable anger. I suppose sex was the motive, or at least the fact that the killer was *denied* sex."

Will Fowler told me Harry Hansen had a secret question, and only Fowler and Bevo Means knew the answer. "But if one word was ever printed or even hinted at," Fowler said, "Harry Hansen would have come down so hard and heavy on whoever spilled the beans, they wouldn't know what hit them!

"There was something physically wrong with Elizabeth Short. She couldn't have sex without medical help. Infantile genitals—an extra thick hymen or something like that, not fully developed," Fowler chuckled. "Think irony... you have to think irony," he said. "Think of this beautiful woman with all the guys after her... and she *couldn't* put out, *couldn't* give them what they wanted."

I thought Will's statements were absurd. I *knew* what Bette looked like. Bette bore no resemblance to any of the photos I'd seen as a child—people with all sorts of hormonal and sexual developmental problems.

But I thought I should check it out. I went to the medical library at the University of California Medical Center in San Francisco. A librarian found some references: women with undeveloped vaginal canals, a condition that occurred once in a million births. I thought of an article I read about Harry Hansen and his comment, years after the murder, that there was information only the killer would know, a "one-in-a-million guess." I thought of Bette's friend back home and Bette's "shocking secret"—the secret the friend would never reveal.

The first book describing the rare genital condition was published in 1953, six years after Bette's murder. The photographs in the book showed very attractive and well-built women.

I contacted Dr. John Money, a leading forensic sexologist with Johns Hopkins University. He informed me that there were variations in this condition, but that all of the women tend to be very feminine and quite attractive. The women also tended to be motherly and nurturing. Mood swings were common. Sometimes the women felt optimistic, as if they would wake up one day and the condition would be gone. Other times they would feel hopeless, as if nothing could change their plight. Dr. Money stated that a famous actress and a well-known model, whose names he could not divulge, had some form of the condition.

Dr. Money said there was not enough information to determine the exact nature of Bette's medical problem. It could have been any number of conditions: imperforate hymen, vaginal agenesis, vaginal atresia, longitudinal vaginal septa, transverse vaginal septa, androgen-insensitivity syndrome, or Rokitansky syndrome.

Muriel Short confirmed that Bette had some "female" problems. She remembered Bette's giant-sized Lydia Pinkham bottle. "But we never discussed what the problem was," Muriel said.

Valerie Reynolds, Bette's niece, became indignant at the suggestion. "Why is it that if my aunt wasn't sleeping around, it has to be attributed to some medical condition, not that Aunt Bette was trying to live a moral life," Reynolds said.

Bette's "strange behavior," her "secretiveness," and her constant moving around gave rise to speculation and rumors of prostitution. Fiction writers and amateur sleuths began taking their cues from the newspaper innuendoes and went a step further by portraying Elizabeth Short as an actress—in porno films.

Harry Hansen scoffed at the speculative dark-side musings of writers and the arm-chair detectives. In a TV interview, Harry told Tony Valdez of Fox TV:

> *There was no record of any solicitation, offering or resorting or prostitution in any way, shape, or form. She was no pushover. She'd bait and take all she could get and give out nothing. She did not put out. Looking at it in perspective, I suppose, the killer did his thing and got away with it.*

With all their digging, within a couple of weeks of the murder, the police and reporters had exhausted their leads. The forty policemen who went door-to-door asking questions were beefed up with Sheriff's deputies to four hundred—and they still turned up nothing. Whatever "sightings" reported between January 9th, when Elizabeth Short was last seen, and January 15th, when her body was found in the vacant lot, appeared to be false. The trail of the Black Dahlia ended at the Biltmore Hotel—until the day Jimmy Richardson received a telephone call that "sent a shiver" up his spine.

On January 24, 1947, a caller made a joking reference to the lagging news coverage and offered his assistance to the City Editor. The "silky" voice on the phone promised to send the *Examiner* a special packet with some personal effects belonging to the victim.

Richardson said he could barely speak. Was this a hoax or

the killer? Richardson managed to ask, "What things?"

"A few things from her handbag," the voice said.

Richardson tried to keep the caller on the line, but there was a click before the switchboard operator, Mae Northern, could trace the call. Other reporters thought Sid Hughes was playing another of his jokes, until the packet showed up a day later.

Large red letters forming the word: "Dahlia's" caught a postal clerk's attention. There was a message and an address of sorts on the over-sized envelope. Odd-sized letters cut from a newspaper formed the cryptic message:

> To Los Angeles Examiner and other papers
> Here is Dahlia's belongings
> Letter to follow

The postal clerk motioned for his line supervisor who took one quick look at the envelope and called upstairs to postal inspectors. After a terse discussion of the US Postal Code, the police and all the Los Angeles newspapers were called. The killer's packet had been intercepted.

Reporters crowded around as the postal inspector put on a pair of gloves and opened the envelope. Out tumbled a Greyhound claim check, Elizabeth Short's birth certificate, a Western Union message signed "Red," some snapshots, a few business cards, a small leather address book with the name "Mark Hansen" embossed in gold on the cover, and a newspaper clipping of Matt Gordon's obituary. Where the clipping said his "bride who he planned to meet and marry in Bedford," the "and marry" was crossed out. The "B" in the word "Bedford" was changed to an "M."

A faint smell of gasoline emanated from the three-by-eight inch envelope. The police surmised the killer intended to burn the packet and changed his mind. Richardson thought differently. He pointed out that a person well versed in "contemporary police science" would know that gasoline destroys the traces of fingerprints.

Captain Donahoe called the address book a "big break in the case." He admitted to the press that "over seventy-five names, both men and women, and some of them *well-known Hollywood personalities*," were in the book. "This book is going to be dynamite!" Donahoe exclaimed. He backed down a day later, expressing concern about "protecting the innocent."

Will Fowler said the reporters looked over the contents of the envelope and press photographers took photos of the various items, "but the names in the address book were *off-limits*."

Before the news blackout, Aggie Underwood revealed the names on the business cards: Carl Bausinger, Jimmy Bufello, Dr. A. B. Bux, Robert S. Geissinger, Wayne Grey, Jimmy Harrigan, E. A. Jack Kleinau, Victor Lewis, and Chet Montgomery, whose name was typed on a *Hollywood Wolves Membership Card.*

"But," said Gerry Ramlow, "it was the name embossed *on* the cover of the address book, Mark M. Hansen, that caused the big stir. The police had routinely questioned Hansen the week before, and Mark Hansen claimed to know nothing about 'the girl.' This, despite the fact she had been living at Mark Hansen's home on Carlos Avenue from August through October of 1946. She shared a room with Ann Toth, an actress, and Mark Hansen's current girl friend."

"This time around, Mark admitted the address book was his. For Christ's sake, his name was on it! But he still wouldn't admit to dating her. He said he didn't give her the book. He said she stole it. 'The book was a gift from some relatives in Denmark,' he said. 'I never bothered with her. She dated hoodlum types.'

"His girl friend, Ann Toth, was sitting beside him, and she got mad when he mentioned hoodlums. Said it wasn't true. Claimed Beth was a 'nice' girl. She was quiet, Toth said. 'She didn't drink, and she didn't smoke.' Toth sent Beth $20 around Christmas time. She admitted that Beth was sometimes cynical about men, and that she'd get herself into hot water but said Beth was adept at getting herself out. Toth lit into us, wanting to know why we couldn't write about the good side of people."

Mark Marinue Hansen, the gray-haired owner of the Florentine Gardens, became major Suspect Number Two. The middle-aged entrepreneur from St. Louis had his connections and his business interests, but he was *not* related to Harry Hansen.

Mark Hansen had been in and out of the newspapers since the 1930s, when he was a movie theater business partner of the Skouras Brothers, Charles and Spyros, in St. Louis. Spyros eventually became head of Twentieth Century Fox Studio, credited with the "Movies Are Better Than Ever" campaign of the 1950s.

Mark Hansen owned Roseland and other dance halls. He was part owner of the Florentine Gardens nightclub with Frank Bruni, and like many influential people in LA, he was rumored to have been involved with some bootlegging during prohibition. Hansen had no criminal record, but the FBI had his prints on file. In June of 1943 Mark Hansen had applied for a Special Deputy Sheriff Commission.

By the end of World War II, Mark Hansen had become a well-respected member of the Hollywood community, a sponsor of the Junior Philharmonic. He left an estate valued at 2.5 million dollars when he died in 1964. With his wife, Ida, Mark Hansen had bought up land in Hollywood. They had been separated for years, but they were connected by business deals. She lived in Beverly Hills. He lived in a large house on Carlos Avenue, directly behind the Florentine Gardens, and rented rooms to aspiring young actresses.

Mark Hansen had more than his share of trouble with women. Some of his girlfriends didn't know he was married. In 1936, stage actress Faith Norris won a breach of promise suit against him. Norris claimed Mark Hansen promised to marry her. Judge Fletcher Bowron ruled in her favor after Hansen was a no-show, but Bowron reserved judgment on the amount to be awarded. The actress asked for $125,000. After a week's recess, Judge Bowron ordered Hansen to pay Norris $100. Bowron was later elected as the "reformist" mayor of Los Angeles.

Two years after Bette Short's murder, Mark Hansen barely survived an attack on his life. Lola Titus, one of his "dime-a-dance girls," shot Hansen while he was shaving. A taxi dancer permit listed her real name as Beverly Alice Bennet.

Police investigating the shooting discovered photos of Bette in Hansen's place. Lola Titus not only claimed Hansen had made love to her and promised to marry her, she also made a bizarre accusation. "Mark is telling people I killed the Black Dahlia," she said. Lola Titus was found guilty of attempted murder and committed to a mental institution.

Nils Thor Granlund, the resident impresario of the Florentine Gardens, kept his eye on the aspiring actresses living in Mark Hansen's house. The young women hoped that NTG or Granny (as he was called by show business people), would "discover" them and give them their "big break." Sometimes NTG's latest "discovery" stayed with him in a small apartment over Mark Hansen's garage, which NTG kept in addition to his large home near the Greek Theater. Rumor had it that NTG and Mark Hansen "encouraged" the girls to "entertain" celebrity guests and special customers.

The penchant of the Florentine Gardens (and Earl Carroll's) for employing underage girls caused legal headaches for the owners. The Gardens put fifteen-year old twins Jean and Dean Stull in the floor show. Dean Stull became sexually involved with a Florentine Gardens regular, an older serviceman, Captain Morrison Wilkerson. Stull's parents, along with the owners of the Florentine Gardens, were prosecuted—for placing their daughters in "unsavory situations."

Impresario Granlund gave Yvonne de Carlo her first break in 1940, when Yvonne was barely sixteen—a featured spot in the floor show. While at the Gardens, Yvonne had her share of men after her, including Hollywood celebrities Franchot "Doc" Tone, Burgess "Buzz" Meredith, Van Heflin, and Orson Welles. Pleading her young age, and virginity ("I'm saving myself for marriage"), she said that most men would take no for an answer. But not Orson Welles.

The year was 1941, and the young and slim Welles was the new "talk of the land," wrote de Carlo in her 1976 autobiography, *Yvonne*. "His *Citizen Kane* had just been released.... When Buzz Meredith introduced him to me, I clung to his every word." Yvonne was flattered that a "genius" such as Orson Welles was interested in her. They were supposed to be going out for dinner. Instead he drove her around, winding up at his home. She couldn't recall if it was in Bel Air or Brentwood. [Welles lived at 426 Rockingham Drive in Brentwood.] De Carlo said she used a bronze Ming sculpture to ward him off. Welles became furious for not getting his way, she said.

Long after Yvonne de Carlo left the Gardens, the programmes still featured her photo in the centerfold. The Garden's playbills gave Nils T. Granlund top billing: *NTG, America's Premiers Cabaret Impresario Presents....* He was credited with discovering a number of beauties: Betty Hutton, Gwen Verdon, Marie "The Body" McDonald, Jean Wallace, and one of Orson Welles' paramours (while he was married to Rita Hayworth), Lili St. Cyr.

Starting out in the 1920s working for Texas Guinan, NTG became a chief scout for the Ziegfield Follies. In 1940, when Granlund took the reins at the Florentine Gardens, the nightclub was in deep financial trouble. The sparkling white building with its palm trees and Greek neon-lit columns was considered a "lesser" club, not having the class acts. The Gardens could only hope to catch the people Earl Carroll's turned away.

Through his New York contacts, NTG booked stars: Beatrice Kay, Sophie Tucker, Paul Whiteman, the Mills Brothers. He livened up the musical revues with his "NTG Beauties," glamorous gals prancing around on stage with little covering their bodies, and the crowd going wild.

NTG created a good-natured chaos, spotlighting the celebrities in the audience and the people on-the-rise, cajoling people to join the singing and dancing on stage. Yvonne de Carlo and most of the showgirls despised the antics of the drunken men climbing over the brim of the top-hat-shaped stage. "We were expected to smile and act as if we enjoyed them pawing at us," she said.

NTG left the Florentine Gardens in 1948. On April 21, 1957, a few months before the release of his biography, *Blondes, Brunettes and Bullets,* NTG's taxicab was sideswiped as it left the Riviera parking lot in Las Vegas. He was thrown from the cab and died a few hours later from a fractured skull and internal injuries. Yvonne de Carlo claimed his body.

The Florentine Gardens was one of Marilyn Monroe's

favorite clubs when she was still Norma Jean and living around the corner in the Studio Club, a well-respected rooming house for actresses.

Occasionally Mickey Cohen and other gangster types could be seen at the Gardens. "Part of the lure," a long-time Hollywood resident told me. The same lure gave rise to the rumors of police corruption and a cover-up to protect Mark Hansen.

A number of people hinted to me about a police cover-up, but it was writer/publisher Lionel Rolfe, who in November 1988, gave me the name of a newsman willing to lay out the whole story. I'd met Lionel Rolfe by coincidence, through Gary Bryson, then-director of the Special Collections Library at the University of Southern California (USC). Gary introduced me to Lionel, who happened by while I was digging through some dusty boxes whose contents were yet to be catalogued and filed away.

"You have to talk to Nieson Himmel," Lionel told me. "He works nights at the *LA Times* on the police beat. Nieson has been around a long time, has some ideas about what happened to the Black Dahlia. You should talk to him. Phi Beta Kappa. Extraordinary memory for details. Call him. Tell him I gave you his name."

Nieson Himmel was friendly on the telephone. He told me that he lived close to where I was staying. "I'll pick you up and we can have lunch," he said.

Nieson, a rotund man, walked with some difficulty. In measured steps we approached the entrance to a Denny's restaurant in Pasadena. Looking straight ahead, he started to speak. "She had a small vagina, couldn't have sex with a man," Nieson said. "There was this guy. Someone I knew. He wasn't a very nice guy. She needed a place to stay. Couldn't pay her rent. Was locked out of her room. He let her stay overnight, tried to have sex with her."

"What do you mean, tried to have sex with her?"

"As I said, he wasn't a very nice guy."

It was cool inside Denny's, air conditioned. We didn't have to wait long for a booth, since the lunch crowd was thinning out.

"Denny's has good soup. The rest of the food is lousy. But the soup is good. I always order two bowls." He motioned for the waitress.

"I had just started working for the *Los Angeles Herald Express* when the 'Dahlia' was killed," Nieson said. "Only been there a couple of months. I was there when Aggie Underwood became the City Editor. I sometimes ran errands for her. She helped me. Taught me a lot. She was a damn good reporter. The *Herald Ex's* top crime reporter. Aggie knew how to get the stories." Nieson paused, gave his order to the hovering waitress—two bowls of soup. I opted for one.

"So you knew the Dahlia?" he asked.

I recognized my cue. I'd been through it before—time to tell my story, or some portion of it—how I knew the woman known as the Black Dahlia and how our bond of friendship had formed. It seemed that each time I finished my story, whoever was listening would stop referring to the "Dahlia" and start calling Bette by her real name. Nieson Himmel was no different.

"It has been so many years," he said, "my memory isn't what it used to be. Your friend... Bette... how can I help?"

"Lionel Rolfe told me you had a theory about who killed her." I said.

Nieson hesitated. "There were a lot of rumors about a police cover-up," he said. "You have to understand, there was a lot of corruption in the police department in those days. People said that Harry Hansen's partner, Finis Albania Brown, was a bookie. We called him F.A. for 'Fat Ass.' Mark Hansen was rumored to be Finis' layoff man, covering Finis on the big bets." He paused as the waitress brought our soup.

"Do you know what a layoff man is?" the newsman asked.

"Never heard the term before," I said.

"He's the guy who covers the big bets. You lay off the bet to him, but you have to pay him back if he covers for you. Anyway, as the story goes, Finis was into Mark for $5,000. A lot of money in those days. Mark Hansen had supposedly been after Elizabeth Short for months, wanting to get her into the sack. As the story goes, she wouldn't come across. Mark became infuriated and killed her. Finis Brown supposedly covered up for

Mark Hansen, cajoling his brother Thad Brown, Chief of Detectives, to protect Finis and destroy some evidence. Hansen, supposedly, then forgave Finis Brown's debt."

Surprised at Nieson's frankness, I focused intently and made mental notes of the details. I was vaguely aware of the restaurant sounds: dishes clanking, voices murmuring, people moving back and forth past our table.

"What about Agness Underwood?" I interjected.

"Aggie would hint that she knew something, but she never told me anything. She died a few years ago. Left her papers to the Journalism Department at Cal State Northridge. You never can tell. She may have left some notes behind."

Nieson paused, and his voice became softer, less strident. "I always felt sorry for the girl. Somehow I thought the whole thing was sort of a sociological phenomena. Her fiancé killed and she's sort of floating around, wandering aimless. Doesn't know what to do. There were a lot of women in that position after the war. Their husbands or the guys they were going to marry, dead. No jobs. Housing shortage. No place to go. There was a big recession in 1948-50, but by 1946 times were already getting tough.

"Some people say Finis went crazy, lost his marbles. He may still be alive. Thad Brown died a few years ago. He was well-respected. Tony Valdez over at Fox did a TV program a few years ago. He mentioned something about police involvement. Maybe you can get a copy of the tape. Sometimes it's so hard to remember details after all these years."

We sat quietly for a few minutes in the now-deserted restaurant. I broke the silence and spoke first, posing another question.

"About Jean Spangler, the actress who disappeared. An actor who knew both Jean and Bette said they were similar, resembled each other. I found a story about Jean's disappearance in October 1949. Was her body ever found? Were the crimes related?"

"All they ever found was Jean's purse at the entrance to Griffith Park," Nieson said. "No one thinks the murders were connected. Most people in the know think the mobster Fratiano was involved, or she might have been killed in a plane crash on a spur-of-the-moment trip to Las Vegas. Her wealthy ex-husband was also a suspect. As I recall, they were involved in a bitter custody battle. There were a couple of other murders around that time, another woman named Jeanne, a nurse, Jeanne French. The 'flying nurse,' I think she was called. And there was an earlier murder, Georgette Bauerdorf. The *Herald Express,* the paper I was with, tried to link some of the murders together, called them *The Werewolf Murders*. Has the werewolf struck again? That kind of crap."

We had been talking for over three hours. The waitress was giving us the evil eye for monopolizing her table. As we left, I slipped a few extra dollars under my plate—rent on the booth. Nieson drove me back to where I was staying. He gave me his home phone number and asked me to keep in touch.

Nieson Himmel had given me plenty of material to check out. He seemed to corroborate the information given to me by Will Fowler—about the "infantile genitals." Strange, I thought, to be the first thing both men had mentioned in my interviews with them. Was that common knowledge among a small select group of people? The many articles and books I had read about the murder did not even hint at the possibility.

Dace Taube, the new director at USC's Special Collections, helped me find some rare news clippings about Thad Brown that could have been the basis for the cover-up rumors. In the late 1940s, Thad and District Attorney H. Leo Stanley feuded over some bloody clothing items that were removed from the police evidence room and destroyed. Stanley leaked the information to the press. Thad Brown issued a statement claiming the police "thoroughly checked them out and decided they had no value." The disputed evidence figured in the Jeanne French copy-cat murder of February 1947, *not* the month-earlier Black Dahlia murder.

I telephoned Gerry Ramlow and asked him about the possibility of a police cover-up to protect Mark Hansen. Gerry told me that rumors had been floating around for years, but that he didn't put much stock in them. "I think the killer mailed the address book to put suspicion on Mark Hansen," Ramlow said.

"I heard that a few pages were torn out of the book. Maybe the killer's name was on one of them. I didn't get a look at the inside of the book, so I never saw whose handwriting was in it—the Dahlia's, Mark Hansen's or both. Mark claimed she stole the book." Gerry laughed. "Well, you know, she wouldn't be the first one to lift an address book to see if there were any important names and phone numbers in it.

"I can't remember when it was, but Finis Brown was soon dropped as Harry Hansen's partner, and Jack McReadie took his place."

Thad Brown and Jack 'Father' McReadie were universally well-liked by reporters and other police, while Finis had more than his share of enemies. "Thad Brown was a cop's cop, well-respected," I was repeatedly told. "Stood up for his men, but with a reputation for being fair and honest." Finis was variously described as "real strange," "couldn't believe anything he said," "had a bug up his ass about one suspect," and "hard to believe he and Thad were brothers, Thad being so smart and all."

Movie stars could count on Thad Brown to be a friend. "I was grateful to Thad Brown—the considerate way he protected me," wrote Kirk Douglas in his autobiography. Douglas was being investigated in the disappearance of Jean Spangler, the stunning movie bit player who bore a striking resemblance to Bette Short. Spangler had worked as a showgirl at the Florentine Gardens. She was linked to Kirk Douglas by the newspapers. Jean Spangler knew many other Hollywood people whose names never made it into the press, including Ronald Reagan. The Jean Spangler disappearance, like the Black Dahlia murder, was never solved.

Finis Brown continued to go out of state chasing 'Dahlia' leads—Florida, Texas, New York, and the Great Lakes region. In 1951 Finis checked out a tip from Chicago police. Records indicated a woman, who might be Elizabeth Short, was referred by a Chicago doctor to an Indiana urologist in 1946. All medical records of women with gynecological problems were routinely checked by the Chicago authorities as possible abortions.

The handwritten medical report listed the woman as B. Fickle from Lexington, Massachusetts, Age: 21, Blood Type:

AB. The indecipherable notations by the Chicago doctor were:

> AB/ND. CO;
> F/21/W/AB
> PLB/H-2/morphylgy
> HERED. GEN.
> Refered to David Stine URO.

By the spring of 1946, Bette had re-kindled her war-time romance with Lt. Gordon Fickling. She was on her way to meet Fickling in Long Beach, California, where he was to be mustered out of the service. En route, Bette would have to change trains in Chicago. Extending her layover in order to consult with a specialist was well within the realm of possibilities.

The name, B. Fickle, written by the doctor could have been a hastily scrawled B. Fickling. Bette's age, 21, was the same as the patient's. Bette had the same uncommon blood type, AB. The note seemed to indicate that the patient had an inherited problem (HERED.) that was either genital (GEN.) or genetic.

I remembered that on occasion, Bette visited with the neighborhood physician, Dr. Landy. Perhaps, I thought, the visits were not social calls but medical appointments. Through Medford sources I found out that Dr. Landy had died and his wife Martha had moved to Tennessee. I spoke to Mrs. Landy on the telephone. "Bette Short may have spoken with the doctor on occasion," she said. "But I really don't know what they discussed or if he referred her to anyone. If there were medical records they'd be so old, they would have been purged by now."

Gerry Ramlow thought at one point the killer was about to give himself up. "But then it could have been another of Sid Hughes' jokes," Ramlow said. "A postcard was mailed to the *Examiner*. A kid's handwriting. A new ball-point pen was used. That was unusual. Most people still used fountain pens." The killer wrote:

> HERE IT IS
> TURNING IN WED.

Jan 29 10 A.M.
HAD FUN AT POLICE
BLACK DAHLIA AVENGER

"I got to City Hall early," said Ramlow. "We waited on the steps. Mostly police and other reporters were there."

Seconds gave way to minutes, to an hour.

"We finally realized the killer was going to be a no-show. Donahoe asked us to take down a statement and print it. He said he believed the postcard was authentic, that it came from the killer, and that the killer had intended to give himself up."

To the killer Donahoe said: "I want you to know that I will meet with you anytime, anywhere, and while I can't promise anything, that you will get fair treatment."

An answer came the next day, pasted-up letters on an envelope:

> HAVE changed my mind, you would not give me a square deal.
> Dahlia killing was justified

Five latent fingerprints were lifted from the letters, but the FBI crime lab in Washington, DC could find no matches. The FBI concluded that the original envelope, which contained items belonging to the victim, came from the killer, but that other communications came from individuals who had "no knowledge or connection to the case."

SEVEN
The Hollywood Connection

By the end of 1988, conducting interviews had become emotionally draining; two a day were about all I could handle. Working late at night became impossible. I'd have nightmares, a strange recurring dream—someone would be calling my name and knocking at the door, but I'd be afraid to answer. Each dream became more intense—the knocking became pounding, then the doorbell, and finally, the insistent ringing of the telephone.

When I made trips to Los Angeles I'd stay with an aunt, Ardys Jefferson. Ardie was a feisty woman, seventy-years old, a chain smoker who, nevertheless, won her battle with cancer. She aptly fit the description of the Little Old Lady from Pasadena. Ardie had to drop out of college during the Depression. She found work as a nanny caring for Mary Astor's children. Ardie became accustomed to the movie people who were in and out of the Astor mansion. Her biggest thrill, she said, was the day Clark Gable gave her a ride to downtown Los Angeles. "He was so nice and charming and tried to make me feel at ease."

Ardie started nagging me about someone she wanted me to call—John Babcock with KABC. "He writes about the history of Los Angeles," she said. "Mostly the political and the criminal aspects. On one of his programs I heard him mention the Black Dahlia. If anyone can fill you in, he sure can. Call him!"

Ardie became tired of my foot-dragging, and one morning she handed me an address and phone number. "I called him," she said. "John Babcock wants to talk to you." I met the award-winning journalist at the Los Angeles television station where he was Head of Special Programs. Babcock had received an Emmy for a TV news series on the political influence of the Times-Mirror Company (publisher of the *Los Angeles Times)*, and the prestigious Peabody Award for his work with Wayne Satz exposing racism in the Los Angeles Police Department. Babcock was writing a book on the department's history.

After a few conversations we realized we'd met previously. He had been the director of a political TV spot filmed in my

Modesto, California home. A bountiful table with a cornucopia of foods grown in the Central Valley was his inspiration. The television spot helped to win a very hot environmental issue—construction of the New Melones Dam which farmers and the local Sierra Club supported.

I mentioned to Babcock my conversation with Nieson Himmel. Babcock, like Gerry Ramlow, had heard the rumors, but had a different take on the situation. "You have to assume that Mark Hansen was well-connected," Babcock said, "considering the people that frequented the Florentine Gardens. And he could have called in his chips, but not only for himself. Maybe he had a vested interest in protecting someone that came into his club. Mark Hansen put pressure on his girls to entertain the good customers. What if he had linked up the Black Dahlia to the guy who killed her?

"Back in the '40s, it wasn't like today, a matter of one or two bad cops. Corruption within the Los Angeles Police Department had become *institutionalized*. LAPD corruption went to the highest levels, operating under a tight system developed over the years. Personalized 'courtesy cards' of the policemen were given out as favors, a form of currency to be redeemed, usable when someone needed *special assistance* to get out of a jam. Possession of a courtesy card became a form of protection against arrest and bad publicity.

"An arresting officer would take the card as payment when he 'fixed' a situation. Sometimes substantial cash would also change hands. The policeman whose name was on the card became obligated to redeem it by doing whatever favor was then asked of him.

"Press agents hired by the major studios maintained a close relationship with LAPD. The agents made money, *big* money, covering up for the stars and keeping the studios out of trouble. The police could be 'trusted,' but not the press. The powerful gossip columnists—Louella Parsons, Hedda Hopper, Sidney Skolsky—precursors of today's tabloid journalists, had their own fiefdoms, a separate system based on informers and friends that occasionally overlapped with LAPD. Reporters were the loose cannons. But the general rule was that the stars were protected—the ones with box office draw, that is. If the studio was ready to cut someone loose, they'd let him sink in his own scandal."

Babcock credited William Parker with cleaning up the police department. "He became chief of police after the 'Brenda Allen Scandal' broke in the newspapers," Babcock said. "There were wholesale firings and transfers. Chief of Police 'Cowboy' Horrall was forced into early retirement. Thad Brown and William Parker fought for the top position, but Parker was chosen. He was a cop's cop and fair, with a reputation for being honest, but hard and demanding. Parker's reign ushered in the years of reform. He started the psychological testing of police recruits."

The arrest of Brenda Allen, LA's top madame, was Gerry Ramlow's big-time exclusive story—two years after the Black Dahlia murder. Ramlow went along on the police bust and found Brenda Allen's trick book. His headline story exposed the connection between Brenda Allen and a lieutenant working in Administrative Vice out of Central. But it was only the tip of the iceberg.

Ramlow confided he always felt he "found" the trick book because one of the cops wanted it that way. Ramlow told me there was a Grand Jury investigation of the police and Brenda Allen in 1949 that also looked into the "Dahlia" case.

Sergeant Charles Stoker from Hollywood Vice became the star witness—he had bugged Brenda Allen's telephone with the aid of Ray Pinker. Even before the final report was issued, firings and transfers had begun. A "partial reorganization" of the Los Angeles Police Department was in the works.

I secured a copy of the Grand Jury Final Report but was told I could not have a copy of the testimony unless indictments were returned. "The testimony used to return indictments becomes a matter of public record," the clerk told me, "but all other testimony is sealed by state law."

The 1949 Grand Jury Report, a slim document of twenty-one pages, uncovered "deplorable conditions indicating corrupt practices and misconduct by some members of the law enforcement agencies in the county... alarming increase in the number of unsolved murders... jurisdictional disputes and jealousies among law enforcement agencies." The Grand Jury also alluded to attempts made to discredit its findings "by some public servants and private citizens."

And there on page three, in the fourth paragraph of this historic document, were the first official words, the first indication that there may have been substance to the rumors of police involvement:

In the closing days of its session, the 1949 Grand Jury probed into the murder of Elizabeth Short, who is known as the "Black Dahlia." This is but one of a number of unsolved brutal murders which have taken place in Los Angeles during the past six or seven years. Testimony given by certain investigating officers working this case was clear and well defined, while other officers showed apparent evasiveness.

In addition to the sadistic murder and mutilation of Elizabeth Short, the record shows that other victims of unsolved murders included Mary Tate, Mrs. Jeanne French, Evelyn Winters, Rosenda Montgomery, Mrs. Laura Treldsted, Gladys Kern and Louise Springer. 'Mysterious Disappearances' are involved in other cases... such as Mimi Boomhower and Jean Spangler. This record reveals, in the opinion of the 1949 Grand Jury, conditions that are appalling and fearsome...

The 1949 Grand Jury has come to the conclusion that something is radically wrong with the present system of apprehending the guilty. [Italics added.]

The 1949 Grand Jury recommended that the Black Dahlia and other unsolved murders be investigated further by the next Grand Jury.

Aggie Underwood had expected an indictment to be returned in the Black Dahlia murder. She had been given a tip that the 1949 Grand Jury was charged with looking into Bette's murder. In Aggie Underwood's old files at Cal State Northridge, I came across a 1949 unsigned memo typed on newscopy:

black dahlia

The "Black Dahlia" death chamber has been located, according to expert investigators, the Herald Express is able to disclose today as the County Grand Jury prepared to probe the butcher murder mystery, still officially unsolved after more than two and one-half years.

Bloody sheets and blood-stained clothes of the same size worn by the "Black Dahlia," Elizabeth Short, 22, are known to have been seen in the suspected death chamber, investigators declare.

The quarters in which Miss Short is believed to have been slain are situated in a structure on a busy street less than 15 minutes' drive from the weed-covered lot in which her mutilated boy was found on January , 1947. [sic]

The lot, on Norton avenue [sic] near Coliseum drive [sic], is situated almost on a bee-line with the quarters where investigators believe Miss Short's gay life was ended in fiendish death.

Officially, Aggie Underwood was *not* covering the Black Dahlia news story. William Randolph Hearst had mysteriously ordered her taken off a few days after Aggie's exclusive interview with suspect Red Manley. A furious Aggie, in protest, brought a large embroidery hoop to the City Room.

Aggie, as the story goes, calmly sat at her desk, pushing a needle and colored thread back and forth through the linen, not saying a word. Every so often, with a flourish, she'd hold the hoop high and flash it towards the other reporters as if saying, "Hey guys! Look at this crime reporter's new assignment!"

On the second day of the stalemate, Herb Krauch, the crusty managing editor, bellowed the length of the newsroom, "Aggie! Get rid of that god-damn embroidery!" He then told her she was back on the Dahlia case.

Aggie's next by-line story, in bold headlines, asked the question: "Will Dahlia Slaying Join Album of Unsolved

Murders?" Aggie had dredged up the unsolved murders of Ora Murray, Georgette Bauerdorf and Gertrude Landon, linking them to the Black Dahlia murder. Photos of all four women accompanied the story.

Two days later, Aggie was given a "promotion." Krauch informed Aggie that Old Man Hearst was making her the *first* woman city editor in the country. The job was a form of punishment. Krauch told Aggie to give all her Black Dahlia notes to another reporter. When she turned the notes over to the reporter, Aggie, it is believed, made copies for herself.

No one had ever lasted more than two years as the *Herald Express* city editor. Aggie Underwood would last seventeen years and became a legend as the most popular city editor in the newspaper's history.

"Aggie Underwood was tough and one of the boys," an old-time reporter told me. "She didn't resort to cussing or idle threats. Aggie kept everyone in line with a baseball bat she banged down on her heavy oak desk, leaving marks—a clear signal she meant business."

Agness Underwood counted gangster Mickey Cohen and his wife LaVonne among her friends and sources.

Aggie helped cub reporters and regaled them with tales of her days on the police beat, telling how she was taken off the Dahlia case, not once, but twice. "Kicked upstairs the second time," she'd say. But she didn't let on that she never gave it up, never stopped working on the Black Dahlia murder.

Rilla Underwood, Aggie's daughter-in-law, said that throughout the early 1950s Aggie met surreptitiously with Dr. Paul De River, the LAPD psychiatrist. They'd meet at Aggie's house late at night and pore over the books de River had written, discussing theories and drawing psychological profiles of people—some who were quite prominent, and others who were low-level hoods and hangers-on. At one point they were talking about extradition. "For a while around 1953-54," Rilla said, "Aggie seemed to behave differently, nervous, and took to carrying a gun. She warned me to watch the children and be extra careful."

"There were grave suspicions about one guy who was

questioned... evidence was almost conclusive. The police had him, and they let him go," Aggie Underwood said years later, adding, "He was no one of much importance."

During one of my meetings with John Babcock I mentioned a *Los Angeles Times* story I had come across about an alleged "smut ring." According to the article, Bette Short and her former roommate, Lynn Martin, had posed nude for a photographer by the name of George Price. I told Babcock I had also picked up rumors of a porno film and was trying to locate the nude photos and film footage.

"You won't find them," Babcock said, "because there aren't any. Not one nude photo or porno film of her ever surfaced—except the photos of her body in the empty lot. Porno films were made in Mexico with prostitutes. Believe me, there's always been a willing market for such stuff, and if any photos or films with the Black Dahlia were around, they would have made a bundle of money for the person who had them. You heard nothing, not even a whisper about porno the first ten or so years after the murder. It started with Dunne's novel *True Confessions*—a mishmash of fact and fiction based on the LA Madame, Brenda Allen, with a murder like the Black Dahlia as a backdrop."

"Didn't he call the victim the *virgin tramp*?"

"Yes. That's what he called her. Dunne always insisted it was a work of fiction and people should not read anything else into it."

"What about Bette's life in Hollywood? Her behavior may have been bizarre for the 1940s, but..."

Babcock cut me off. "Listen," he said, "her behavior was *not* bizarre for those days. She was fun-loving and going out night-clubbing, just as everyone else did."

Babcock said he'd help me by writing a newspaper article asking anyone with information to contact me. He handed me a slip of paper with some names and phone numbers. "These are people who went out with her," he said. "You can use my name."

I told Babcock that when we talked I'd get an image of Bette as this beautiful woman swimming in a sea of sharks.

"Be careful," he said. "The sharks are still there."

The first person on Babcock's list denied knowing Bette. "It couldn't have been me," Lam said. "I was married at the time." He admitted that Beth went out with his friend. Lam was reticent, but he did remember his friend talking about some Greek businessmen from out of town. "She went along to the night club, dinner and dancing. She usually was pleasant company, fun to be around."

During the interviews, I noticed that when I asked people to forget about the murder and think of Bette when she was alive, they would relax and smile or laugh a little. They all told me more or less the same thing. She was fun and seemed "interested" in people. "Beth was Beth," they said. And if she did get moody, it was easy to forgive her, because times were rough with the returning GIs, the strikes, and the housing shortage; and she never had "unkind" words. Her politeness seemed to make a lasting impression.

"But she wasn't shy about asking if you 'could stake her,' and you'd want to help her if you could," said Fred, who met Beth when he lived at a residential hotel on North Orange Street in Hollywood, the Hawthorne. "I was separated from my wife at the time," he said. "Beth was living marginally, employed off and on as a waitress and sometimes a hat model. She was taking care of a man on the first floor who was trying to lick the bottle—he was going through the DT's. She asked me if I'd look in on the guy while she was gone. Beth wanted to go away for the weekend, but didn't want to leave the guy. The guy may have been helping her out and keeping the manager at bay. Can't remember the manager's name. Think it was Scotty Wolfe—might have been the owner—white-haired. Moved a few months after the murder. Would provide rooms to some of the gals in exchange for 'favors.'"

Someone else thought the owner's name was Jack Richmond and he had gone to Israel shortly after the murder. "Jack knows who killed her," the person said.

At the Hawthorne, Beth shared a room with Margery Graham, a friend from back east, and Lynn Martin, who later proved to be a sixteen year-old runaway from Long Beach,

Linda Meyer. Margery Graham said she was "staking" Beth while Beth tried to break into the movies. When Margery Graham left in the autumn of 1946 because jobs had become scarce, Beth decided to stay in California. She told Margery, "I'd rather die than go through another New England winter."

According to newspaper accounts, Lynn Martin was heard sobbing in a Ventura motel the night the story broke about Bette's murder. Lynn told police her boyfriend "Duke" Wellington, a forty-year-old entrepreneur, had urged her to go to the police because she had lived with Beth and maybe could help with the investigation, but Lynn was afraid. She hadn't seen Beth Short since September, Lynn said, and they really were never friends. Other people disagreed, claiming Beth had befriended Lynn.

Former neighbors of Duke Wellington, who watched over Wellington's home when he was out of town, told me that they saw Lynn Martin and other women visiting Wellington. But the neighbors could not recall ever seeing anyone resembling the Black Dahlia.

A couple of guys who lived in the Hawthorne, Donald Leyes and Harold Costa, said they would often fix Beth up with a guy when they were going out to dinner—help her get something to eat. They remembered her as being broke and skipping meals. Talk about Beth was "outrageous," they said. "She was classy, but down on her luck, often times lacking food money."

Another man, who dated her a few times, said he really like her. "But it was going nowhere, and she'd borrow money a few dollars at a time," he said. "She wouldn't lower herself. If she had been willing to, money wouldn't have been a problem for her." He thought she avoided "bad situations" by leaving when she found herself in "over her head."

One person, who was stationed at Fort McArthur in 1946, recalled having a date with Beth in September of that year. They went to see the Tony Martin radio show at CBS and then to dinner at Tom Breneman's supper club. He was impressed that the head waiter at Breneman's seemed to know Beth and that they didn't have to wait in line for a table. The soldier said Beth was very well dressed and gave the impression of being an actress. He overheard people at neighboring tables comment that Beth might work at RKO or one of the other studios. The soldier told police that he stayed overnight with Beth in her room in the Figueroa Hotel. He said she was rather "cold," but that he was "successful" in his conquest. He asked for another date, but she refused to go out with him again.

People in Hollywood remembered Beth as resourceful with a bag of tricks to maintain a well-groomed look: burnt cork to freshen her suede shoes, candle wax to make her teeth shine and to fill the cavities in her teeth, clear fingernail polish to stop runs in her stockings.

Cheryl Coates, Beth's roommate in the Chancellor Apartments on Cherokee Street, worked as a make-up artist for Max Factor. Cheryl was critical of Beth's make-up. "Too extreme," she said. "Her eyes were her best feature. But the powder was too light and made her look like a geisha. Sometimes she'd keep us awake nights coughing, and I had to be up early on the lot, by five for the make-up calls."

Cheryl remembered a short, swarthy man who drove a dark sedan paid Beth's rent a couple of times. Once Beth asked Cheryl to accompany her to Crescent Drive in Beverly Hills. "Beth said she was owed some money and didn't want to go alone. I was too busy," Cheryl said. "I don't know how it turned out."

Beth was "secretive," her roommates said, and hinted at her "contacts," but she rarely told people where she was going or whom she was seeing. A man named "George" called a few times, and a radio announcer named "Maurice," who was helping Beth with her voice and diction.

Bartenders at the clubs where Beth hung out, said she rarely drank liquor and would spend hours dawdling over a coke.

For a few weeks, the actor Paul Burke lived in the same rooming house as Beth on McCadden Street. "One year I lived in seventeen different places," Burke said. "We all moved around in those days."

Paul Burke, who made his mark on television as Captain Gallagher in *Twelve O'clock High* and as a featured performer on *Dynasty,* was a struggling young actor in the 1940s.

"During the war it was illegal to stay more than five days in a hotel," he said, "and afterwards, the housing shortage was severe. Rooming houses would rent a room out from under you, give it to someone willing to pay a little extra on the side, more than rent control allowed.

"We all hung out at the same places—all of us trying to break into the movies. It was an exciting time. We'd have our daily coffee klatches, trade information, and gossip. There were a couple of cops who'd join us on their break. They wanted to get in the movies. We'd talk about who was putting out. We knew she wasn't sleeping around—'look, but don't touch' was the word. She was pretty much known on the Boulevard.

"At the McCadden place I was staying with Alex Constance, a dress extra who wanted to be a hairdresser. He'd do the girls' hair for practice. We called him 'Alex the Gleam.' The police picked him up and kept him about three days. When he asked the cops why, they said it was because of the *gleam* in his eye. Alex said Beth worked for a while in a restaurant out in the Valley, a family-owned business. The joke was that you could find the most beautiful waitresses in the world out here.

"Alex warned Beth about playing one guy against the other. He said that Beth sometimes had crying jags, but usually she was happy-go-lucky and friendly. Alex said that she wanted to make her mother proud of her and show that she could make it on her own."

Paul Burke drove me around Hollywood and pointed out the old hangouts: Don the Beachcomber's, The Mayflower Coffee House, Boardner's, the Coconut Grove, the Florentine Gardens, and the Palladium.

"Hollywood *was* motion picture people with a carefully delineated social strata," he said. "Everyone went night clubbing—the Stars to the supper clubs: Ciro's, Trocadero, Mocambo, Coconut Grove. People on the rise went to Earl Carroll's and the Florentine Gardens, while the 'kids,' like me and my friends, and those watching their wallets, had the Palladium with its cheap prices and four bands nightly. See and be seen was the name of the game.

"Hollywood was a company town, and the industry was the

movie business," Burke said. "If there was a strike or any other ripple at the studios, it would affect everyone in the whole Los Angeles basin."

During World War II Hollywood became a boom town, grinding out patriotic movies for the home front and training films for the armed forces. The studios used ingenuity to get around the shortages—and not just of materials. Many of the actors and technicians either joined the service or were drafted. It is estimated that by 1942 close to 3,000 movie people, including top stars like Jimmy Stewart, Henry Fonda, and William Holden, were in the armed forces. Those who weren't in the service were on the road, entertaining troops and helping with war bond drives. Actress Carole Lombard, Clark Gable's wife, was killed in a plane crash returning from a war bond drive.

The materials for sets were rationed during the war. A limit of $5,000 per film was allowed to cover the set construction. Film was also in short supply. Ingenious directors rehearsed each scene longer to cut down on the number of takes and eliminated the need for scarce building materials by shooting on location.

When the war ended, so did the blackouts. War slogans were replaced with talk of returning to normalcy and worry about the movie strikes. Pre-war scripts were taken off the shelves—westerns, comedies, "quickies"—anything to turn a dollar. "Extras"—gals in slacks and dark glasses with bandannas protecting their freshly waved hair—wandered back and forth across Sunset Boulevard, hanging out and shopping in "Columbia Square" on Gower Street near Columbia Studios.

Almost overnight the servicemen disappeared from Hollywood Boulevard, but the bars and lounges that had catered to them were still in full swing. The twelve o'clock curfew was lifted, and when the bars closed, the people moved to the all-night restaurants and the All Night Theater next to the Four Star Grill. At two in the morning, the Mayflower Coffee House was packed, serving up its specialty of waffles. Over on Vine Street, between Hollywood and Sunset, in the area known as Jazz Street, Coffee Dan's catered to the song pluggers, show girls, and gag writers from the nearby music and radio studios.

Day and night, people strolled along Hollywood Boulevard. By evening the promenade would be in full swing—the boulevard crowded with showgirls, actors, actresses, and the hopefuls dressed in their glamour outfits and gimmicky costumes competing for attention. Sometimes a dog would be spotted, a basset hound dressed like Sherlock Holmes. He'd trot nonchalantly down the boulevard wearing a Sherlock hat and coat and carrying a curved pipe in his mouth. But no one could remember what his master looked like.

One of Autry's "cowboys" often strolled the boulevard; he was a tight-lipped, thin man with an unusually pale complexion, adorned in turquoise and silver jewelry. As he passed the actresses he'd raise his hand, tilt his Stetson slightly, and say, "M'am" without cracking a smile or blinking an eye.

When Paul Burke, Bette Short, and other movie hopefuls strolled Hollywood Boulevard, the street scene was vastly different than today. It would be all the people in "the business" out for a walk and making contacts—when "the business" was the movie industry and the biggest financial game in town.

Everyone dressed up to go out in the 1940s, and "a date" meant dinner and dancing, or maybe a movie, not a business proposition in the back seat of a car or in an alleyway. A "working girl" was a show girl or actress, not a prostitute. A woman could expect to walk Hollywood and Sunset Boulevards until the wee hours of the morning without fear in those days.

EIGHT
The Saint and The Magician

I hesitated contacting the Los Angeles police. The Black Dahlia murder had already attracted more than its share of crackpots and weirdoes. Again, it was John Babcock who, in January of 1989, helped me out, putting in a "good word" with John St. John, the detective in charge of the case since 1980.

John St. John had inherited the Black Dahlia case from Buck Pierce, who had inherited the case from Danny Galindo, who had inherited it from the team of Jack McReadie and Harry Hansen. Each succeeding detective held little hope of solving the murder and developed a caretaker attitude, locking the files to keep the voyeurs out and responding to "tips."

Shortly after Mark Hansen died in 1964 (of natural causes), Detective Danny Galindo received a call. The anonymous tipster said evidence linking Mark Hansen to the Black Dahlia murder was "hidden inside a wall" of Hansen's soon-to-be-demolished house at 6024 Carlos. Police working side-by-side with the wrecking crew tore open the walls and found nothing.

Detective John St. John was not surprised at the results of the search. He believed the killer was a younger man, not someone middle-aged, as Mark Hansen had been at the time of the murder.

John St. John had a nickname, "Jigsaw John"—the man who puts the puzzles together—literally. St. John's moniker came from his first major case, a quickly solved dismemberment.

St. John wore Badge #1 with pride, staying with homicide for more than forty years, long after he should have retired—always for "just one more year." He was credited with solving two-thirds of the 1,000 homicides he was assigned during his tenure with LAPD. St. John was instrumental in bringing William Bonin, California's "Freeway Killer," to justice. The 1976 television series *Jigsaw John* was based on his exploits.

I'd always meet St. John on his turf at Parker Center. The building was a far cry from the Central Headquarters of the 1940s, when post-war overcrowding forced Robbery and Homicide to set up shop in the City Hall basement. The detectives of that bygone era found it easier to come and go through a large window rather than meander through a labyrinth of corridors.

At the new Parker Center, three policemen served as receptionists, talking to people from behind a large, four-sided wooden counter. They called upstairs to confirm appointments and handed out visitor passes specifying on which floor the visitor was allowed. A couple of policeman stood guard, watching the people come and go.

Parker Center was named after the legendary William Parker of "clean-up" fame. The Center housed the offices of Administration, Internal Affairs, and Personnel, as well as the Chief of Police and Deputy Chief. The special detectives who handled major cases or who had particular expertise worked out of Parker Center, on tap in case the area divisions needed help. There were also holding cells for short-term prisoners who were booked and waiting to be transferred to County Jail. The ubiquitous reporters had their press rooms hidden away on the main floor, to the rear.

Original records from all the area divisions were copied and put on microfiche for easy retrieval and kept at Parker Center, along with fingerprints and the photo lab. All the other scientific labs had moved over to Piper Tech on Ramirez Street.

Sitting in a bare, sound-proof interrogation room across the table from me, St. John gave the appearance of being a much larger man. Except for a few outbursts (his way, I imagine, of keeping me off guard), St. John's gravelly voice was usually well-modulated. We seemed to hit it off when I said, "Bette didn't always wear black."

St. John asked me what other colors Elizabeth Short wore.

"Pink was Bette's favorite color, and light blue," I said. "I remember a black, pink-flowered print dress."

"What did she talk about to you?" he asked.

I thought a moment and said, "She told me never to go in the candy store."

St. John laughed. "Good advice."

We danced around various subjects—give and take. "You know what sadists do to their victims, do you?" And then he'd proceed with a graphic description. St. John would toss out a few facts and ask my opinion. "She wasn't a prostitute. She was a tease. What do you think?"

It was in the throw-away remarks that names and information surfaced. "I just had lunch with John Babcock," or "I had coffee with so-and-so at the coroner's," he'd say. Checking in with Babcock (or whomever St. John casually mentioned) inevitably yielded additional hard facts. The inquest transcript which I had been told was "lost years ago" materialized after one such exchange.

I raised the subject of a police cover-up and repeated the rumors I kept hearing about someone close to the investigation, most notably the Brown brothers. St. John didn't give much credence to the cover-up theory. "Too many people involved in the investigation," he said. "Cover-up can be suspected when a couple of people are investigating and they keep things very close and private. Then it might be possible. With so many people checking things out, like in the Elizabeth Short murder, it would be next to impossible to monkey around." He said he personally liked Finis Brown.

We discussed the packet mailed by the killer—the fact that it had been soaked in gasoline.

"Those kooks," St. John said. "They always know about those things. It's in books and magazines."

St. John referred to Bette as "Elizabeth." When we talked, I would imagine Bette alive, walking down the street and smiling. But I felt the image St. John had was of a mutilated corpse in a vacant lot.

I asked St. John about Harry Hansen.

"Harry wanted to solve this murder, like no other," St. John said. "It was a real sore point with Harry. He never gave up on it."

St. John did not like to "inherit" cases. "When you go to the scene and take it in, you see things that might never make it into the report you file," he said. "Small details, that register somewhere in your head and that might seem insignificant at the time, but that later, in your mind, form some link. And this information never gets passed on to the next detective. So I like to be there at the very beginning." St. John, a rookie at the time of the Black Dahlia murder, was recruited for the door-to-door work.

St. John talked to Babcock about me. He told Babcock that of all the people who had made their way to LAPD's door to give tips or discuss the Black Dahlia murder, I was the only one who seemed concerned about the victim.

Every time I met with St. John he'd ask me about the people I had interviewed. He seemed interested in keeping tabs on the old-time reporters. At one point I let slip that a former Hearst reporter had given me, in strict confidence, a movie script. The author used the curious pseudonym of Ibycus Crane. Checking a book on Greek mythology, I learned that Ibycus was the name of a beloved poet who, when traveling to a theater in Corinth, was waylaid and murdered by bandits. A flock of cranes flying overhead were the only witnesses to the crime. The cranes followed the bandits to the theater. As word of the crime rippled through the audience, the cranes circled over the bandits, revealing the identity of Ibycus' killers.

The script named Chet Montgomery as the killer of the Black Dahlia and placed the murder scene in a leather factory deserted because of a strike. (Chet Montgomery was the name typed on the *Hollywood Wolves Association* card included in the packet mailed by the killer.) In the script, a Jacque shear table (also known as a jackknife table) was used for the bisection. The table, a mechanism for cutting volumes of leather, had a large, sharp, cantilevered blade much like that of a paper cutter.

When St. John casually asked to see the script, I demurred, saying the script had been given to me in confidence and I didn't feel right passing it on. St. John put pressure on me—calling me at my home and at my work every few days and asking to see the script. He became more and more aggressive—and persuasive. He gave me the telephone numbers of his home and his vacation cabin. St. John told me to call him if I changed my mind. I suspected that St. John thought someone connected to Hollywood and the movies might be involved in the murder. I wondered if St. John was suspicious about the Hearst reporter who had given me the script.

I called John Babcock for advice. "I'd like to get a gander of that script," he said. "But look, I think you should show it to St. John. If there's something in it that can help with the case.... He's due to retire, and he's giving the case another look. I know he'd like to close it. Keep your perspective. Policeman don't give out their phone numbers to just anyone. There's a trust, here. You have an obligation to your source, but there's a bigger obligation."

"I know what you mean," I said. "My only real obligation is to Bette Short."

"You got it!" Babcock said.

The graphic descriptions in the screenplay weren't consistent with the autopsy report, St. John said. "But I'd sure like to know who wrote it. That is one sick mind."

I told him that Ibycus Crane was a pseudonym for a woman, adding, "I think she also writes children's books. I also think the old-time reporter helped her to write it."

St. John let me experience first hand some of the craziness the detectives deal with. He gave me a few phone numbers of recent Black Dahlia "tipsters"—psychics, arm-chair detectives, a cryptologist. "It is amazing," he said, "how many people offer up a relative as the killer."

St. John had checked with the individuals before passing on their names and phone numbers. One psychic said the killer was living in Maine, was not crippled, and for some reason the name Anderson kept popping into her head. Another said she was willing to channel Elizabeth's spirit because Elizabeth wanted to talk to her mother. The third psychic said her spirit guide was Beth and that Beth wanted to contact me. I was instructed to visualize myself as a white whirlwind to be "receptive." A woman who wanted Elizabeth Short's birth certificate turned out to be an astrologer who hoped to reveal the killer by doing Bette's astrological chart.

The amateur cryptologist told me to carefully check the pasted-up message from the killer and to look closely at the word "follow." I told him to wait a minute while I retrieved the blown-up photo from my files. "Yeah," I said, "I'm looking at the word."

"Look carefully at the 'O' and the 'W'," he said. "Notice they are *larger* than the other letters in the word."

I stared at the photo of the pasted-up letters. The guy was right. They were larger. I also noticed that the two letters were *exactly* lined up, and of the same typeface and color—white letters on a black background.

"That's the clue," he said. "The 'letters to follow' are the O and the W. Do you know anyone with those initials?"

"Well," I said after thinking a moment, "Oscar Wilde comes to mind, or Orson Welles."

After the call, I sat and studied the photo, noticing the spacing of the pasted-up letters. Someone with a trained eye, I thought. The left-hand margin was justified; the layout was balanced. The O and W letters had been particularly difficult to line up as they had been part of an italicized word in a movie advertisement. All the words and letters (except the *Examiner's* masthead and the word "Dahlia's") had come from the movie section of the *Los Angeles Herald Express*—the January 23, 1947 edition.

I was developing an appreciation for the frustrating work of police detectives. I joked with St. John about the results of my phone calls.

"Now you know," St. John said. "Now you know."

St. John talked a lot about corroboration. "You have to have corroboration," he repeated over and over again. An "open mind" and "probable cause" were other key phrases of St. John.

Usually stone-faced, St. John once displayed a hint of emotion. He was describing what it was like to be on the stand while a defense attorney tried to tear his investigative work to shreds. "You work your butt off, running down leads, getting your evidence, being careful, going by the book," he said, "and then this guy, this lawyer, tries to make you look incompetent, tries to make you into a buffoon. It's enough to make you sick."

We discussed Steven Nickel's book *Torso,* about the New Castle/Cleveland murders that spanned twenty years. Cleveland Detective Peter M. Merylo had contacted Harry Hansen and raised the possibility that the "Cleveland Butcher" had killed the Black Dahlia. Some of the victims of the Cleveland killer were bisected in a manner similar to Elizabeth Short. The killer taunted the Cleveland police just as LAPD had been taunted by Elizabeth Short's killer. Merylo forwarded to Harry Hansen a copy of the crudely typed letter received by the Cleveland Chief of Police and postmarked Los Angeles, December 21, 1938. The message, arriving the day after Christmas, read:

> Moved to California for the winter Head minus features will be buried in gully on Century Blvd between Western & Crenshaw

"There was no connection," St. John said. "That had been checked out thoroughly. The Cleveland killer had a particular *signature*. All the Cleveland victims were killed *quickly*, and *decapitated*. Those were the two elements which *never* deviated."

St. John explained. "Signature is different than MO," he said. "Signature is the *extra* things a perpetrator does, the *obsessive* things he *needs* to do that aren't *necessary* if his objective is just to kill someone. Killing quickly was the Cleveland killer's MO; the decapitation was his *signature*. Torture and posing of the body was not involved, like in the Elizabeth Short murder."

St. John said the murder of Elizabeth Short was unique. "There was *never* one like it before, and there hasn't been one like it *since*. The perpetrator combined a number of elements that have never been seen together—a *unique* signature." St. John was adamant. He believed the killer struck only once. St. John said that Finis Brown and Harry Hansen were the only people who watched the autopsy being performed—no reporters or other policemen were present. St. John hedged when I asked him if the killer had medical training or had used medical equipment.

"I can't get into that," he said and then laughed. "Our job is to get information, not give it... The perpetrator may have had some knowledge of anatomy, but he wasn't necessarily in the medical profession."

In February of 1947, a month after the murder, the question

of medical expertise had led to an investigation of all medical and dental students attending the University of Southern California. (The university is located about thirty blocks from the crime scene.) The FBI ran background checks on three hundred students and came up with three who had criminal records. LAPD investigated further and could find nothing that linked the three students to the crime.

Five years later, in 1952, the LAPD asked the FBI to check out the serviceman who had posed as a surgeon during the Korean War. Although the impostor had no formal medical education, he entered the navy as a surgeon-lieutenant and allegedly performed numerous surgical operations. He had used the credentials of another doctor. The FBI's investigation placed the impostor outside of California at the time of the Black Dahlia murder.

"All we can know for certain," St. John said, "is that the perpetrator had a car or access to a car, and that he most likely was between twenty and thirty-five years of age because those are the ones more apt to use knives. He was very powerful, judging by the force of the blows. But he may not have set out to murder anyone. He may have been operating on a short fuse and something could have set him off, driven him over the edge. You find where she was on the missing days, from January 9th, when she was last seen, to January 15th, when her body was found, and you have her killer."

St. John introduced me to newsman Norm Jacoby and brought up the name of Tony Valdez, mentioning the same TV program as Nieson Himmel and John Babcock. "Maybe he'll show you the footage," St. John said.

Taking St. John's advice, I finally called Tony Valdez. Valdez said he could meet me around five o'clock the next day at the Fox TV station (Channel 11 in Los Angeles). The television station was located on Sunset Boulevard, close to Gower Street.

I was traveling around Los Angeles by bus, allowing plenty of travel time between destinations. I'd often arrive early and wait in a restaurant, preferably an older one like C. C. Brown's or Clifton's. I'd read a book or go over my interview notes. On this particular day my stopover was a Denny's located in Gower Gulch, a neighborhood shopping center that looked like a western frontier town. The waitress told me the stores were actually an old movie set. "Check out some of the old westerns," she said, "and you'll recognize the buildings."

Fox TV reporter Tony Valdez is also host of his own show called *Mid-day*. He has an unforgettable voice. His special segments on the Black Dahlia murder have aired on the station's ten o'clock news.

We were in a small room when he ran the broadcast tape. The segment had been taped eight years earlier, in 1981. I sat on a high stool while Tony stood near the monitor. Music from the 1940s played as a clip from *True Confessions*, a film based on the murder, opened the segment. The lead actor, Robert Duval, wore a gray fedora; he resembled Harry Hansen.

Tony's voice-over described the murder. The camera panned to a seated Harry Hansen, retired and much older, talking about the victim. "She was not a prostitute, in any way, shape, or form," Harry said. A few more words came from Harry before Bette's sister, Virginia West, lying in a hospital bed, came on the screen. "We were devastated," she said.

When Mrs. Short next appeared on camera, Tony noticed a change had come over me. He stopped the tape. "Are you okay?" he asked.

"No," I told him. I'm not sure of the exact words I used. I said I felt strange, very confused. "Like I'm not sure of *where* I am." I *knew* I was at the TV station, but at the same time I *felt* as if I was back in Medford and that the murder had just happened.

Mrs. Short's face had taken me by surprise. I hadn't seen her for years, not since a few days after the murder. I recognized her immediately, and seeing her face confused me.

I asked Tony to continue playing the video. Near the end of the tape Mrs. Short said, "I am not one to hold a grudge, but I wish it were all over."

I felt stunned, incapable of voluntary movement. It seemed as if an iron door was crashing down inside my head and wouldn't let thoughts in or out.

Tony offered to drive me home. I told him I knew I was

staying in Pasadena but couldn't remember exactly where. I had difficulty conversing with Tony as we walked to the parking lot. Once in the car, Tony started asking me questions, trying to draw me out, but I could not respond.

As we neared the Pasadena off ramp, I began to remember street names. "I'm staying on Dominion Street," I said. "I think the street is on the far side of Pasadena, near Altadena." Tony said he knew the area.

When we finally arrived at my destination, Tony parked the car and we talked for a while. I still felt strange, as if I was encased by an iron wall. At one point, Valdez looked straight ahead for a few seconds and then turned to me. "I think you're having a flashback," he said. He told me he had become interested in the problems of Viet Nam Vets and had researched post-traumatic stress syndrome. "I think you're experiencing something similar." he said. "I think this murder affected you very deeply." After a few days, the strange feeling began to dissipate, and I almost felt normal again.

Whenever I made a trip to Los Angeles, I'd be sure to touch bases with Tony Valdez. Tony gave me the telephone number of Jan Knowlton, a woman who was causing quite a stir. Knowlton claimed that she had witnessed her father killing the Black Dahlia, but had repressed the memory. She said her memory of the traumatic event had recently surfaced.

On the telephone, an overwrought Ms. Knowlton described a grotesque scenario that bore no relation to the actual murder. I tried to reassure Ms. Knowlton that her repressed memories were not consistent with the facts in the "Black Dahlia" killing. During our conversation, Knowlton posed a number of questions to me, always referring to Bette as "Elizabeth." She asked me to describe "Elizabeth."

"I never knew her as Elizabeth," I said. "I called her Bette."

Knowlton then quizzed me about my relationship to "Bette."

"Bette was ten years older than me," I said. "She went to school with my brother. Bette befriended me when I was a kid. I guess you could say she was like an aunt."

A few months later I saw Ms. Knowlton on television. She was discussing her father and the Black Dahlia murder.

Knowlton now referred to Elizabeth Short as "Aunt Bette." Her recovered memories had grown to include a number of unsolved murders. She "recalled" with graphic detail how her father had killed various women and babies.

One time I casually mentioned to Tony Valdez the 1942 Sleepy Lagoon murder on which the movie *Zoot Suit* was based. He wanted to know who had discussed Sleepy Lagoon with me. No one in particular, I told him, just a strange coincidence.

A few months earlier, in March of 1989, when I was looking through the Aggie Underwood boxed files at the Urban Archives (California State University, Northridge), a student brought me an extra box. I pointed out the mistake and he said, "Maybe you'll find something of interest." While waiting for some of the Underwood papers to be copied, I decided to look through the carton. It was the Sleepy Lagoon/Union file. The unions were helping to raise funds to defend the Hispanic youths on trial for the murder of Jose Diaz, who died during a fist fight near a reservoir. The top folder containing a light blue brochure c. 1943 caught my eye:

> TALK OF THE TOWN...
> Did 22 Mexican-American Boys Commit Murder?
> Can the fifth-column knife cut Los Angeles in half?

I had become inordinately sensitive to use of the expression, "cut in half." I put a copy of the pamphlet, which had been written by Orson Welles, in my Serendipity file with other off-the-wall references to cutting in half.

In the summer of 1989 I moved to Pacific Beach in Southern California and stayed for a few months, checking out Bette's last known address on Camino Pradera and the places she had frequented. The war-time housing development where she had stayed was gone. Her favorite coffee shop, Sheldon's, had moved across the street from its original location. I found people who remembered reading about the murder, but I could find no one who had known Bette Short. I went by the Aztec Theatre in San Diego, the place where Dorothy French had met and befriended Bette. The marquee was the same, but the theater now showed adult films.

In the public library I looked at the old San Diego newspapers on microfilm. I hoped to pick up bits of information about Bette and her murder that might not have been covered in the LA newspapers. I had limited success. I then browsed through the stacks in the art and theater section of the library, checking for books that might supply background information about Hollywood. A book written by Otto Friedrich with the intriguing title, *City of Nets*, caught my eye—a five-hundred-page book focusing on the Hollywood of the 1930s and 1940s.

Midway through reading *City of Nets,* one particular paragraph caught my attention. During the 1940s, in a circus tent set up on Cahuenga Boulevard in Hollywood, Orson Welles entertained servicemen with his *Mercury Wonder Show*. The highlight of the performance was a magic act—Welles cutting his wife, red-headed sex-goddess Rita Hayworth, in half—until an infuriated Harry Cohn, head of Columbia Studios, put a stop to it. Welles then substituted various volunteers—Johnny Carson was one of them. Finally, Welles recruited Marlene Dietrich for the performance. Welles, in a cameo role, performed the magic trick with Dietrich in the 1944 movie *Follow the Boys*. I photocopied the information for my Serendipity file.

Other Welles trivia is sprinkled throughout *City of Nets.* The break-up of Welles' marriage is blamed on Welles attitude towards women. Friedrich portrays Welles as a misogynist, using a quotation from Welles—"All women are dumb, some dumber than others"—to make the point.

Friedrich briefly touches on the troubles Welles had with two movie studios, RKO and Republic. In May of 1946, RKO gained control of the Welles' South American film *It's All True*, after Welles failed to repay a $200,000 loan. The following year (1947), executives at Republic Pictures became upset when Welles left for Europe before the editing of *Macbeth* was finished.

The timing of Welles' departure from Hollywood piqued my curiosity. He left a few months after Bette's bisected body was found in the vacant lot. I thought of the conversation I had with the cryptologist, and the magic act of Welles. They were coincidences, most likely, but I thought I should check a little deeper. I began to read books about the actor/director.

The biographers of Welles paint a disturbing picture—a charming and charismatic man, but prone to violent outbursts; a "sadistic megalomaniac" who "dabbled in causes," "aspired to be President," and often conducted himself "as a king with disdain for those around him."

Welles, who was born on May 6, 1915, had a mentally ill older brother, Richard Ives Welles. In 1926, Richard was diagnosed as a schizophrenic and spent ten years in a mental institution before securing his own release on a writ of habeus corpus. Richard Welles surfaced in Los Angeles in the mid-1940s. During one of Orson's magic performances, Richard volunteered to help Orson cut a woman in half. From time to time, Welles would send his brother money.

Richard was more than a nuisance to Welles, according to Barbara Leaming, the authorized Welles biographer. Richard was "a loathsome and distorted image of his [Orson's] own strangeness." A troubled Welles told Leaming of "the other Orson," the less rational side of his personality—an entity that he referred to as "Crazy Welles" or "Imperial Welles."

Welles, according to another biographer, Frank Brady, was fearful that he suffered from "the agonizing strains of the Welles clan," fearful that he might go "crazy" and become incarcerated like his older brother.

John Houseman, perhaps the first to recognize the full potential of Welles' creative talents, saw also the other, darker side—Welles' destructive and violent tendencies. Houseman, in his book, *Run-through, A Memoir*, tells of his thoughts when first seeing the young Welles perform on stage—"a monstrous boy... obscene and terrible" with "an irresistible interior of violence."

Houseman exerted control and direction over Welles from the early days of the Federal Theater Project in the 1930s through the completion of the masterpiece *Citizen Kane* in 1941. Houseman ran interference and spared the young director from the fallout of his own capricious actions.

Welles, according to his biographers, habitually left in his wake unfinished projects, grandiose schemes, financial chaos, and broken furniture. Strung out on Benzedrine, Dexedrine, and cocaine, he'd work for days without sleep, then collapse or disappear, leaving his actors and projects in chaos.

Biographer Charles Higham describes Orson's childhood as "Gothic." In the downstairs rooms of a large, Victorian home, the sounds of classical music mingled with the intellectual musings of salon conversation. Upstairs, the moans and screams of his grandmother dying from stomach cancer echoed through the halls.

Orson, it is said, claimed his grandmother practiced witchcraft; he also claimed, "half-jokingly," to be a descendent of the pagan magician, Aleister Crowley. Sometimes the story would change, and his claim was of a family tree that included Harry Houdini, Henry Thurston, or Horace Goldin, the renowned magician who developed the illusion called "The Divided Woman"—the magic act of sawing a woman in half.

Orson, prone to violent temper tantrums as a child, cut the dress of his nanny to shreds when he was five. I viewed a school book defaced by the ten-year-old Orson—pages torn by violent scribbling and pencil jabs, his name and doodles throughout the book.

Dr. Maurice Bernstein, the orthopedic surgeon who attended Orson's grandmother, was infatuated with the boy's mother, Beatrice Welles. The doctor, rather than Beatrice's alcoholic husband, Richard Welles, became the major influence in young Orson's upbringing. Dr. Bernstein, who considered Orson a "genius," had him tutored at home for a couple of years and arranged for psychological testing to determine Orson's full intellectual and creative potential.

When Beatrice Welles died in 1924, a few days after Orson's ninth birthday, Dr. Bernstein took complete charge of the boy. And when Orson's father, Richard Welles, died six years later, in 1930, the doctor became Orson's legal guardian. Later, it would be Dr. Bernstein who supplied Welles with drugs. Welles called Dr. Bernstein "Dadda," while in turn, Dr. Bernstein called Welles by his childhood nickname, "Pookles."

In 1925, at the age of ten years, Orson began his formal

education at the Washington School in Madison, Wisconsin. That lasted one year. According to Barbara Leaming, Welles was discovered playing "doctor" with neighborhood girls. One mother became hysterical and complained to Orson's father, "You know that Leopold and Loeb case... this is something just like it. That's what this child of yours is doing with my daughter!" The girls' mother was referring to the 1924 kidnapping and murder of fourteen-year-old Robert (Bobbie) Franks, by two "mentally gifted" university students, Nathan Leopold and Richard Loeb.

When Loeb and Leopold confessed to the murder, they declared they killed the boy for the "exhilaration of planning the perfect crime." During the course of the trial, it was revealed that Loeb and Leopold had a "secret" pact—Leopold agreed to collaborate in Loeb's criminal fantasies, if Loeb took part in Leopold's sexual fantasies. Loeb and Leopold were saved from the electric chair by Clarence Darrow, a criminal attorney famed for his oratory. In the 1959 film *Compulsion*, based on the infamous crime, Welles portrays the Darrow type attorney who defends the killers.

Dr. Bernstein placed Welles in the well-respected Todd School for Boys the same year that Orson's older brother was declared a schizophrenic and committed to the Kankakee State Institution (1926). The school became Orson's haven—his eccentricities were allowed free rein. Under the tutelage of Headmaster Roger Hill and his wife, Hortense, Orson became a star of the school.

According to author Charles Higham, in December of 1946, Orson Welles was on location shooting *Black Irish* in San Francisco. The film, released by Columbia Studios under the title *The Lady from Shanghai*, is based on the Sherwood King novel *If I Die Before I Wake.*

Perusing through the book *Orson Welles, A Critical View* by André Bazin, I came across a photo of the *crazy house* set which Welles helped construct for *The Lady from Shanghai* and which Columbia Studios edited out. The outtake shows Rita Hayworth standing in a room with dismembered female mannequin parts hanging from the ceiling, wall murals resplendent with violent scenes, and grotesque anatomical diagrams, including a cow flayed to its mid-section. A woman, who appears to be cut in half, is lying on top of the cow. A clown head is imprisoned in a metal bird cage, another hangs on the wall.

According to Higham, on January 6, 1947 (eight days before Elizabeth Short's murder), Welles returned to Los Angeles from San Francisco. Ten days after the murder, Welles applied for a passport but did not leave the country immediately.

Higham states that in October of 1947, a month before Welles' departure from Hollywood, an ambivalent Welles contacted the California College of Mortuary Sciences. He was sent a list of the requirements for admission, details for earning an embalmer's license, and the prospects for employment as an apprentice in a mortuary.

I was struck by the bizarre movie set and the strange actions of Welles around the time of the Black Dahlia murder. I recruited Matt Evans, a Welles aficionado who was living in Southern California, to aid in research. "By coincidence," Matt informed me, "there is a sealed Welles file that is due to be open soon, on November 18, 1991." The file was part of a collection given to UCLA by Richard Wilson, a special assistant to Orson Welles from 1937 to 1951 and associate producer of two films, *The Lady From Shanghai* and *Macbeth*. Wilson had stipulated that the Orson Welles file remain sealed for ten years.

Evans made an appointment to go through the documents the day after the file was unsealed, becoming the second person to view the collection. After perusing the files, Evans told me I needed to go by the library and read all the correspondence. "The people at Republic Pictures were angry because Welles left Hollywood," he said. Evans sent me his notes and copies of a few letters written by Richard Wilson, Orson Welles, and Lou Lindsay in 1948 and 1949.

The correspondence between Richard Wilson and Welles indicated that at first Republic Pictures was pleased with the rushes from Welles' *Macbeth* (filmed the summer of 1947). But the studio became furious when Welles went to Europe a few months later, in the fall of 1947, before he completed the editing of the film. Republic wanted the director/actor to return immediately and finish. Welles insisted on remaining in Europe. On March 26, 1948, Richard Wilson wrote to Welles:

> ...Yes, Newman [Chairman of the Board of Republic Pictures Corporation], and Feldman [Charles, producer of *Macbeth*] want you in Hollywood right now.... It was most certainly understood by all concerned that you were to return when the music was finished.

An April 6, 1948 letter from Richard Wilson reiterates the anger of Republic executives:

> The agitation is again beginning about your coming back--and what tangible forms it will take other than telegrams, etc. I don't know. Newman told me yesterday that he wanted to find out when you're coming, as "They weren't fooling around."

In a letter dated April 26, 1948, Richard Wilson relays to Welles that the situation was deteriorating.

> ...it was my understanding that you would be back shortly, but I couldn't guarantee that you'd be back for the scoring. I said I did know that you would be here for the dubbing. Mr. Newman commented prettily: "He must be here for the scoring, too." I said, "Surely we aren't going to wait just because he isn't here the first day of the scoring." To which he answered, "Oh yes he is -- or that will mark the end of you guys working on the picture. If he isn't here, when we're ready, we intend to take the picture over entirely from the first day of scoring on."

After *Macbeth's* disastrous Boston premiere in October of 1948, Richard Wilson again pleaded with Welles to return to Hollywood. "I think it's tragic that you're not here personally," Wilson wrote, "because I'm absolutely and sincerely convinced that if you were around for the next three or four openings to lecture, meet the critics, women's clubs and all that, you could put this [*Macbeth*] over the top and turn it into a controversy such as the industry has seldom seen.... I think that you would have tremendous popular sympathy and understanding if you went on the road in behalf of MACBETH."

Bad reviews forced Republic to withdraw the film for re-editing and re-dubbing. Since Welles still refused to return to Hollywood, film editor Lou Lindsay was dispatched to Europe, where, according to his correspondence, he feared having a nervous breakdown trying to re-edit *Macbeth* with Welles. Upset at the lack of proper equipment and Orson's often irrational behavior and squandering of money, Lindsay sent a litany of complaints to Richard Wilson and threatened to quit. The European experience of trying to work with Welles was so shattering that when Lindsay returned to the United States he gave up the editing of films and became an agent with the William Morris Agency.

If, as author Frank Brady states, "Welles, like Griffith and Eisenstein, saw the editing as 'one of the most crucially creative acts in the production of the film,'" the refusal of Orson Welles to return to Hollywood and finish the editing at Republic's behest seems all the more bizarre. As some of his biographers point out, it didn't make sense for Welles to go to Europe in 1947. The United States had the technical expertise and the equipment for the kind of films Orson Welles wanted to shoot. A politically unstable post-war Europe, devastated by World War II, lacked the equipment, facilities, and tools he needed.

Movieland mythology has projected the image of Welles as a misunderstood genius, driven out of Hollywood and destroyed by William Randolph Hearst because of the film *Citizen Kane*. According to this scenario, Welles, unable to realize his artistic vision, became a reluctant wanderer in Europe, begging for money to finish his film projects. But according to even his most loyal admirers, it was a self-destructive Welles who brought the difficulties on himself.

Welles' sexual affairs fragmented his energies, believed John Houseman, and they were the "beginning of Welles' troubles." In restaurants, Welles habitually sent messages to women who caught his fancy, trying to arrange a rendezvous.

Welles married for the first time at the age of nineteen. His bride was Virginia Nicolson, a young socialite described as a "porcelain-skinned beauty..." who friends feared was a "bit too fragile" for Orson. He carried on multitudinous affairs in a separate apartment in New York City while his wife maintained their home twenty miles up the Hudson River at Sneden's Landing.

According to author Barbara Leaming, Welles admitted that he paid $20,000 to hush up a rape charge in 1945 (a substantial sum, equivalent to $300,000 in today's dollars).

For a while, Welles became obsessed with ballerinas. He had, writes Leaming, "discovered the unmatched beauty of the dancer's body." Orson claimed he fell madly in love with Dolores Del Rio, and later, Rita Hayworth, when he viewed their photographs. But his first love, said Welles, was the Irish actress Betty Chancellor. In an interview with Barbara Leaming on May 21, 1984, an "obviously still smitten" Welles discussed his obsession with the actress he performed with many years before in 1931, at the Gate Theater in Dublin:

> *She was one of those absolutely black-haired girls, with skin as white as Carrara marble, you know, and eyelashes that you could trip on, and all that." She played Jew Suss's daughter, and I had to rape her—that was offscene—and I came on disheveled, practically unbuttoned, having had my way with her.* [Italics added.]

A chill ran through me as I read the paragraph. The description of Betty Chancellor could have been that of Bette Short.

I searched through theatrical archives for photographs and information about Betty Chancellor, with no success. Richard Pleuger, a free-lance journalist from Germany, offered to help me. Richard covered the film and entertainment news for German publications. We had met when he interviewed me after reading John Babcock's article. Richard, who was returning to

Europe for a few months, said he'd stop in London to check out Betty Chancellor. The clippings he sent back showed photos of a woman with penetrating eyes and soft dark curls reminiscent of Bette Short.

Richard Pleuger helped me in other ways. At the end of his interviews with Hollywood personalities, he would bring up the subject of the Black Dahlia. Whatever information he garnered he would pass on to me. Richard called me one day with the name of a very prominent person who agreed to speak with me under the condition of anonymity.

The woman told me she was attending Hollywood High School in 1946 and working part time as a waitress at Brittingham's, the restaurant in Columbia Square at the corner of Sunset and Gower.

"After the murder, police came to the restaurant and questioned all the waitresses two and three times," she said. "They took out photographs of the body and asked if we could identify her. I was terrified, had nightmares. Benny, the manager, was furious at the police and argued with them. I was just a kid, and no one could have identified her from those photos.

"People from Columbia and CBS came in all the time. Big wigs sat in the booths and other movie/radio people would sit at the counter. Beth would come in often. We knew she wasn't a hooker. Not the type. She was a woman of mystery. People always noticed her and wondered about her. Soft, feminine, and fragile. She never laughed loudly. Pale face, always wore black, about 5'5" tall. I spoke to her a few times in the powder room."

I asked the woman if she could remember when Bette was frequenting Brittingham's.

"Exact dates are hard to remember," she said. "But it was around the time Orson Welles was shooting *The Lady from Shanghai*. He was one of the regulars, also Jeff Chandler and Nina Foch. Rumors were that Beth was going with someone who worked at Columbia—someone named Max or Mac."

When I mentioned Orson Welles to St. John, he told me that he couldn't comment, then added, "I hate Hollywood types."

St. John's reluctance to discuss Welles puzzled me. He had

always been quick to point out why he thought a particular suspect wasn't the Black Dahlia killer. He readily eliminated Robert Manley, Mark Hansen, the Cleveland Butcher, and other lesser suspects. But for Orson Welles he would only say, "No comment."

NINE
The Plot Thickens

I wrote to the Welles biographer, Charles Higham. He quickly called me back. We discussed the book and he told me that Welles was not pleased with the biography, but did appreciate Higham's extensive genealogical research.

I asked Higham about Welles' application to the embalming school. "Evidently he decided not to pursue it," Higham said. The author couldn't hazard a guess why Welles would want to delve into mortuary science.

I explained to Higham that I was a home-town friend of the woman known as the Black Dahlia, and that I was doing research on her murder. During the course of our conversation, Higham said, "You should talk to John Gilmore. I believe that Gilmore knows who killed the Black Dahlia."

I told Higham I was trying to track Gilmore down. My research had turned up a January 1982 article with a photo of Gilmore standing in front of a vacant lot—the location where Gilmore said the murder took place. The article mentioned a "Mr. Smith" and a "Mr. Jones."

Higham gave me John Gilmore's telephone number, and I called Gilmore in New Mexico. We talked on the telephone for well over an hour the first time, in January of 1990.

"The Black Dahlia is something I keep working on, no matter how busy I get with my other writing projects," Gilmore said. "I always keep coming back to this one, turning up more information."

I asked him why he was so interested in this case. "I met her once," he said, "when I was a kid. She was at my house. No one in my family talked about it after the murder. My grandmother knew a lot of movie people, and friends of my grandmother's, a hairdresser and a movie projectionist, gays, brought her by the house." Gilmore explained that his grandmother's sister was married to a man named Short, and "Beth" thought they might be related.

"I just remember her seeming very glamorous, dressed in black," Gilmore said. "She was wearing a black hat with a veil that covered her eyes, and her lips were bright red. I was surprised that she talked to me, included me in the conversation." Gilmore was about ten years old at the time. He took Beth out back and showed her where, as a very small child, he had put his hands in the cement.

"She made some comment about the Chinese Theater," he said. "I remember her driving away in a big sedan with large chrome-backed oval headlights, waving goodbye, her black glove in the window. I guess I stood there until the car disappeared from sight. And then a few months later they found her body. It became something you didn't talk about—that she had been by, because of my father being a cop and the hairdresser. Just wouldn't be good for a cop.

"My father was a beat cop, not Homicide. But because of him I met a lot of cops when I was growing up, mostly in robbery."

For weeks after the murder, Gilmore's father drove by the vacant lot on Norton Avenue. Sometimes Gilmore would be with him in the patrol car, while at other times they'd be in the family car, an old Buick.

I told Gilmore I had known Bette for about ten years. "She went to school with my brother," I said. "I was much younger. I really can't say she was my friend, because she was so much older than I was. Maybe she was more like an aunt. I guess you'd say she was my idol when I was growing up. She was very kind to me."

Finally, I summoned the courage to broach the subject of why I had called. "Charles Higham told me you know who killed her," I said. "Is that true?"

"Yeah, well, maybe," Gilmore said. "At one time I thought I did. Now, I'm not so sure. It's a very, very strange story."

Gilmore explained he had a source that he talked to "off and on over the years." The source, named Arnold Smith, kept where he lived a secret. Gilmore said that Arnold always called out of the blue to touch base or to give some information he said he just remembered.

Gilmore said that Arnold Smith was dead; he died in a mysterious fire in February 1982, less than two weeks after the newspaper article about John appeared in the *Los Angeles Herald Examiner*. "Everything spun out of control," Gilmore said. "The radio stations picked up the story about a break in the 'Dahlia' case."

Gilmore told me that he first met Arnold Smith in 1966. Gilmore said he was living in Los Angeles then and being interviewed on a talk show about a new book he had just written, *The Tucson Murders*. "Near the tail end of the interview, I was asked what else I was working on," Gilmore said. "I mentioned a couple of things including the *Black Dahlia*. By the time we were off the air, a woman had called the station saying there was a person I should talk to, someone who knew the Black Dahlia. The woman left her phone number. I called her back, and she set it up for me to go over to her apartment for dinner and meet her friend.

"The house was on Sayer Lane. Two other people were there that night—a heavy-set Indian guy named Eddie, and my source, a tall thin man who told me his name was Arnold Taylor. He didn't say too much, but he showed me a nightclub photo. Eddie called Arnold 'Jack' a couple of times that night. Arnold later told me it was just a figure of speech, like saying, 'How's it going, Jack?' He also told me his name was Smith, not Taylor. It turned out he never gave me his real name. Later, I had Smith followed and found out where he was living—one step above skid row in the Holland Hotel."

Gilmore said that Arnold kept calling off and on. Sometimes Arnold called for days in a row, and then Gilmore might not hear from him for months. Usually they'd meet for drinks or a meal. Sometimes they'd wind up hopping from bar to bar. "I would pick up the tab," Gilmore said, "while Arnold talked about the forties, living in Hollywood, the people he knew—some of them were pretty shady—and the Dahlia. Sometimes when he talked I'd get a strange feeling, like he was still living in the forties, that he was stuck there. I'd look at him and think of a snail, inching along, carrying the years on his back—like a snail with its shell."

Gilmore said they lost contact for a couple of years when Gilmore was going through a divorce and moving around—a year back east, time in San Francisco, a couple of trips to Europe, then finally back to Los Angeles. In November of 1981, Gilmore's ex-wife, Celia, phoned him and said Arnold Smith had called a few times.

Arnold told Celia he had important information for John and left the telephone number of a bar where he could be reached. It took John Gilmore a few days to make contact with Arnold.

"Arnold told me that he had *very* important information that he knew I'd want, but that he needed money," John said. "I told him maybe, but I had to know what he had. He said he didn't want to talk about it over the phone just then, but to meet him the next day at a bar on South Main Street."

John Gilmore was collaborating on a Black Dahlia manuscript at the time with Ron Kenner, a writer who had been on the Metro staff of the *Los Angeles Times* during the late sixties. Gilmore and Kenner had previously written a book about the Manson Family, *The Garbage People*, published soon after the trial in 1971. Kenner told me that by coincidence he was working the police beat on the day that Charlie Manson was arrested. "I had just returned to the *Times* as a vacation replacement after a two-year stint co-managing a Copenhagen press bureau," Kenner said. "We like to think that we intelligently direct our lives, but circumstances often dictate what we fall into.

"I was with Gilmore a couple of times when he met Smith. They'd go off by themselves and talk. Smith wouldn't talk in front of me. He was very tall and emaciated. About six-foot-four and walked with a limp. He seemed paranoid. Didn't want to say anything while I was around. Once, John asked me to bring a tape recorder. But when I set the tape recorder on the table—they were still fairly large-sized in those days—Smith clammed up and wouldn't say a word."

Ron Kenner came up with fifteen hundred dollars, which was given to Arnold by John Gilmore—a couple of hundred dollars at a time.

According to the Gilmore account, over the next couple of months, Arnold re-told a story he claimed had been originally told to him by a third party, someone named Al Morrison.

Arnold showed Gilmore an old See's candy box held together with two rubber bands. "This is all I have left of her," he told Gilmore. Arnold took out some bobby pins, a couple of old yellowed newspaper clippings about the murder, a small silk handkerchief trimmed in black lace with an American flag embroidered in the corner, and a photograph of a group of people, a four-by-five night club shot. "Late 1945," Arnold said.

The photo showed three women and three men. "The woman, who looked like the Black Dahlia, was smiling," Gilmore said. "As I remember, she was wearing a dark high-necked dress, and a flower was pinned over her ear. Her hands were under her chin, elbows leaning on the table. Arnold said he was the man in the foreground of the photograph, the man in profile. Arnold tapped one of his fingers on the man who was facing the camera and said, 'This is your man.' The man's hair was slicked back, and he was wearing a flowered tie."

Gilmore usually met Arnold in Main Street bars. Sometimes they'd meet in the upstairs room at Clifton's Cafeteria on Broadway, near the fountain with the tableau of wildlife. Kenner remembered another place on Olympic Boulevard near Alvarado. He and Gilmore waited for more than an hour in a restaurant that had a glassed-in menagerie with trees, monkeys, birds, and a running brook.

"Arnold was late and pretty drunk when he finally wandered in," Kenner said.

I wondered why Gilmore and Kenner never finished their book about the Black Dahlia murder. Kenner acknowledged that he and Gilmore received apparent death threats made of pasted-up newspaper letters, crude imitations of the original packet the killer had sent. Ron thought they might be a practical joke because he hadn't been mentioned in the newspaper story when John was interviewed by the *Herald Examiner*, and only a couple of friends knew of his collaboration with Gilmore. The gist of the note, Kenner said, was a warning to stop pursuing the story. Ron suspected, as one likely possibility, that the pasteups, mailed separately to John and him, might have been sent by Arnold himself—perhaps a way of indicating that the two were on the right track, getting hot, and that more money for Arnold, the informant, would be well-spent.

Gilmore and Kenner went back and forth trying to makes sense of the notes. For a fleeting moment I wondered if Gilmore was behind the pasted-up notes. Kenner laughed when I posed the question to him.

"It was difficult to know what to make of it," Kenner said. "The threat bothered my wife, Mary, and I wasn't too thrilled with the communication, either. But John and I kept working on the story."

Gilmore and Kenner visited various sites where the "Dahlia" was known to have stayed or frequented. "We talked into the tape recorder as we drove around," Ron recalled. "Those are the only tapes I know about. We made one trip from Chinatown to South Los Angeles. Then we made an 'eerie trip,' surreptitiously checking out one place where supposedly she might have been murdered. We visited a hotel off Hoover Street where John was told she stayed briefly during the 'missing week,' then took the inevitable trip to the vacant lot near Crenshaw in South Central Los Angeles where her body was found.

"One time, John had a meeting set up with Arnold in a cheap bar down town. John sat there drinking beers or whatever, so as not to look too conspicuous. But Arnold showed up so late that by the time he arrived, John, tired and drinking so long, had difficulty remembering some of what Arnold told him. John had to go over that information in another meeting."

Kenner recalled that he and Gilmore sent a draft of more than one hundred pages to the publisher Lyle Stuart, who had published an earlier book by Ron, *Max the Butcher*, the biography of Max Block, the colorful union organizer of meatcutters in New York and New Jersey. Stuart told Ron that the story on Elizabeth Short was compelling and well-written, but that it would be too difficult to revive interest in a 35-year-old murder.

"We hung in there for a few months after Arnold Smith died, in February, 1982." Gilmore told me, "but once he was dead, we sort of lost our impetus."

By the end of 1982, Kenner had moved on to other writing projects. A few years later, Gilmore discovered that Smith's real name was Jack Anderson Wilson and that Wilson had a four-page rap sheet with a number of aliases and three social security numbers. Most of the arrests were for drunkenness (fifty-five), a few begging and mooching, a couple of assault and battery, a dozen theft and burglary, and one "crime against nature." (In Tennessee, Wilson was caught having sex with another man in a park.) The rap sheet listed Los Angeles as Wilson's birthplace with two dates of birth: August 5, 1920 and August 5, 1924.

John Gilmore and I discussed pooling our information and collaborating on a book. When I finally met Gilmore face to face, the silver-haired author struck me as a cross between Clint Eastwood in *Dirty Harry* and Christopher Lloyd in *Back to the Future*.

I mentioned the research I was doing on Orson Welles. "Interesting," Gilmore said, "but I think you're dealing with coincidences that aren't worth pursuing." Gilmore was insistent that we focus on Jack Anderson Wilson. I was eager to collaborate with an experienced writer like John Gilmore. Dropping the Welles line of inquiry and going in another direction brought a sense of relief—Orson Welles was too much of an American icon.

Gilmore said that Jack Anderson Wilson aka Arnold Smith claimed to have been part of the "McCadden Group," a loosely connected robbery gang that hung out at Al Greenberg's cafe on McCadden Street in Hollywood. The McCadden group supposedly did "scores" for Maurice and Gail Reingold. Gail owned a jewelry store on Wilshire and employed Maurice. In 1942, Maurice Reingold was fined $2000 for perjury involving his "acquisition" of twenty-five stolen diamonds valued at $12,000.

On January 6, 1947, three days before Bette Short was last seen at the Biltmore Hotel, the Mocambo nightclub was held up. At 10:30 a.m., three men wearing raincoats and brown felt hats made off with the weekend receipts of $10,000 and $7000 worth of jewelry that had been on display at the Mocambo. The jewelry belonged to the Reingold Brothers. One of the bandits was described as 6'4" with a "scar" on his face. Rounded up immediately were: Robert Savarino, age 28 (admitted Mocambo robbery), Elijah R. Soza, age 22 (Savarino's brother-in-law), Abel Soza, age 30 (Savarino's brother-in-law), and Henry F. Hassau, age 27.

Arrested in a second round-up on January 15, 1947, the same day Elizabeth Short's body was found, were: Marty Abram (alias Marty Abrams), age 50, Louis Abrams, (alias Louis Brams) age 47, Al Greenberg (alias Al Green), age 42, and Harry Bruno (alias Harry Burns alias Harry Burnell), age 31. The six-foot-four bandit was never caught.

According to Gilmore, Wilson said he was the unidentified Mocambo bandit and "stayed low" after the first round-up. After the second round-up, Wilson went to San Francisco. He told Gilmore that Elizabeth Short was a friend of Henry Hassau's wife. During the "missing days," Bette was supposedly staying with the Hassaus on Sycamore Street.

On January 13, 1947, according to what Wilson told Gilmore, Bette left Hassau's place on Sycamore with the killer and went to a "safe house" at 244 31st Street. Trouble started when she wanted to make a phone call and leave the hideout. (Wilson also told Gilmore that the killer knew he wanted to kill her from the first time he met her. And that was the only reason he kept seeing her.)

Gilmore gave me copies of the transcripts of the conversations he had with Jack Wilson (aka Arnold Smith). A number of pages on the case, including Wilson's statements, had been typed and edited by Ron Kenner from Gilmore's notes. Jack Wilson's statements rambled in places, but the account was chilling. At one point Wilson said, "The first thing you've got to understand is, you couldn't fuck her."

Wilson sounded drunk in parts. He gave his account of how "the separation" took place. Although he claimed that all this had been told to him by "Al Morrison," many of the details revealed by Wilson in his roundabout "telling" of the murder seemed like eye-witness accounts, or bizarre fantasies.

In one instance Wilson made a comment, almost an aside. "If you look at the map of the city," Wilson said, "and you see where she was put, where the body was placed, it is the only section of the city that is shaped like a woman's pussy."

I checked my files and pulled out a copy of a 1945 Los Angeles street map and located 39th and Norton. From another file I pulled a copy of a sketch Gilmore had sent me. Gilmore said the drawing on the cocktail napkin was made by a detective (not St. John), and depicted the markings carved in the victim's pubic area after she was dead. I put the drawing and the map side by side, studying them. Only a devious perverted mind could have come up with that, I thought. I called Gilmore.

"John," I said, "have you ever checked a map of the area where the body was placed? He admitted he had not. "Well," I said, "if the detective was half-way accurate in the depiction of the markings in the pubic area, they could be a crude drawing of a street map."

In June of 1990, I called Gilmore again. "John," I said, "Maybe we should send the transcripts of Wilson's statements and the report from the inquest to some experts. I have a couple of people in mind, if it's okay with you. What do you think?" Gilmore thought it sounded fine. He also had some contacts in the Sheriff's Department and some other experts that he would check out.

Dr. Money, a forensic sexologist associated with Johns Hopkins University, hedged on the telephone. He wasn't sure what he could do. "Just your opinion," I said. "Whatever your opinion is. That's what we want."

Dr. Money responded with a letter dated July 18, 1990, reiterating the opinion he expressed during our earlier telephone conversations. "There is insufficient information," he wrote, "to be able to arrive at any conclusion regarding Ms. Short's genital status." He ventured the opinion that the various known medical conditions would *not* have rendered Bette incapable of eventually having a normal sexual relationship, possibly even giving birth, depending on the condition of her uterus and other female organs. "Some patients have a blind vagina which, although short, is progressively lengthened over a period of time, as a sequel to repeated penile penetration, with the penis acting as a dilator."

Referring to the Gilmore notes of Arnold Smith (Jack Anderson Wilson) and comparing them to the *partial* autopsy information in the Coroner's Inquest report, Dr. Money states, "Despite the incoherency of parts of the interview, the overall content is consistent with the possibility that Ms. Short met her death as the victim of a lust murderer. Lust murder is one of the 40 different paraphilias. Its Greek name is erotophonophilia... I think it is very likely that Arnold Smith himself was the murderer of Ms. Short."

The Chief of Autopsy Services at the University of California Medical Center, Dr. Finkbeiner, looked at the same documents. "The transcripts of Arnold's statements are consistent with the information in the Coroner's Inquest report, Dr. Finkbeiner said. "That's how it could have been done—the body bisected. And that's how a layman, someone without medical training, might have described it." Dr. Finkbeiner qualified his statements by adding that he would have to see the *complete autopsy report* and look at detailed *photos* to give a definitive opinion.

I showed John St. John the letter from Dr. Money. St. John said he'd look at the transcripts and whatever else John Gilmore and I had. "But what we need," he said, "is *corroboration*—a photo, a witness, something that would *link* Wilson to Elizabeth Short."

St. John told me he had been on the Black Dahlia case for only a year when John Gilmore's story caused a mild furor in the press. St. John said he couldn't just go and pick up Wilson without the all-important *corroborating* evidence. St. John explained: "We needed *probable* cause. Once we picked him up, he would be *legally* a suspect. And once he was *officially* a suspect, then it's a whole new ball game. You have to keep an *open mind*, because the very *instant* you begin to suspect someone, you have to *read them their rights*. It is a very important *legal* issue. We couldn't just pick up this Wilson guy, because of what someone *told* us he said. But if Wilson had *voluntarily* come in and talked to us, that's different. At the time, I was busy on the Bonin case. It was coming to trial."

Bringing William Bonin, the serial killer of boys and young men, to justice took precedence over the thirty-five-year-old Black Dahlia case. Waiting another couple of weeks didn't seem unreasonable. But who could have predicted the fire that engulfed room 202 of the Holland Hotel?

All that remained was a charred corpse in a fetal position, some loose teeth, a belt buckle, and part of a one-dollar bill. Everything else in the room had been completely destroyed—no See's candy box filled with mementos, no photos, no evidence proving that Wilson had ever known Elizabeth Short.

A few months after my conversation with St. John, Gilmore and I were scheduled to be interviewed for a segment on the syndicated television show, *Entertainment Tonight* (ET). Two minutes of an hour-long interview aired. The ET interviewer was hostile in his questioning. Gilmore's theory was based on the fact that Smith had information about the physical condition of Elizabeth Short that was never made public, but which I seemed to verify. The ET interviewer kept raising the point that if I was able to obtain the "secret" information, couldn't Jack Wilson (Arnold Smith) have come by the information in the same way?

Will Fowler had told me two other Hearst reporters knew of Elizabeth Short's physical problem: Bevo Means and Sid Hughes. But Nieson Himmel also knew. Maybe it wasn't *public* knowledge, but it was not exactly a secret.

The interviewer asked Gilmore if he had tapes of his conversations with Wilson. Gilmore said the original tapes had been lost, but he had a photograph of them. The interviewer became skeptical. He wondered why anyone would take a *photograph*, but not make *audio* duplicates of audio tapes. The interviewer became more skeptical when Gilmore could not produce a photograph of Wilson. "How do we know this guy even exists?" he asked off-camera.

Immediately following the ET interview, I headed for the east coast to meet with Bette's sister, Muriel Short. Muriel had written to me after an article about my book project appeared in the Medford newspaper.

Muriel picked me up at the bus station. Forty-four years had passed since we had last seen each other, but I recognized Muriel immediately, she looked so much like her mother. "Let me take you to dinner. I know a great seafood restaurant," she said.

We sat quietly in the dark-paneled booths, ordered our Captain's Plates, and began to reminisce about Medford: the band concerts, the parades, the old neighborhood, and the hangouts in Medford Square.

"Nonie and I stayed in Medford for a couple of years after Bette's death. But it was hard," Muriel said. "Reporters wouldn't leave us alone. Every time there was something in the paper.... People have said such horrible things."

"Not those who *knew* her," I said. "They wouldn't talk to the reporters. Everyone who knew her, liked her. Bette never hurt anyone. And even *if* she had slept around, it seems blatantly unfair in this day and age to still be judging her by 1947 standards."

"I never thought of it that way," Muriel said.

"Yeah, but I've since found out, that none of it, none of it is true. She'd leave, flee from touchy situations. Harry Hansen, the detective who had the case for over twenty years said, to use the vernacular, that Bette didn't *put out*.

"And I don't think Bette was exactly broke at the time of her death. Gordon Fickling said he sent Bette a hundred dollars a couple of weeks before she left Pacific Beach. Another twenty dollars came from Ann Toth. Considering what prices were like in 1947, that would be like having fifteen hundred dollars in your pocket. And since she left her luggage at Greyhound, I think she might have been planning to take a bus somewhere, maybe Chicago, like she had told a few people."

"There were so many stories. We tried to ignore them," Muriel said. "We never understood why people wrote those things. It's gotten worse over the years. I'd go and visit your Aunt Dot. I don't know what I would have done without her. We'd have coffee and talk."

After dinner we returned to Muriel's home. On her living room mantle was a photo of Bette, the often-published one—Bette smiling slightly with a curl falling over her forehead.

"Mama's favorite photo," Muriel said. "My children and the other grandchildren don't know the story, don't know that Bette is called the Black Dahlia. They only know their aunt died very young."

Muriel went to her bookcase and retrieved a photo album. We sat side-by-side on the couch as Muriel turned the pages. She picked up a small photo and handed it to me.

"That's my brother Richard!" I said.

"I used to have a big crush on him. Kept it all these years. Maybe he'd like to have it," Muriel said. "I don't have many pictures of Bette. Only these two photos of us as kids. And this one Bette sent from Miami." Muriel turned the photo over. "Bette wrote on the back—'Hubba, hubba.' You can use the photos if it will help."

I told her I'd make copies and send the originals back. "Meanwhile I have something for you," I said. I fished into my large black purse and pulled out a photo of Muriel's father. "You said you were interested in knowing something about him. I came across this photo in a special collection at UCLA," I said.

Muriel thanked me for the photo. "My father did write a couple of times about wanting to come back," she said. "But Mama told him, no. Mama was working in Boston, a bookkeeper with Stone and Webster. Nonie was a secretary with Liberty Mutual Insurance Company, and I had a part-time job after school. Mama thought we had become independent and were doing quite nicely without him. Mama never forgave him for leaving the way he did—business bad, owing creditors, not able to meet the payroll. When he died, the government sent Mama a flag, but she took it into the back yard and burned it.

For the next couple of hours we talked about Bette. "Every year just before school started, Bette would take me shopping," Muriel said. "Bette carefully planned the shopping trip: lunch at the Medford Cafe—I always wanted the baked macaroni. Then we'd go to a matinee at the Square Theatre, and after the movie, to W. T. Grant's on High Street. I'd worry about money, so I'd always choose the less expensive pencil box which had only one drawer. But Bette would see me sneaking glances at the bigger pencil boxes with two or three drawers, and Bette would say, 'Maybe this one is better, the one with two drawers. It has more room. Why don't we buy this one?'"

Muriel said Bette wasn't the only one in her family with health problems. "Nonie and I also had asthma. When the three of us were having trouble breathing, we'd take turns in the rocking chair. Sometimes Mama would send for Doctor Beck, and he'd come and give each of us a shot of adrenaline. In those days it wasn't known about allergies to cats and dogs. That's probably why Bette always felt better in Florida and California—no pets."

"My Aunt Dot told me you and your sisters used to fight," I said.

Muriel laughed. She could remember fighting with Ginnie over the radio. "On Saturdays, when the Met started broadcasting, Ginnie would want to listen to the opera, and Bette and I would want the popular music," Muriel said. "Even when Ginnie babysat, she'd turn on the opera and make the kids listen. Bette had a fairly decent voice, but she rarely sang around the house like Ginnie. Ginnie played the violin in the school orchestra and sang in church. She later gave concerts at Jordan Hall.

"When we were growing up, Mama was very particular about how we looked—especially going to church on Sundays. Mama had a Saturday night routine—ironing, fixing hair ribbons, polishing shoes—making everything neat and pretty.

"It was so hard to believe that something like this could happen to our family—to my sister."

Muriel became quiet for a moment, then she said, "Mama had a premonition. Mama told me she knew something was wrong—before the phone call and before the police knocked on the door. The night Bette was murdered, Mama came home from work very tired and went to bed right after supper. Around midnight, Mama felt her blanket being yanked off the bed and woke up with a cold chill. Thinking the wind had blown it off, she went over to close the windows. But the windows were shut. Mama said that she knew then that something was wrong, that something had happened to Bette.

"Mama was unusually quiet at dinner the next day, despite the fact that Dottie was home on leave. After dinner, Mama said that she'd clean up and that we should visit. Nonie, Dottie, and I went into my bedroom, the one I shared with Bette when she was home. We were laughing and making plans for the coming weekend. Mama almost didn't hear the knocking at the front door. Mr. Weir from the downstairs flat stood on the landing in his bathrobe and slippers. He told Mama there was a phone call from *California*, from a *newspaper*, something about Bette winning a beauty contest. 'I don't know how they got my phone number,' he said. We still didn't have our own telephone because of the post-war shortages.

"We were making quite a ruckus when Mama came back from Mr. Weir's. Sometime later, maybe a half hour, we heard the buzzer and saw Mama walk slowly towards the back door. We quieted down when we saw Mama and a policeman walk past the bedroom towards the parlor. We strained to hear what Mama and the policeman were saying, but we couldn't make anything out. Finally, the policeman left and Mama came to the doorway of the bedroom. 'I've just been informed that something happened to your sister Bette,' Mama said. 'Bette is dead. She was murdered in Los Angeles, in California.'

"I can't remember who ran the three blocks through the icy snow for the minister. But our pastor, Reverend Henderson, seemed to be there almost from the minute Mama told us. He stayed through most of the night and prayed with us.

"Everything seemed so unreal. I couldn't believe it. I must have been in shock."

"When did it hit you," I asked. "When did you *know* in your heart that something had *really* happened to Bette?"

"It was at the airport," Muriel said, "with all the photographers running backwards in front of us, crouching down, taking photographs. It was then, with strangers blocking my way and the flashes of light blinding me, that I suddenly realized my sister was *dead*—my sister Bette had been *murdered*.

"I can never forget that night. Mama was going to California by herself, but we accompanied her to the airport. We left through the back door, walked quickly down the alley, and crept through a hole in the back fence of the old cemetery. Dottie gripped Mama tightly while Nonie and I linked arms.

"We walked in the dark, the four of us. I remember the crunching sound as we walked on the crusted snow—through the cemetery, past rows of tombstones, to the Cross Street entrance. Through the high, wrought-iron gate I could see the exhaust from Reverend Henderson's waiting car."

"I know Mama's faith helped her through it. Mama and my sister Ginnie had to identify Bette. They didn't want to, but the police insisted. Mama said that Ginnie's husband, Adrian, walked between them towards the window when they went to view Bette's body. Adrian held each of them by the arm. When the attendant moved the gurney in front of the window, Mama started to feel light-headed, about to fall. She said she could feel her knees giving away. Then Mama felt a very light touch on her other arm, a pressure that grew stronger. She thought that someone was on the other side helping to hold her up. Mama turned to say thank you. But no one was there. Mama could feel the pressure getting firmer. Mama said she knew then that she'd be all right—that she'd have help to see her through the ordeal.

"In one of Bette's last letters home, Bette wrote that a movie director was going to give her a screen test."

"Do you remember the director's name?" I asked.

"No, I just remember he was someone important."

At the end of our conversation Muriel said, "We try to protect Mama, and we never discuss it among ourselves. But Mama does believe that someday the truth will come out and Bette will be exonerated."

A strange, sad comment, I thought—the need to *exonerate* Bette, the need to *exonerate* the person who was the victim of such a fiendish crime.

On the way back to California, I stopped by Nashville, Tennessee, where Bette's niece, Valerie Reynolds, lived. An aspiring singer and songwriter, she was Nonie's daughter, born a few years after her aunt's murder. Valerie had emerged as the family's public spokesperson. Like her aunt, Valerie had beautiful translucent blue eyes, which I found unsettling.

"I never knew my Aunt Bette," Valerie said. "But I know how Aunt Bette's death affected our family. Even now, there are days when my mother goes off by herself to another room, and I hear her sobbing."

Valerie agreed to accompany me to Johnson City,

Tennessee, where Wilson, aka Arnold Smith, had been arrested for a "crime against nature." On the drive to Johnson City, Valerie told me about a strange experience that her mother believes was an omen. "It was during the war," Valerie said. "My mother had come home from work and saw her friend Ginger sitting on the front steps. Ginger had been there for hours, clutching a telegram from the War Department. Her husband was missing in action. Ginger told my mother that she had to find out what happened and begged my mother to go with her to the gypsy's—there was a clan of gypsies in Medford, and the grandmother told fortunes. Ginger couldn't face going alone, she said, so my mother and my Aunt Bette went with her.

"The gypsy told Ginger that her husband was a prisoner, but that he'd be back. Then she talked about children and happy events that would transpire in Ginger's and my mother's lives— events that later proved to be true. My mother said that Aunt Bette waited expectantly for her turn. But when Aunt Bette sat down to have her fortune told, the gypsy said that she was very, very tired, and that there was nothing she could tell Bette. My mother thinks the gypsy sensed something terrible was going to happen to Aunt Bette."

At the small police station in Johnson City a major communication problem developed. Everyone spoke English, but I had a Boston accent and the policeman in charge had a thick Tennessee drawl. We could not understand what each other was trying to say. I kept pointing to Wilson's CII form with the Tennessee arrest listed on it, while Valerie, leaning against the wall and taking it all in, created the impression of being a bored police woman. Finally the policeman threw up his hands in frustration and signaled the clerk to check the computer. The print-out of Wilson's arrest record listed his birthplace as Canton, Ohio, not Los Angeles, California. I was so excited about the purloined information that I forgot to ask for a mug shot.

I immediately called John Gilmore. He had relatives in Canton who could obtain Wilson's birth certificate, he said. A few days later a hand-corrected document arrived in the mail. The name on the certificate was Grover Loving Jr. with a birthdate of August 5, 1920. The name of the father, Grover Loving, was crossed out, and the name of Alex F. Wilson written in. The mother was listed as Minnie Buchanan. Both mother and father gave North Carolina as their place of birth. An attached affidavit signed by Minnie Buchanan and dated November 10, 1942 listed Jack Anderson Wilson as the correct name of the child with Alex F. Wilson as the correct name of the biological father.

Upon my return to San Francisco I visited a library that specializes in genealogy—the Sutro Library. Looking through old census tracts, telephone books, and city directories I traced the whereabouts of Jack Anderson Wilson and his mother, Minnie Buchanan Wilson. I found a trail of listings that placed Minnie Wilson in the city of Wilmar, a suburb of Los Angeles, between 1939 and 1942. Her name disappeared from the telephone books and city directories in 1943. The 1940 Los Angeles City Directory listed a Jack A. Wilson living on Hill Street in Los Angeles. The 1941 and 1942 city directories had a Jack A. Wilson working at Cogar Brothers Sign Company in Los Angeles with a residence in Wilmar. All the information, with exact dates and addresses, I passed on to John Gilmore.

John obtained Wilson's military file. Wilson had been in the army from January 12, 1944 to March 15, 1945. I created a chronology combining Wilson's arrest record with the new information, but a major gap appeared—no paper trail existed for Wilson's whereabouts between his entry into the army and his arrest in 1948 for vagrancy and lewd behavior. There was nothing to indicate whether or not Wilson was in the Los Angeles area when Elizabeth Short was murdered.

A friend visiting from Oregon, Shirley Launder, volunteered to take a detour through Medford on her trip home and try to obtain Wilson's mug shot. After a grueling drive, Shirley arrived in Medford, Oregon at three o'clock in the morning. She parked her car outside the police station and cat-napped while waiting for the station to open. A week later I held Wilson's mug shot in my hands.

John Gilmore checked out a "hot" tip he had received from a person who used the name "Just Plain Bill." The call came in

February of 1991, a few days after the "Black Dahlia" segment aired on *Entertainment Tonight,* "Just Plain Bill" suggested that John and I look into two unsolved murders—the victims were Georgette "Georgie" Bauerdorf and Karyn Kupcinet. Both were unsolved cases of the Los Angeles Sheriff's Department (LASD). "Just Plain Bill" claimed that the Sheriff's inspectors thought the Bauerdorf and Kupcinet cases were connected to the Black Dahlia murder, but Harry Hansen had his own theory and wouldn't cooperate in a joint investigation.

The first victim named by the tipster, Georgette Bauerdorf, age 20, was murdered in her "swank" apartment on Fountain Avenue in West Hollywood on October 12, 1944—almost three years before the Black Dahlia murder. The heiress was found face-down in an overflowing tub of warm, bloody water. She was clad in her pink rayon pajamas top. Her teeth were clenched tightly around a piece of crepe tetra bandage (eight inches wide) that had been forced down her throat and then torn off. Georgette's lips had a heavy coating of lipstick. She was dead when placed in the tub.

Reporters surmised that Georgette had been raped in the bedroom as "she lay dying." Across the hall from the bathroom, a smeared blood stain on the bedroom floor indicated that someone had attempted to wipe it up, possibly with the missing piece of cloth. According to the *Daily News,* the bloodstain was still damp.

Georgette, the newspapers reported, had "struggled fiercely." The knuckles of her right hand were smashed, and a contusion, possibly from a fist blow, was found on the right side of her head. Another bruise was found on her abdomen, and a bruise on her right thigh was in the rough shape of a hand. The cloth had been jammed down with such force that her lips were torn at the corners.

Georgette's missing automobile, a 1936 Green Oldsmobile coupe, was found out of gas on East 25th Street. The keys were in the ignition.

The bulb to the entryway light (eight feet from the ground) had been unscrewed so that it could not be switched on, leaving the area outside the door in darkness. There was a print on the bulb; the prints on the steering wheel of the car were smudged. The height of the person who unscrewed the light bulb was open to conjecture. He could have stood on one of the metal lawn chairs clearly visible in the newspaper photos.

On the day of the murder, Georgette went on a shopping spree with her father's secretary, Rose Gilbert. At 6:30 p.m. Georgette parked in front of the Hollywood Canteen and knitted while waiting for the Canteen to open. June Ziegler joined her in the car. Georgette said she was nervous and asked June to spend the night. (Georgette had been a regular hostess at the Canteen, located at Sunset and Cahuenga, since April 23, 1944.)

Georgette left the Canteen and headed home about 11:30 p.m., stopping to pick up Sgt. Gordon R. Aadland, a hitchhiking soldier. She drove him from Vine Street to a block east of Laurel off Sunset. According to Aadland, Georgette seemed nervous and excited about a trip the next day to El Paso, Texas. She told him she was rushing home so she wouldn't miss a call from her boyfriend, Jerry (Private Jerome M. Brown stationed at Fort Bliss), a soldier she had met six months before at the Hollywood Canteen.

Georgette Bauerdorf had fixed a snack and made an entry in her diary, a small red book. It was speculated that while preparing for bed, Georgette was interrupted by either the doorbell or someone who had a key. There was no forced entry.

Actors, actresses, hostesses, and other people associated with the Hollywood Canteen were questioned. They described Georgette as refined, pleasant, friendly, and generous to servicemen—"giving them rides, entertaining them at night clubs and giving them money." Georgette thought her "participation in the Hollywood Canteen a service to the country."

Too many fingerprints and too many keys hampered the investigation. Georgette had given out several duplicate keys to her apartment. According to the newspapers, she would sleep upstairs while she let servicemen sleep on the living room couch and floor.

Although suspects numbered in "the thousands," the ones mentioned in the newspapers were: the hitchhiker, a jitterbugging soldier who had kept cutting in that night, and an unidentified man described as a friend of the soldier. People said the man was noticeable because he was over six feet tall, maybe six-foot-four, unusually tall for those days. Georgette told friends she didn't like the tall guy; he was too persistent. Both soldiers were able to prove they were back at camp at the time of the murder. Robbery was ruled out as a motive.

"Georgie," the newspapers reported, graduated in 1941 from the exclusive Westlake School for Girls. Her father, George F. Bauerdorf of 299 Park Avenue, New York City, and Reno, Nevada, was an independent oil man and goldmine owner. He also was a friend of William Randolph Hearst. Georgette aspired to be a reporter and worked for a while at one of the Hearst papers.

Treatment of Georgette Bauerdorf by the press was in stark contrast to the treatment of Elizabeth Short. The Bauerdorf story dropped from the front page after a couple of days, and coverage disappeared altogether after a week.

Aggie Underwood resurrected the story of the Bauerdorf murder. Aggie was a close friend of Sheriff Biscailiz, and it is surmised that he put the bug in her ear. It is also surmised that Aggie was "kicked upstairs" because she was making waves prying into the Bauerdorf murder, and Hearst wanted his reporters to pursue other angles.

The second victim named by the tipster, Karyn Kupcinet, was murdered on November 27, 1963—the week following the assassination of President Kennedy, sixteen years after the Black Dahlia murder. The body of auburn-haired Karyn Kupcinet was found in her second-floor Hollywood apartment. She was the twenty-two-year-old daughter of Chicago columnist Irv Kupcinet.

Actor Mark Goddard and his wife, Marcia, who discovered Karyn's body, had become concerned that Karyn was not answering her telephone. The evening of November 30, 1963, they drove to Karyn's Hollywood apartment on Sweetzer Avenue, arriving around 7:30 p.m. They noticed three newspapers, a couple of magazines, and a book, *The Tropic of Capricon*, lying outside her door. Mark rang the bell, and when no one answered, he tried the doorknob. The door was unlocked. They entered the darkened apartment and saw the outline of Karyn lying on the couch, illuminated by a television set that had its sound turned off. When Mark switched on the lights, it became apparent that something was wrong with Karyn.

Sheriff deputies who arrived on the scene noted the signs of a struggle: an overturned coffee pot and cigarette container were lying on the floor; a spoon, pink-and-white panda bear, and throw pillow were nearby. Across the room on a stand was a cup of coffee, half-filled. A bathrobe was thrown over the back of a living room chair. Karyn's nude body was face down on the couch with her head turned towards the television set. In the kitchen, three cups were in the dish drainer.

In the apartment, inspectors found a notepad containing names, addresses, and memos of telephone conversations—mostly of other budding young actors and actresses. "It was not exactly a diary," Detective Lieutenant George Walsh told reporters, but he indicated that the "notes were extensive and gave valuable insight into Miss Kupcinet's private life." Karyn had a wide circle of "drop-in" acquaintances.

An autopsy indicated Karyn Kupcinet had been dead about three days. The newspapers reported that she was beaten about the face and manually strangled with such force that one of her vertebrae snapped. The killer, the autopsy surgeon said, used only his left hand. It was noted that Karyn was not sexually assaulted and her body was very clean, as if she had just showered or taken a bath.

Marcia and Mark Goddard told inspectors that Karyn had been quiet at dinner on November 27th, the last time they saw her. Karyn's career was going well; she had just performed in a Perry Mason TV episode. But the Goddards thought Karyn was still upset about her breakup with actor Andrew Prine. Karyn said Prine felt it would be best if they did not see each other as often. He was dating other women.

Two other witnesses came forward, the last known persons to see Karyn Kupcinet alive. Writer Edward S. Rubin and actor Robert Hathaway said they visited Karyn after she returned from her dinner at the Goddards' home, in Coldwater Canyon. They had coffee and cake, the friends said, watched television and chit-chatted for a couple of hours. When Karyn went to bed they continued to watch TV until the end of a program, then left, locking the door.

Andrew Prine told investigators he had called Karyn twice the night of her murder, trying to smooth over their differences. His first call was at 6:30 p.m., and then he called at 11:30 p.m. after he had returned from a date.

William Mamches, another actor, said Karyn was "very upset and frantic about her broken romance."

The writer Edward Rubin and the three actors, Mark Goddard, Andrew Prine, and William Mamches, were given polygraph exams. All passed.

During questioning, Prine gave a hot lead—death threats made of pasted-up letters that he and Karyn had received. Prine turned several of the notes over to detectives. The lead fizzled when Karyn's fingerprints were found on the backside of the sticky tape that sealed the notes. She had sent the notes, it was surmised, in a futile attempt to resurrect her romance with Andrew Prine.

Friends and family described Karyn as "enthusiastic," "bubbly," "intelligent," and "beautiful"—her career as an actress well on its way. Karyn's television credentials included appearances on *The Red Skelton Show, U.S. Steel Hour*, *Hawaiian Eye*, the *Donna Reed Show,* and twenty-six episodes of the *Gertrude Berg Show.* Karyn had a small part in the Jerry Lewis movie *The Ladies' Man* and had just finished her work in a *Perry Mason* episode.

Karyn Kupcinet, like Georgette Bauerdorf, came from a socially prominent family and attended private schools. After graduating from Wellesley College, Karyn studied "method acting" with Lee Strasberg.

Illuminaries (including Mayor Daley and Illinois Governor Otto Kerner) attended Karyn's funeral services. Unlike the funerals of Georgette Bauerdorf and Elizabeth Short, which were private, in Chicago more than 1,500 persons heard Karyn Kupcinet eulogized as "born to be a star."

As the years passed and the police were unable to find the

killer, Karyn's mother, Esther Kupcinet, turned to psychics. "When you're desperate, nothing is too far-fetched," she said. Karyn's father, Irv Kupcinet, told interviewers, "We have a good idea who did it, but nothing we could ever prove."

In a November 1998 magazine article, writer James Ellroy puts forth the theory that Karyn hadn't been murdered, but had died from an overdose of sleeping pills. Ellroy theorizes that her snapped vertebrae came from a botched autopsy.

Inspectors in the Sheriff's department believed the murders of Karyn Kupcinet, Elizabeth Short, and Georgette Bauerdorf could be connected. The victims were about the same age and similar types—fun-loving, outgoing, and friendly, but well-mannered and polite. They were pretty and dark-haired; Karyn's hair was auburn and Elizabeth Short's naturally brunette hair had reddish highlights. Water was part of the scenario in all three murders. Powerful force was used on all three victims; and in all three cases, the number of acquaintances and leads hampered the investigation.

Gilmore said the inspector in charge of the Sheriff Department's old unsolved murder cases planned to compare Jack Anderson Wilson's fingerprints to the prints taken from Bauerdorf's light bulb. But when the inspector went to the Bauerdorf files, not much evidence was left. The fingerprint samples had disappeared. No comparison could be made.

LAPD detectives in charge of the Black Dahlia case insisted there was no connection between the murders. Three different killers who had three different MOs were the perpetrators. The Bauerdorf murder was sexually motivated with anger a secondary factor. The killer had forced cloth down Georgette's throat to quiet her during an attempted rape. On the other hand, the Kupcinet murder was motivated by anger; the powerful left-handed killer snapped Karyn's neck with one hand. Sex was not a factor.

"Whoever murdered Elizabeth Short only struck once," insisted St. John. "Elizabeth Short was killed by a sadist, pure and simple. He never struck again."

Larry Harnisch, a reporter and copy editor for *The Los Angeles Times* became highly critical of John Gilmore's theory about the Black Dahlia murder. Harnisch touched off a minor controversy when he criticized Gilmore's book *Severed* on the Internet. Harnisch commented that "*Severed* is 25% facts, 25% mistakes and 50% fiction." Harnisch, who had written a newspaper article on the 50th anniversary of the murder, created his own web site. On Bette's seventy-fifth birthday he went on-line revealing his theory and naming a suspect.

To St. John, without corroborating evidence, Jack Anderson Wilson became just one more person added to the long list of people who had confessed to the Black Dahlia Murder.

TEN
The Signature

A short distance from the old neighborhood, near Washington Square, stands a granite-and-bronze memorial for Elizabeth Short. When Kyle J. Wood, a producer of documentaries, first approached the Medford Historical Society with the idea of erecting the monument for the woman known as "The Black Dahlia," then-president Dr. Valerini had misgivings. But he did not expect the plaque for Elizabeth Short to be quite so controversial. Members of the community, including a former classmate of Bette Short, protested that honoring a murder victim as "infamous" as the "Black Dahlia" would cast a blight on Medford's good name.

Kyle J. Wood paid for the monument, saying he "did not want to exploit Elizabeth Short's name without giving something back in return." Kyle had produced and written a documentary about the murder.

I first met Kyle in 1995. One year later we combined our research files and donated them to the Medford Historical Society. Jay Griffin, the new president, said he was delighted that the historical society would finally have comprehensive research material on the Black Dahlia—the subject for which the society receives the most phone calls.

I took Kyle on a tour of the old neighborhood and showed him where Bette's apartment house had once stood. Kyle later visited me in California, and we went by Mountain View Cemetery to place flowers on Bette's grave.

My odyssey, it seemed, had come to an end.

A major motion picture was in the works, based on my collaborative efforts with John Gilmore. The movie company that optioned our rights, the Edward R. Pressman Film Corporation, had an impressive track record: *Badlands*, *Reversal of Fortune*, *The Crow*, *Das Boot*, and *Wall Street*. Richard Pleuger, the young German journalist, played a part in bringing about the movie deal.

Over the years, Richard had become my confidant of sorts. Whenever I was in Los Angeles, we'd get together and have dinner at Musso Frank's, a Hollywood landmark that still retained its 1940s flavor.

On one such trip I accompanied Richard as he conducted research in the library of The Academy of Motion Picture Arts and Sciences. On a whim, while waiting for Richard, I requested *The Lady From Shanghai* stills. I was given white gloves to wear and a file containing a number of glossy photos: Welles and Rita Hayworth in Mexico and San Francisco, waterfront shots from Sausalito, close-ups of Everett Sloane, and then a photo that startled me. Orson Welles and a man (whom I later identified as makeup artist Bob Schiffer), were posed as if working on a mannequin's head. The head/skull was mutilated in ways similar to the injuries Bette had sustained: teeth knocked loose and cuts from ear to ear below the zygomatic arch.

The similarities troubled me. I showed Richard the photo. Over dinner and wine we discussed the coincidences. "Don't get carried, away." Richard cautioned me. "What are you thinking?"

"I don't know," I said. "I'm wondering if maybe I should get off my duff and check some of the things about Welles that I never got around to. That photo disturbs me."

But I hesitated, afraid the research would take over my life again and lead me to a place I definitely did not want to go. A couple of years had passed since my work with Gilmore. The book had been published. My notes and research materials were packed up and shipped out. I was in the middle of a new series of paintings.

A comment of Bette's niece, Valerie Reynolds, started haunting me. "No stone should be left unturned," she once said. I thought of my last conversation with Muriel, telling her that I would do right by Bette. But in my heart I felt I had not.

My nightmares started up again—a few snake-in-the-grass dreams, a few dreams about something undone, unresolved. They were followed by the most disturbing of all my nightmares.

I seemed to be in a twilight state—half asleep, half awake. A gray amorphous "spirit" with a greenish glow appeared in the corner of my bedroom. The spirit was moving, undulating as if trying to take form. I woke up disoriented and quite afraid. For a few seconds the spirit seemed to be hovering in the room.

I did not want to delve into an explanation of the dream. I sensed that something inside of me was desperate to communicate—an embryonic idea, half-formed, that needed to take shape.

I made a few trips to Los Angeles—going back over old territory and venturing into new areas—picking up the threads of my earlier research. The American Film Institute was high on my list; my previous work indicated the complete archival collection of Columbia stills was housed there. After a long walk up a steep hill I discovered Columbia Studios had removed the entire collection.

I had better luck in the basement of the Charles E. Young Research Library at UCLA where I perused the Richard Wilson file and made copies of all the correspondence from 1947 to 1951 for further study.

Under the Freedom of Information Act, I requested the file of Orson Welles from the FBI. Since I had waited two years for the Elizabeth Short file, I did not expect prompt action.

Next I recruited a few friends to help me with research: Jeanne Jabbour, Sonia Rummel, and Pia Mogollón. Jeanne became my assistant and invaluable sounding board.

Sonia Rummel watched videos of Orson Welles' films with me. We divided a list of his biographies to read. There were a couple of new ones on the market, and some revised editions of previous work. Sonia made notes, concentrating on the years 1946 through 1951.

During one of our many discussions about Welles, Sonia remarked, "If Welles was ever going to crack-up, it would have been around 1946 and 1947—when he was filming *The Lady From Shanghai.*" Rita Hayworth was divorcing Welles; Harry Cohn, the head of Columbia Studios, was hassling him about the film; Welles' stage production of *Around the World in Eighty Days* was a flop; creditors and the IRS were after him; and he was heavily into drugs. A number of his projects were in disarray, yet Welles explored the possibility of taking on new projects.

With so much pressure, a crack-up would have been well within the realm of possibilities. Throughout his life, Welles had what appeared to be periodic breakdowns. A July 1938 *New York Times* article implied that Welles was either drunk or close to a breakdown when he gave a rambling speech to the National Council of Teachers of English.

According to Charles Higham, during the 1939 stage production of the *Five Kings*, Welles kept erratic hours, drank heavily at late-night parties, and used amphetamines to keep his weight down. "The dangerous lack of control that was soon to mark his [Welles'] career had manifested itself."

Biographer Simon Callow describes Welles as a man with "a barely controlled feverish energy that suggests the centre cannot hold, that things will fall apart."

And, according to Pauline Kael, the center did fall apart—when Welles "lost his collaborative partnerships that he needed....

"He was alone, trying to be 'Orson Welles,' though 'Orson Welles' had stood for activities of a group. But he needed his family to hold him together on a project and to take over for him when his energies became scattered. With them, he was a prodigy of accomplishments; without them, he flew apart."

The winter of 1940, Welles became disoriented while on a lecture tour. He couldn't remember where he was supposed to be and bought tickets to the wrong destination. In March of 1941, two weeks after the opening of *Native Son* at the St. James Theater, Welles checked himself into a sanitarium.

Another breakdown occurred in 1942 while Welles worked on a film in South America. Upon returning from Brazil, Welles immediately checked himself into a sanitarium again.

The year 1950 brought more mental confusion. Welles' drug of choice that year was Dexedrine, but it did not help with weight loss. The six-foot-two expatriate Welles, reportedly eating as many as six lobsters at one sitting, ballooned from a trim one hundred and ninety-five pounds to an obese three-hundred-plus pounds. Charles Higham wrote, "The sight of the naked Welles [in a bathtub] —like a beached whale, a mass of quivering blubber—reciting speeches through several days of stubble and a Havana cigar was almost too much even for his admirers."

During the editing of Welles' last Hollywood film, the 1957 *Touch of Evil*, according to author Frank Brady, "Welles was so crushed... that control of the film had been virtually taken away from him that he went on what might be considered a month-long psychological bender—not quite a nervous breakdown, but a serious withdrawal from the concerns of the world and all personal responsibilities."

While Sonia and I worked our way through a myriad of Welles biographies, Pia Mogollón, who lived in Indianapolis, traveled to the Lilly Library in nearby Bloomington and looked through the primary information in the library's extensive Orson Welles Collection. Pia had some correspondence and photographs copied and sent to me. "There is so much here, you've got to go through the files yourself," she said. "I'm afraid I'll miss something that you'd find significant. There are four *Lady From Shanghai* scripts, one titled 'Scenes as Shot,' with dates, but only ten pages can be copied, unless you get permission from Columbia Studios. Something to do with copyright law."

I had written previously to Columbia Studios requesting an appointment to view *The Lady From Shanghai* shooting schedule, outtakes, and stills—with no success. I wrote again, asking if the Lilly Library could copy the shooting scripts for me. The answer: a faxed letter with a resounding "no," and a warning about copyright infringement.

I tried another avenue, having someone with connections try to gain access for me. The person was given two different stories: 1) "The fun house outtakes were destroyed by Harry Cohn so that Welles would never be able to use them," and 2) "The crazy house outtakes were not destroyed, but are so deep in the vault that they are difficult to retrieve." In either case, it meant the outtakes were not available for viewing.

From other sources, including the Margaret Herrick Library of the Academy of Motion Picture Arts and Sciences and Hollywood memorabilia stores, I acquired various stills of the expurgated *crazy house*. Columbia Studios would not give permission to reproduce the photos in this book. Artist renderings have been substituted, with a notation of where the original photos may be available for viewing.

In one photo, Welles is posed near a painted backdrop of a bisected skeleton. The left leg of the bisected skeleton is arranged in the same way as the left leg of Bette's bisected body. A spear-like object protrudes from the skeleton's left thigh, approximating where Bette's left thigh had been mutilated. (Orson once claimed that during his attempt at bullfighting in Spain, his left thigh had been gored by a bull.)

Another *crazy house* photo shows Rita Hayworth wearing a dark suit, posed near the entrance. Dismembered mannequin arms frame the entryway, and mannequin legs hang down from the ceiling; on the wall is a painting of a woman lying on a cow that has been flayed to its mid-section. The woman appears to be cut in half; a screw protrudes from the left breast with blood dripping down, approximating the location where Elizabeth Short's left breast had been mutilated. At stage right there is a tableau with a doll cut in half and mutilated. In the entryway, a banner reads: "Stand Up Or Give Up." What appears to be wire or string laces the entryway. A clown's head hangs on the wall at stage left.

As I looked at the photos, I recalled the conversation with St. John when he emphasized the *unique* signature of Bette's killer. I understood well the meaning of signature—each artist possesses one. There is no mistaking a painting by El Greco, Van Gogh, Giotto or Motherwell. A Segal sculpture would never be confused with a Giacometti or a Kienholz.

In the signature work of the artist who created the *crazy house* set, I recognized many of the same ritualistic elements contained in the signature murder of Elizabeth Short. There were the obvious figures cut in half, and there was the mutilated face of the mannequin. But most significant, in both the movie set and the crime scene, was the repetitive use of a knife for cutting—a rare signature that has become known to homicide detectives as "picquerism."

Dr. Robert D. Keppel, chief criminal investigator for the Washington State Attorney General's Office, explains picquerism as the act of gaining power and deviant sexual satisfaction "by the process of penetration... cutting and stabbing, slicing, or biting... animals and/or fleshlike materials...." The killer's deviant obsession compels him, according to Dr. Keppel, "to slice, carve, dig, and gouge, and let the blood drain from his victim."

In his book *Signature Killers* Dr. Keppel states that a posed victim is a clear sign that the perpetrator is a signature killer. Posing is very rare, only about one percent of all killers pose the body. Signature killers, according to Dr. Keppel, are sadistic killers, most often necrophiles who express their ultimate control over their victim's dead body. Explains Dr. Keppel: "The deliberate act of posing involves positioning the body or its parts just as a photographer would arrange all aspects of a subject for a photo shoot.... There is hardly a stronger statement of domination than a killer exercising control over not just the victim, but the victim's individual limbs or parts....

"This is what signature killers are all about, whether they commit only one homicide or an extended series. They exist in a world of anger-driven sexual fantasy and emerge periodically into real life to thrive upon domination by controlling their victims through sexual degradation and mental humiliation."

Dr. Keppel uses the term "diphasic personality" to describe signature killers. "A diphasic personality," explains Dr. Keppel, "is one in which there is a split development into two phases. One phase consists of a construction and retreat into a fantasy world where it's safe and the child is in complete control... the other phase of the child's development takes place in the real world....

"As a child who has developed a diphasic or two-pronged personality, progresses through elementary school,... how much mental energy the child imparts to the fantasy [world] helps determine how much he will grow out of it.... Overindulged children are just as likely to have problems as children who experienced a deprivation...

"In the direct proportion that his fantasy replaces reality and creates false reality, does his behavior become increasingly deviant—which is not to say it's criminal, only deviant...

"Some adolescents may become violent; others seek control in different ways.... Many an entertainer has described a difficult childhood and adolescence in which his or her only means of control was to always keep them laughing. They may survive quite nicely in the paranoid world of show business by the very skills that helped them when they were children.

"Not all diphasic personality types cross over the threshold into criminal behavior. In fact, the overwhelming majority of potentially violent people find their needs satisfied at a point somewhere between the edge of normalcy and the borderline of criminality...."

As described by Dr. Keppel, the diphasic personality has a short fuse, is quick to anger, and overreacts when its authority is challenged. The deep-seated anger that drives the diphasic personality can manifest itself, not necessarily as murder, but as a form of psychological abuse—routinely degrading or instilling fear in others. The person can function as a petty tyrant with a support system that allows him to escape the consequences of his actions. But if that support system collapses, perhaps through death, divorce, loss of status, or loss of work, it can be the trigger mechanism which unleashes the fantasies.

"If the person has lived within society's conventions for most of his life," states Dr. Keppel, "his fantasies don't get much beyond violent thought.... It is only [a] tiny percentage in which the fantasies turn to reality and the beast within unleashed....

"Whether they actually cross the great divide between fantasy and reality to commit criminal offenses depends on many, many factors such as how close are they to the line. Do they act out fantasies with people in their daily lives without actually committing a crime? Have they found a safe niche to enable them to act out fantasies without consequences?... Do they medicate themselves with drugs or alcohol to a point where they diminish the inhibitors that keep them from causing violence?"

Dr. Keppel likens a signature killing to a vicious psychodrama played out in three acts. In Act One, the killer sets the situation up by "creating a real or imagined sense of being wronged by the targeted victim." Act Two is the implementation of the killer's fantasy system and the process of the murder, the satisfying of the killer's "angst and hostile aggression." The killer exerts his ultimate control in Act Three. With postmortem rituals and posing, he degrades his victims, reducing them "from human beings to statues or objects."

With death, explains Dr. Keppel, the signature killer has transcended the moral plane, and his unfettered fantasies become realized with impunity.

"Signature killers believe that some murders are okay.... In fact, they may even see their own murders as art, especially the killers who gratify themselves by posing their dead victims.... Once dead, the victim becomes a tableau for the killer to express visually the message he had for the world in general, and women in particular, leaving a distinctive signature of transgression and defilement."

The killer operates from a script. The actors and the scenery may change, but the script remains the same. "Each drama as if it were some bizarre form of Greek tragedy must be built upon the three D's of sexual sadism: dread, dependency and degradation."

Dr. Keppel's comments made me recall St. John's heightened interest when I informed him of the script given to me by the old-time reporter. The grotesque fantasies in the script were far removed from the actual circumstances and facts of the Black Dahlia murder. But the fantasies depicted in Welles' *crazy house* set appeared remarkably close.

Studying the *crazy house* stills again, I looked closely at the tortured figures, the slashed figures, and the figures cut in half. I noticed that in one photo, Rita Hayworth's arms are posed in the same way that the killer had posed Bette's. I looked again at the photo of the bisected skeleton—the left leg painted in the same pose as Bette's left leg. I stared at the protruding arrow that seemed to point to the location where the killer had mutilated Bette's left leg after she was dead. I thought of the clown's smile carved into her face and the clown faces painted by Welles. One clown's head had a curl over the center of its forehead. Bette wore a curl over the center of hers. I thought of the circus tents set up on the open field close to the spot where the killer later placed Bette's bisected corpse. I thought of Orson Welles performing his magic act in a circus tent on Cahuenga Boulevard—creating the illusion in which a woman cut in half, is made whole again. But the figures in the Orson Welles set, like Bette's corpse, were no illusion and remained cut in half.

In February of 1997, I left for my final research trip to Indiana. I spent four days at the Lilly Library in Bloomington going through the Welles collection of letters, memos, and photographs—more than forty boxes. I also checked the much smaller Darryl Zanuck collection. Charles Higham, I was told, had also visited the library. Many of the Lilly documents had been his primary source of biographical information. I found the letter from the mortuary college mentioned by Higham, as well as various memos, letters, telegrams, and California registrations for two automobiles.

Welles bought a tan Cadillac in January of 1944, and a black Plymouth in March of the same year. In 1946, Welles had a "slight accident" that caused minor damages to Dick Powell's car. After Welles left for Europe, Shorty Chirello, Welles' right-hand man, sold one of the automobiles. Telegrams and letters indicated that Shorty was "not cooperating" and withheld the money from Welles. Although Welles told Barbara Leaming that "he never drove another inch" after he paid off the woman in 1945 to keep the alleged rape attempt quiet, he did drive during the shooting of *The Lady From Shanghai*.

At the Lilly Library, I watched a video in the archives entitled *Orson Welles: What went wrong?* In the documentary by Robert Guenette, photographs and footage from films are interspersed with live interviews. Guenette comments that Welles did not like connections to be made between his work and his life, connections that Guenette readily makes. He portrays Welles as a conjurer and a magician, his life, like that of the fictitious character, Charles Foster Kane, a jigsaw puzzle with one missing piece. Guenette asks, "Was there a Rosebud in his life? Was there some link, some key event, some secret, that would explain the strange life of Orson Welles?" (Guenette, again, is referring to the movie *Citizen Kane* and the enigmatic words Charles Foster Kane utters just before he dies.)

On camera, Welles muses about his childhood. "I was

groomed to be different, special. As a child, I never heard a discouraging word. Everything I did was the best and the greatest there ever was. If I wrote a story, it was wonderful! If I did a painting, it was marvelous!"

Welles, according to his authorized biographer, Barbara Leaming, had plans for art school until, at age sixteen, he bluffed his way onto the stage of Dublin's Gate Theater. On October 13, 1931, Welles made an impressive acting debut and met his first "love," Betty Chancellor. For another year, Welles traveled and acted in Ireland. Under the pseudonym of Knowles Noel Shane, he wrote a newspaper column that praised his own performances.

In the same year, 1932, Roger Hill and Welles co-authored *Everybody's Shakespeare* (published by Todd School). Orson's next endeavor, *Bright Lucifer*, a play about a teenage boy obsessed with the "dark side," was never staged. According to Charles Higham, the undercurrents of homosexuality and necrophilia in *Bright Lucifer*, and the forceful speeches by the Faustian hero, Eldred, seem to stem from a "tormented mind." Higham speculates that the play is a pointed reflection of "Welles' disordered subconscious... more so than anything the director subsequently wrote."

Higham notes that the gifted and mercurial Welles "unwittingly reminded even his admirers that he had been denied by the fairy godmothers at his cradle the one gift without which all gifts are finally useless: discipline."

Author James Naremore considers Welles to be "too complex of a man to hold a naïve belief in 'Christian Law and Order'.... He repeatedly dealt with the same issue...: a conflict between the will to power and the need for orderly constraints."

In a discussion of the proposed film *Heart of Darkness*, Naremore touches on Welles' inherent duality. "An important theme... is the irrational drive to evil that can be detected in the most humane of men...."

The many biographers of Welles have claimed that the work of Welles is *about* Welles. The major Wellesian characters have been narcissistic tyrants—megalomaniacs who feel above the law and who justify their mania and contempt for humanity as a reaction to a corrupt society—qualities that seem to reflect the arrogant extremes and excesses of Welles.

James Naremore considers the film *Citizen Kane* to be more a profile of Orson Welles than of William Randolph Hearst. "It was Welles, after all," writes Naremore, "who was known as the *enfant terrible*, and this may account for Kane's emphasis on infantile rage. It was Welles, not Hearst, who was raised by a guardian, and the guardian's name has been given to a character in the film."

Pauline Kael claims the similarities between Welles and the character Charles Foster Kane are no coincidence. In her essay, "Raising Kane," Kael states that Herman Mankiewicz, the original screenwriter, "wrote the capricious, talented, domineering prodigy [Welles] into the role, combining Welles' personality and character traits with Hearst's life."

Naremore points out the Freudian psychology used in the film. "Kane can be typed as a regressive, anal-sadistic personality..." says Naremore, "as an adult he 'returns' to what Freud describes as a pre-genital form of sexuality in which 'not the genital component instincts, but the *sadistic* and *anal* are most prominent,' (*General Introduction to Psychoanalysis*, 1917). Thus throughout his adult life, Kane is partly a sadist who wants to obtain power over others, and partly an anal type, who obsessively collects zoo animals and museum pieces."

Bernard Herrmann, composer of the musical score for the film suggests that *Citizen Kane* was a "dream-like autobiography of Welles." Robert Guenette uses the term "mirror image" when comparing the central character of Charles Foster Kane to Orson Welles.

According to John Houseman, who worked with Mankiewicz on an earlier version of the script, "the deeper we penetrated beyond the public events into the heart of Charles Foster Kane, the closer we seemed to come to the identity of Orson Welles..."

Welles relished controversy, claims Houseman, but was not prepared for the intensity of William Randolph Hearst's response to *Citizen Kane*. According to Charles Lederer (nephew of Marion Davies and husband of Welles' ex-wife,

Virginia Nicolson), Hearst didn't care what was said about him. Hearst was furious about the depiction of the female lead (played by the soon-to-be blacklisted actress, Dorothy Comingore, who resembled Marion Davies, Hearst's long-time mistress).

A *New York Times* article, "Trouble Ahead?" (September 7, 1941) reports that despite Fox-West Coast buying the film, *Citizen Kane* would not be shown in the circuit's 514 theaters. The theater chain had bowed to a directive from William Randolph Hearst: Nationwide, in the Hearst newspapers, there would be no publicity and no advertising space for *all* of RKO's releases, the producers of *Citizen Kane*, or the theaters that *exhibited* the film. En masse, fearful theater managers canceled showings.

Old-time Hearst reporter Will Fowler told me that when he worked for the *Los Angeles Examiner,* there was a "standing order to get *anyone* who had anything to do with *Citizen Kane.*"

During the filming, Welles seemed to live the part of Kane. The rage of Welles became all too real as the cast watched him tear apart "Susan's room."

"You felt as if you were in the presence of a man coming apart," said actor William Alland. "Welles staggered out of the set. His hands were bleeding, his clothes torn, his face flushed, his eyes misted. He almost fainted. 'I really felt it,' Welles mumbled, wandering off in a daze. 'I really felt it.' "

Welles' absorption into his roles became almost a legend. "Like Jack, the actor in *Bright Lucifer*," writes James Naremore, "he [Welles] seemed to feel a Faustian temptation behind his talent, a danger of becoming the role he played...."

While portraying Brutus in the much-acclaimed 1937 New York stage production of *Julius Caesar,* Welles who also directed, insisted on using a *real* knife; the other actors had rubber knives. During a performance, Welles stabbed Joseph Holland, the actor playing Caesar, in the chest, severing an artery near the heart. The actors, according to author Frank Brady, were slipping on the blood spurting from Holland's wound as the curtain came down. Holland was rushed to the hospital, and it was months before he returned to the stage.

Eartha Kitt told of Orson getting "carried away" on the London stage while performing in the "Helen" segment of the 1951 *Time Runs,* which he also directed. Welles bit her lip so hard during a stage kiss that she bled profusely on stage and her face swelled. Eartha Kitt said she didn't know what she had done to make Welles so angry with her.

In that same year, 1951, Orson Welles caused an international furor—during the strangulation scene in *Othello,* he lost control and banged Gudrun Ure's head violently against the bedpost. Welles apologized to the audience for his actions, commenting that he seemed to have become caught up in the play. The actress playing Emilia in the same play suffered a severely swollen face that lasted weeks when Welles threw heavy coins at her for "realism." During the performances, the six-foot-two Welles wore four-inch heels so that he would tower over all the other actors.

According to Frank Brady, the rehearsals for *Othello* were legendary, with Welles "wielding an enormously long stick from his seat in the front rows to direct and guide his actors where he wanted them to move; disappearing for days before opening night; forgetting his own lines; changing his own entrances... without telling his cast where he would appear."

Orson Welles, it seemed, had many of the characteristics of the diphasic personality as described by Dr. Keppel. Throughout Welles' life, drugs and alcohol seemed to be a major part of his problems. Welles became known for his violent outbursts—in public and private. In a 1940s syndicated column, Jimmie Fiddler wrote of a New York incident: "Wotziz anent [What's this about] Orson Welles being requested to leave the Algonquin Hotel in New York recently because of alleged 'rudeness' to the hired help?"

Chasen's, a Hollywood restaurant, recorded a couple of volatile incidents in the 1940s. Welles became enraged and overturned a serving cart when he was given some bad financial news by Albert Schneider. Welles hurled flaming sternos at Schneider and John Houseman, barely missing them and setting the drapes on fire. In the same restaurant, Welles botched a reconciliation with Rita Hayworth when he flew into a rage and his estranged wife walked out.

A megalomaniac Orson Welles, it has been reported, hated to give full credit to his collaborators. It was Howard Koch, not Welles, who adapted *War of the Worlds* for the famous 1938 radio broadcast. (Koch went on to receive an Academy Award as co-scriptwriter for the classic film *Casablanca*.) In 1940, Welles tried to persuade sociologist Hadley Cantril, who was writing a book about the panic caused by the *War of the Worlds* broadcast, to drop Howard Koch's name. When Cantril would not comply, Orson went on a rampage at his rented house on Rockingham Drive. He was billed for the damages by the landlord.

In 1942, Orson's uncontrollable rages caused him trouble in South America. He was called back by RKO before filming was completed on *It's All True*. It was not just that his rages were bad for the "Good Neighbor" policy—Welles would become infuriated if dignitaries did not meet him at the airport—he was also accused of squandering precious war-time resources. RKO was furious at a $6,000 bill for a private airplane Welles used to scout locations—an expense they considered unconscionable while operating with the constraints of war-time spending limits.

The antics of Welles were reported back to RKO weekly by a man named Vargas. A crockery-breaking binge with dishes flying out the window of Welles' hotel room and narrowly missing passers-by made headlines in the Rio de Janeiro newspapers.

The death of the Brazilian hero, the fisherman Jacaré, during a re-enactment, finally shut the film down. According to a memo from Richard Wilson to Jack Moss, the Rio de Janeiro and Fortaleza newspapers criticized RKO and Orson Welles for "their failure to live up to their promises" to the family of the deceased hero Jacaré. RKO finally made a financial settlement of $3,500 (approximately $24,000 in today's dollars). Welles' Mercury Theater was thrown out of its offices at RKO. When Welles returned to Hollywood, RKO issued a terse press release that Welles had entered a private sanitarium due to "exhaustion."

A number of actresses, in addition to Yvonne de Carlo, told

of having problems with Welles. During the filming of the *Magnificent Ambersons* in 1941, Anne Baxter claims to have fought off a drunken Welles while she was driving. Using leverage, she pushed Welles out of the car, and he, along with Miss Baxter's bra, wound up in the gutter.

A few years later, the Italian actress Lea Padovini used a heavy-duty doorstop against a raging Welles. He became "hysterical with rage" when she broke off their engagement. Terrorized, the actress hit the mammoth Welles with the doorstop, knocking him off balance. She fled to her hotel, packed her clothes, and with her maid, immediately left Venice. She never saw Welles again.

Movie historians claim that the films of Welles reflect his misogynistic attitude towards women. French film critic André Bazin speculates that in the movie *The Lady From Shanghai*, director Welles turned Rita Hayworth into a "glorious martyr" and "one of the first victims" of the American cinema's budding misogyny.

The red-headed actress had been separated from Orson Welles for over a year when they began filming *The Lady From Shanghai*. She claimed there was no reconciliation in the works; Hayworth was making the film to ensure Welles had money to pay child support for their daughter, Rebecca Welles.

By fall of 1946, Welles' financial position had become tenuous. His radio program had been canceled. IRS and his creditors were demanding payment, and a pending divorce from his wife, Rita Hayworth, ended his presidential aspirations.

His grandiose stage production of *Around the World in 80 Days,* which closed in August of 1946, was a financial disaster. Mike Todd had been a backer of *Around the World*—until a fight with Welles over one climactic scene. Welles envisioned a huge oil derrick center stage spouting black oil—*real* black oil—as people danced around. Todd pointed out that the oil would ruin the expensive costumes and pose a physical danger. Welles insisted the gusher was necessary to realize his artistic vision. Todd pulled out. Money from Harry Cohn allowed the play to open as scheduled (*sans* gushing oil derrick).

But Welles, in September of 1946, was not yet an outcast in

the Hollywood community. Jesse Lasky of RKO sought Orson's opinion of a screenplay that RKO was about to produce. Warner Brothers offered Welles the starring role in the film *The Unsuspected*. Police Chief C. B. "Cowboy" Horrall requested Welles' attendance at a special screening of a "Safe Driving" film.

Welles began filming *The Lady From Shanghai* for Columbia Studios later that same month. A number of publicity stills show Welles working on the *crazy house* set with the assistance of his valet/chauffeur, George "Shorty" Chirello, a slightly hunched-back man fifty-six inches tall.

Biographers Brady and Higham claim that when Welles ignored the union craftsmen and insisted on painting the *crazy house* set himself, he sparked a strike that shut down Columbia Studios. According to records in the Union Files of the Urban Archives at California State College, Northridge, Columbia Studios was shut down on October 7th—three months before the Black Dahlia murder. Picketing members of the Conference of Studio Unions (CSU) used automobiles to block the entrances to the studio. Hundreds of the strikers were beaten by police, arrested, and jailed overnight.

This was around the time, fall of 1946, that aspiring actress "Beth" Short frequented Brittingham's, the restaurant in Columbia Square, and was rumored to be the girlfriend of someone connected to Columbia Studios.

On October 17th, Welles and the *Lady* cast left for location shots in Mexico and San Francisco. In Mexico, the cast and film crew worked under dangerous conditions. Local swimmers were hired to keep the barracuda away as Rita Hayworth swam in the infested waters. Actors were collapsing from the heat during the day and were plagued by insects at night. The assistant cameraman, Don Corey, died of a heart attack, and his body was flown back to Hollywood.

In the Lilly collection files, there were notes and messages referring to the drugs Welles used during that period: sleeping pills, Dexedrine, and proloids. Welles admitted to Barbara Leaming that he also used cocaine.

Author James Naremore states that it is with *The Lady From*

Shanghai that Welles' films became more "bizarre and circus like," moving from "consciousness to subconsciousness; from ports to crazy houses..."

A dubbed-in voice-over opens the film, Orson Welles speaking with an Irish brogue:

> *When I set out to make a fool of myself there is very little that can stop me. If I'd known where it would end, I'd probably not have let it get started. If I'd been in my right mind that is. But once I'd seen her, once I'd seen her, I was not in my right mind for quite some time.*

Various biographers offer conflicting dates for the completion of location shooting and the return of Welles to Los Angeles, placing his arrival between December 30, 1946, and January 6, 1947. In the Lilly collection, I found a copy of a telegram from Welles to Roger Hill dated December 12, 1946. The telegram indicated that Welles had just arrived back in Hollywood.

Bette Short, returning from San Diego, was dropped off at the Biltmore Hotel in downtown Los Angeles around 6:30 p.m. on January 9, 1947. After making a few telephone calls, she left the hotel and disappeared from sight. Her severed body was found in the vacant lot six days later, January 15th. On her death certificate, the date of death is written as: "1/14 or 1/15/47," implying that death occurred around midnight on the 14th of January.

For the next thirty-five days, the Black Dahlia murder dominated the headlines of the Los Angeles newspapers. *LIFE* magazine ran two features: the issues of February 3, 1947, and March 24, 1947.

In the Lilly Library I found a copy of the script titled "The Lady From Shanghai: Scenes as Shot," dated February 1947. Every page had a date when the scene was filmed—except the *crazy house* scene. The scenes-as-shot script depicted problems in the filming schedule at the studio around the time of the Black Dahlia murder. The film was shut down: Tuesday, January 14, Thursday, January 16, and from Saturday, January 18 to

Tuesday, January 21. There was an attempt to shoot scenes on Wednesday, January 22. Filming was officially suspended the following day, January 23, for four weeks.

The next day, January 24, 1947, Welles applied for a passport—the same day the killer of the Black Dahlia called the editor of the *Los Angeles Examiner* promising a package in the mail.

Filming on *The Lady From Shanghai* resumed February 17th for ten days of retakes. More retakes, mostly close-ups, were made two days in March.

Viola Lawrence, the top film editor at Columbia Studios, edited the film under the direction of Harry Cohn, the head of the studios. The original script called for a corpse (which is later revealed to be a wax dummy), to fall on Welles in the crazy house scene. A memo in the Lilly Collection titled MR. COHN'S CHANGES outlines his editing instructions for a number of reels. Cohn specifies drastic cuts for "Reel 10, Crazyhouse"—"Go from slide to mirrors, cutting out closeups of girl with mask, also following shots." A set that had cost $60,000 (more than half a million dollars in today's economy), was virtually eliminated from the film.

While Viola Lawrence edited the film, Welles tried to drum up work in Europe. His next project was *Macbeth,* the Shakespearean masterpiece that explores the psychology of murder and guilt. In a telegram to European film director and producer Sir Alexander Korda, Welles suggested filming *Macbeth* in Scotland. When Korda did not respond, Welles went ahead with a stage adaptation of *Macbeth* in Salt Lake City (April 1947), then began shooting *Macbeth* as a low-budget quickie for Republic Pictures. (Coincidentally, Jeanette Nolan, who played the role of Lady Macbeth in the film, was cast as the mother of the Black Dahlia killer in the January 12, 1988, TV episode of *Hunter.*)

In the fall of 1947, William Wyler asked Welles to join the Committee for the First Amendment. The committee planned to send a contingent to Washington in support of the Hollywood writers and actors who were being called to testify before the House Un-American Activities Committee (HUAC). An "anxious-to-leave" Welles declined, saying he was leaving the area because he had pressing commitments in Europe. "In reality," pointed out author Otto Friedrich, "Welles had only one commitment—in Hollywood with Republic Pictures."

The Ronald Colman film, *A Double Life,* was about to be released. In the movie, Colman portrays an actor who becomes so immersed in his role of Othello that he cannot separate fantasy from reality and strangles a woman. In the opening scene the camera follows Colman as he leaves the theater and stops to talk to various theater people. On the sidewalk he exchanges brief comments with two actresses. The actress on the left is an uncanny double for Bette Short, except the hair color, which is blonde. One major ad for the forthcoming film announced: "Behind the cloak of his greatness, he nurtured a hidden madness, which, when fanned by the flames of genius turned his greatest triumph into his greatest sin!" Another large ad read: "Behind the hypnotic charm of his smile... a surging torment drove him to *live* the strange desire of his greatest stage role!" A third newspaper ad announced: "His greatness turned to madness and drove him to actually live the evil of his most terrifying portrayal."

Welles left Hollywood in such a hurry that he forgot his false noses, and they were airmailed to him. Welles, who hated his small upturned nose, wore a more aquiline nose when acting and being photographed.

The hounding of the Internal Revenue Service and creditors has often been given as the reason Welles left the country. But correspondence in the Lilly collection indicates settlements were being worked out—payment to IRS of $10,191.29, an amount substantially lower than what Welles owed, with all penalties dropped, and payment to creditors of sixty-cents on the dollar.

When a Korda film agreement did not materialize, Darryl Zanuck helped facilitate Orson's departure. A cablegram to Welles states that Edward Small came up with an idea that would hasten Welles' departure from Republic Pictures. Zanuck had arranged through Small for Gregory Ratoff to give Welles the starring role in the film *Black Magic* to be filmed on location in Italy.

Nancy Guild said Welles was volatile during the shooting of *Black Magic,* and that she became frightened of him. "He was excessively fretful and edgy during the entire period." Welles became immersed in his starring role as Cagliostro, the eighteenth-century magician and charlatan. He remained in character, both off and on screen, speaking as if he actually was from the eighteenth-century. Welles insisted on authenticity during the filming. For a burying-alive scene, he demanded that Nancy Guild lie in the grave as dirt was shoveled on top of her, not a dummy as called for in the script.

There were moments of lucidity interspersed with Welles' manic episodes. A "contrite" Welles "on his best behavior" responded to Carol Reed's ultimatum to appear for filming by October 17, 1948, or lose his role as Harry Lime in *The Third Man.*

Welles made a brief visit to New York in the early 1950s, and in an interview, a seemingly paranoid Welles made vague accusations of Hearst trying to frame him on some unspecified criminal charges.

In preparation for a meeting with a Welles historian, I wrote a ten-page synopsis, *The Strange Coincidences in the Life and Work of Orson Welles and the Black Dahlia Murder.* The historian read the synopsis and studied the photos of the *crazy house.* He admitted that he didn't know what to say. "I'm at a loss for words," he said. "Orson Welles?"

"But what *if?*" I asked.

After a few moments of silence, the historian spoke. "Speaking hypothetically, it would have been disastrous for Hollywood. Harry Cohn would have done something. Pulled strings. Covered it up. Maybe met with some other studio head he trusted to figure out what should be done. Can you imagine what the discussions would have been? Get Welles out of here. The press agents would earn big money on this one. With Welles married to Rita Hayworth, Columbia's biggest moneymaker.... And the crime—so heinous."

"William Randolph Hearst hated Orson Welles," I said. "He would have liked to get something on Welles."

The historian said he could envision a frantic scenario:

Hearst locked into a behind-the-scenes fight with Harry Cohn, the two Titans battling it out, pulling all the strings they could muster. "Elizabeth Short would have been a big problem if she was connected to the studios. Another Fatty Arbuckle Scandal, only worse.... Welles going over the deep end, bringing Rita Hayworth and Columbia Studios down with him. Who knows what the ripple effect would have been?

"Once Welles left the country, he'd be out of reach. He'd be someone else's problem, not Hollywood's.... What happened to Welles? That's always been a big question.

"Comparing the stills to the murder photos, it would be safe to say that Welles at least was *influenced* by the killer's handiwork... Maybe what you have is a mirror image, the reflection of two souls... mirror images, one creative, one destructive... both tapping into the same current that runs deep in the American psyche. It gives one something to ponder: Welles venting his anger on a movie set, the killer venting his anger at a murder scene."

"But what if the creative and destructive elements existed in the *same* person?" I asked. "There are so may points of convergence between the *crazy house* set and the Black Dahlia murder. They seem to stem from the same fantasies."

The historian proposed another scenario: a guilt-ridden and paranoid Welles, strung out on drugs and alcohol *afraid* he might have committed the murder. "Welles, overworking, drinking, the amphetamines. He could have had a blackout and *thought* he did it. Paranoia, that's why he left this country. Hard to believe that Welles would cross the line."

Orson Welles ended his expatriate status with the 1956 New York stage production of *King Lear*. He then moved to the Riviera Hotel in Las Vegas, where he performed some magic shows, quipping that he had asked his wife to let him cut her in half, but she demurred.

Welles returned to Hollywood a few months later to direct *Touch of Evil* and became embroiled in yet another Hollywood controversy—trying to claim sole credit for the script. Welles, according to Frank Brady, "going off on tangents," was barred from the final editing of the film.

In 1970, Welles received an honorary Oscar. "Welles could not bring himself to go," John Huston told Robert Guenette. "So I picked it up for him and gave a little speech saying Welles was out of the country. Then I went back to his hotel room. He seemed very sad. Honored by people who refused to work with him. I could see tears in his eyes and he left the room."

When the American Film Institute gave Orson Welles a Lifetime Achievement Award in 1975, Ingrid Bergman jokingly commented about Welles' notorious European escapades, saying, "Europe ran out of countries."

Four years later, Orson Welles delivered the eulogy at the funeral services for Darryl F. Zanuck. Welles began in the usual way by recounting Zanuck's many achievements. Then, praising Zanuck as a true friend, Welles commented:

> *If I did something really outrageous, that if I committed some abominable crime, which I believe is in most of us to do under the right circumstances, that if I were guilty of something unspeakable, and if all the police in the world were after me, there was one man, and only one man I could come to, and that was Darryl. He would not have made me a speech about the good of the industry, the good of the studio. He would not have been mealy-mouthed or put me aside. He would have hid me under the bed. Very simply he was a friend.* [Italics added.]

The Los Angeles detectives say the Black Dahlia murder will never be solved. Too many years have gone by—key people are long since dead, and there wasn't much hard evidence in the first place. Detective Brian Carr, who now has the files, stated the original detectives had a couple of good suspects but were never able to build a case. When Tony Valdez asked Detective Carr if the police could have been close with one of the suspects, the detective would only say, "Perhaps."

Kris Mohandie, the police department's psychologist, like Dr. Keppel, seems to believe that the answer to the question who murdered the Black Dahlia lies not in the life style of the victim, but in the psychology of the killer. Mohandie ventured the opinion that the killer of the Black Dahlia was someone who needed power and control. "Someone," Mohandie said, "who thought he was superior in intellect and who thought his values were superior to that of the rest of the world. He was arrogant. The killer fantasized about this a long time before circumstances presented a victim and an opportunity to fulfill his fantasy."

* * *

I am a different person today than the woman who started her search for answers twelve years ago. In some ways, I feel as if I've carried on a tradition—sorting through fabrics and colors to piece together a special mourning quilt. Some of the colors in my mourning quilt are painful and dark, others reflect light. But I have tried to faithfully construct a work, that when finished, would conjur up the image and the life of the person for whom I have mourned. This book, then, is my finished mourning quilt. And the act of piecing the bits and pieces of information together has caused a change deep inside of me. But when people ask me to describe the change, I am at a loss for words. For now, I can only say that I am no longer afraid of the dark.

Memorial to Elizabeth Short placed by the Medford Historical Society under the auspices of Kyle J. Wood. *Photo: Author's collection.* The plaque reads:

"THE BLACK DAHLIA"

This plaque has been placed in memory of Elizabeth Short, the victim of one of the nation's most infamous and unsolved crimes.

"Betty" was born on July 29, 1924 and lived at 115 Salem Street, the site now occupied by the interstate #93 rotary. She attended Medford High School until June of 1940 and then moved to Hollywood to pursue an acting career. Her strikingly attractive features, jet black hair and penchant for dark attire earned her the name of "The Black Dahlia."

On January 15, 1947 her severed and mutilated body was discovered in a vacant Los Angeles lot. Newspapers, books, magazines, motion pictures, and television have chronicled her story. The slaying of Medford's "Black Dahlia" continues to remain a mystery.

Afterword

A former prosecutor read my manuscript. He said to me, "Sure, there is such a thing as a coincidence. But just how many coincidences do you need before it becomes something else? Much of the information you've uncovered about Orson Welles has only recently surfaced and was not available to the original detectives. They had no way of seeing the coincidences that were piling up. And when the coincidences begin to pile up, you have what we call *credible suspicion*. Once you have credible suspicion, you have a *viable* suspect. That usually means it's time to take a *closer* look and launch an offical investigation of the person.

APPENDIX A
The Crazy House Set From the Columbia Studios Film
The Lady From Shanghai

Striking studio workers shut down Columbia Studios, October 7, 1946. According to his biographers, Orson Welles precipitated the strike by working on the crazy house set for his film *The Lady From Shanghai*. Photo: *Courtesy of Department of Special Collections, Charles E. Young Research Library, UCLA*.

Note: Columbia Studios would not give permission to reproduce the publicity stills of the crazy house set. The following artist sketches have been substituted with a notation of where the original photographs may be viewed.

Sketch by Ethan Fitch of publicity still for *The Lady From Shanghai*. Photograph may be found in the Margaret Herrick Library of the Academy Foundation in Hollywood, California and the Film/Stills Archives of the Museum of Modern Art in New York City.

Original photo caption issued by Columbia Studios reads: "ORSON TAKES ON ANOTHER JOB... Orson Welles, man of many talents, was producer, writer, director and co-star with Rita Hayworth in Columbia Pictures' thrilling love mystery, 'The Lady From Shanghai'. But apparently he didn't feel his time was fully occupied, so he took brush in hand, and while George 'Shorty' Chirello held a paint pot, Orson personally decorated much of the scenery for the amusement park scenes himself. 'Shorty' Welles' valet, chauffeur and general factotum, also has a small role in The Lady From Shanghai."

Author's rendering of entrance to the crazy house, a publicity still for *The Lady From Shanghai*. In the film, the entryway was severely cropped by Viola Lawrence, lessening the impact of the set. Lawrence edited the film under the direct orders of Harry Cohn, head of Columbia Studios. Photograph may be found in the Film/Stills Archives of the Museum of Modern Art in New York City.

Author's rendering of publicity still for *The Lady From Shanghai*. Photograph may be found in the Margaret Herrick Library of the Academy Foundation in Hollywood, California and the Film/Stills Archives of the Museum of Modern Art in New York City. The photo is reproduced in the André Bazin book, *Orson Welles, A Critical View*.

Original caption issued by Columbia Studios reads: "WHITE FOR EVENING ... Rita Hayworth, co-starring with Orson Welles in Columbia's 'The Lady From Shanghai' wears this lovely marquisette creation by designer Jean Louis against the background of an amusement park 'fun house.' It is there that one of the most dramatic sequences of the picture takes place."

Sketch by Ethan Fitch of publicity still for *The Lady From Shanghai*. Photograph may be found in the Margaret Herrick Library of the Academy Foundation in Hollywood, California.

Original caption issued by Columbia Studios reads: "GROTESQUE!!.. Orson Welles supervises as Bob Schiffer, makeup expert, applies a grotesque makeup to a skull for an exciting scene in Columbia Pictures', 'The Lady From Shanghai', a story of love and crime which co-stars Rita Hayworth and Orson Welles." Note: Mutilations to mannequin's face are in exact location as mutilations to Elizabeth Short's face.

Rendering by Ethan Fitch from publicity still for *The Lady From Shanghai*. The photo is reproduced in the André Bazin book, *Orson Welles, A Critical View*.

Welles, who designed the set, helped with the painting and construction; scenes wound up on the cutting room floor. Note: The arrow-like object protruding from the leg of the bisected skeleton in background. The wound approximates the location of the triangle mutilation to the body of Bette Short. The angle of the left leg is at the same angle as the victim's left leg. (See following page.)

Photo of crime scene at 39th Street and South Norton Avenue. Note that the angle of the left leg is the same as the angle of the left leg of the bisected skeleton in the fun house set of *The Lady From Shanghai*. (See preceding page.) *Photo: Courtesy of Will Fowler.*

APPENDIX B
Photo Album

View of Medford Square c. 1940. Street to the left with trolley tracks is Salem Street; street to the right is Riverside Avenue. Author's home at 101 Salem Street and the adjacent Shorts' apartment building at 115 Salem Street are towards the top of the photo, just below the horizon. *Photo: Courtesy of Medford Historical Society.*

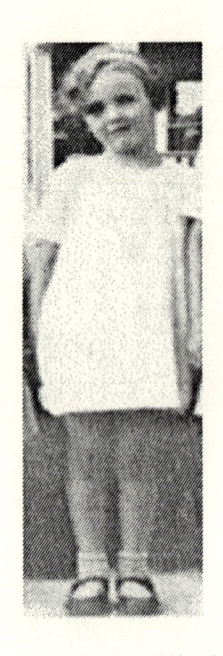

Left: Elizabeth 'Bette' Short c.1931. *Right:* Bette in Medford, Massachusetts c. 1936. *Photos: Author's Collection.*

Two unidentified drum majorettes and the author in 1939 at age five, a month before the neighborhood boy took her into the field. *Photo: Author's Collection.*

The author with her cousin, Ron Hernon c. 1942. *Photo: Author's Collection.*

Ron Hernon in his back yard. The Short family lived on the third floor of the three-decker in the background. Braided rugs can be seen on the balcony of the Short's apartment. *Photo: Author's Collection.*

Elizabeth "Bette" Short in 1945. Photo: *Courtesy of the Medford Historical Society.*

Elizabeth "Bette" Short with unidentified man—taken in a five-and-dime photo machine c. 1945-1946. *Photo: Courtesy of the Medford Historical Society.*

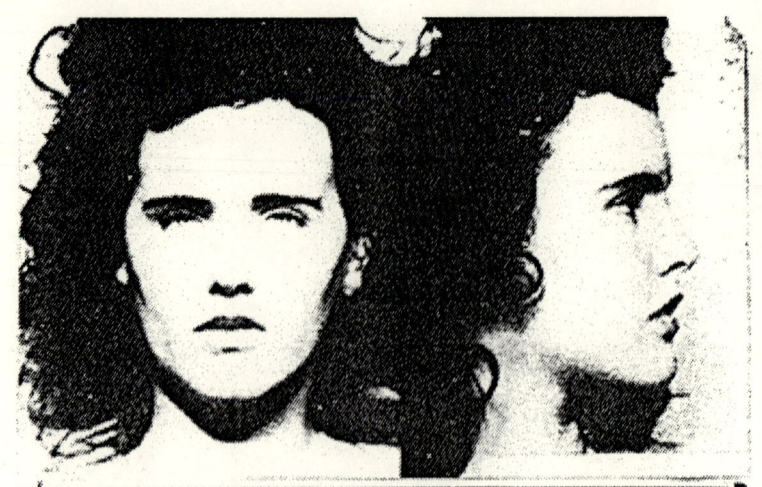

WA -142 - 1/15/47 - CREDIT: I.N.P. SOUNDPHOTO - WASHINGTON, D.C..INTER-
NATIONAL NEWS SOUNDPHOTOS OF FINGERPRINTS OF THE TEEN-AGED GIRL WHOSE
BODY WAS FOUND HACKED IN TWO IN A VACANT LOS ANGELES, CALIF., WERE RUSHED
TO THE FBI IDENTIFICATION SECTION HERE TODAY AND IDENTITY OF THE MURDERED
GIRL WAS ESTABLISHED IN RECORD TIME. COMPARISION OF THE I.N.P. SOUNDPHOTO
WITH FBI FINGERPRINT FILES PROVED THE GIRL TO BE ELIZABETH SHORT OF SANTA
BARBARA, CALIF. PHOTO ABOVE IS FROM THE FBI IDENTIFICATION FILES.

Camp Cooke photo ID from the FBI files in Washington, DC. Photo with accompanying text was sent over the wire.

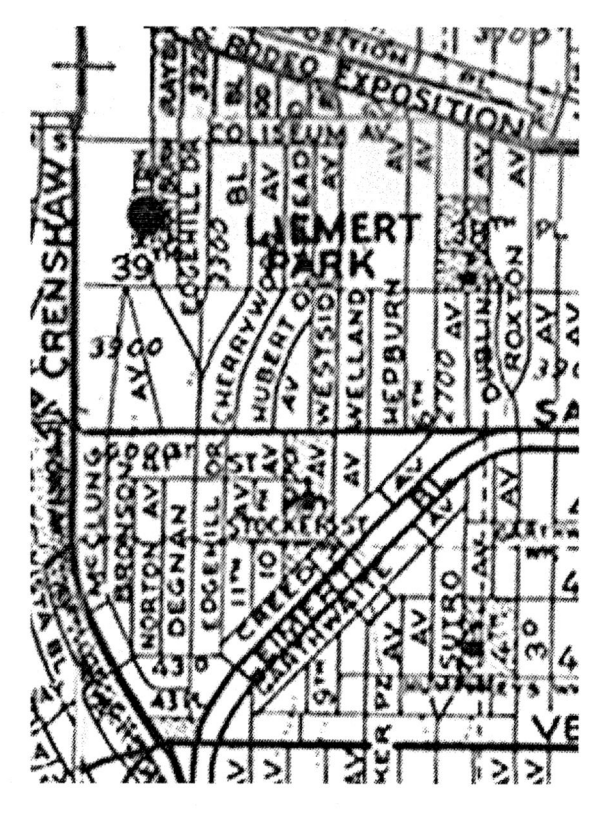

1945 Los Angeles Street Map. Dark circle indicates where the body of Elizabeth Short was placed (South Norton Avenue between 38th Street and 39th Street). In September of 1939 and 1941, the Ringling Bros. and Barnum & Bailey Circus used the open tract of land between South Norton Avenue, Crenshaw Boulevard, and Exposition Boulevard to set up their tents for "The Greatest Show on Earth." *The New Renié Commercial Atlas, Los Angeles City and County.*

Agness Underwood, top Hearst crime reporter and first woman city editor of a major newspaper in the country, c.1959. *Photo: Courtesy of Herald Examiner Collection/Los Angeles Public Library.*

Aggie Underwood, editor of the *Los Angeles Herald Express,* leads a conga line of city editors at their December 1955 meeting in the Ambassador Hotel. Jack Massard, President of the Press Club, stands directly behind Aggie with his hand on her shoulder. Following close behind are: (right to left) Frank Piazzi, *San Francisco Examiner,* Jack McDowell, *San Francisco Call Bulletin,* Jim Richardson (who took the telephone call from the Black Dahlia killer), *Los Angeles Examiner,* Bud Lewis, *Los Angeles Times,* Abe Melinkoff, *San Francisco Chronicle,* Pete Lee, *San Francisco News,* Paul Speegle, *President of the Fresno Press Club,* and Jim Bassett, *Mirror-News. Photo: Courtesy of Los Angeles Examiner Hearst Newspaper Collection, Department of Special Collections, University of Southern California Library.*

Harriett Manley reconciles with her husband, Robert Manley, at the Hollenbeck Police Station. *Photo: Courtesy of Herald Examiner Collection/Los Angeles Public Library.*

Harriett Manley, William Morris Manley (Robert Manley's father), Mrs. Phoebe Short and her daughter Virginia West wait in the witness room as Robert Manley testifies at the inquest. *Photo: Courtesy of Department of Special Collections, Charles E. Young Research Library, UCLA.*

Envelope containing Bette Short's birth certificate and other personal items mailed by killer to the newspapers. The word, "Dahlia's" was cut from the red headline of the January 21, 1947 edition of the *Los Angeles Herald Express*. Most of the other letters and words were cut from the movie section of the January 23rd edition. *Photo: Courtesy of Department of Special Collections, Charles E. Young Research Library, UCLA.*

A card included in the packet mailed by the killer. *Photo: Courtesy of Herald Examiner Collection/Los Angeles Public Library.*

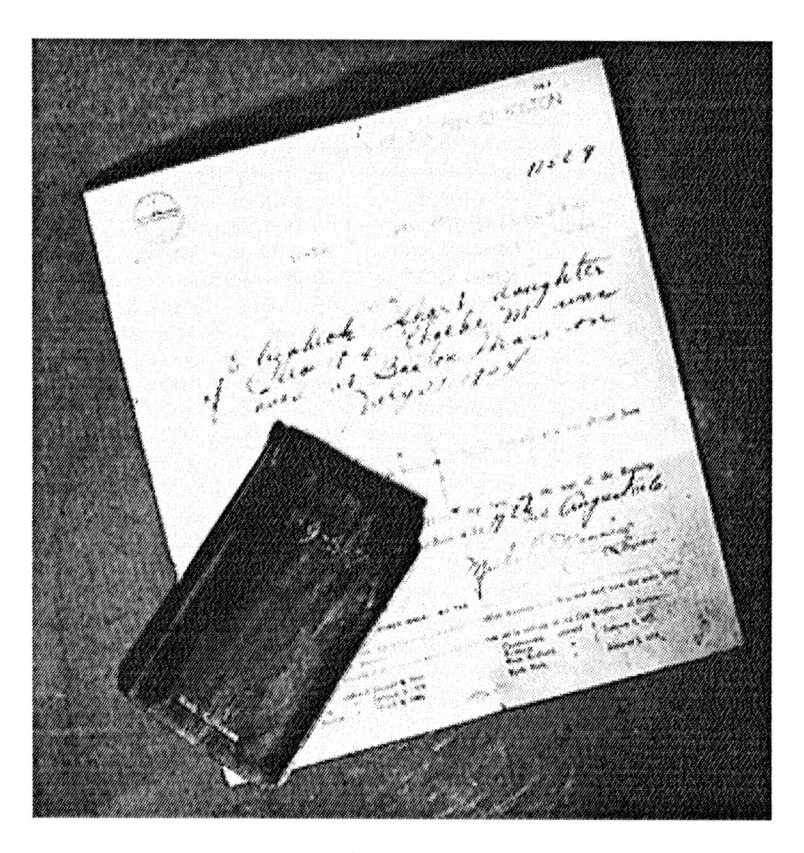

Elizabeth "Bette" Short's birth certificate and Mark Hansen's worn address book with the name Mark M. Hansen stamped in gold letters on the dark brown cover. The items were included in packet mailed by killer. *Photo: Courtesy of Department of Special Collections, Charles E. Young Research Library, UCLA.*

Mark Hansen, part owner of the Florentine Gardens nightclub with Frank Bruni. Hansen also owned Roseland and other dance halls. He rented rooms to young, aspiring actresses. Bette Short stayed at his house on San Carlos for a few months in 1946. *Photo: Courtesy of Herald Examiner Collection/Los Angeles Public Library.*

The Florentine Gardens, one of Hollywood's popular night spots in the 1930s and 1940s; owned by Mark Hansen and Frank Bruni; frequented by the likes of Henry Fonda, Orson Welles, and the soon-to-be-discovered Norma Jean. *Photo: Courtesy of Security Pacific National Bank Collection/Los Angeles Public Library.*

Tom Breneman's, a popular restaurant frequented by Bette Short. A popular radio show, *The Hollywood Breakfast Club*, was broadcast live from the restaurant. *Photo: Courtesy of Security Pacific National Bank Collection/Los Angeles Public Library.*

Photograph of Det. Sgt. John St. John, Badge Number One. Each stripe on the arm of his uniform indicates five years of service with the Los Angeles Police Department. St. John was in charge of the Black Dahlia case for over ten years. *Photo: Courtesy of Richard Pleuger.*

Left: photo of Bette Short, noted for her contrasting jet-black hair and white flawless complexion; in 1946 she frequented the same restaurant as Orson Welles—Brittingham's on Sunset at Gower, during the period *The Lady From Shanghai* was being filmed. *Photo: Author's collection. Right:* photo of Betty Chancellor, the Irish actress whom Orson Welles acted opposite when he made his debut and who was his first infatuation. Welles described Chancellor to Barbara Leaming as: "...one of those absolutely black-haired girls, with skin as white as Carrara marble, you know, and eyelashes that you could trip on..." *1931 Photo: Courtesy of Mander & Mitchenson Theatre Collection, Beckenham, Kent, United Kingdom.*

Sketch by Ethan Fitch from photograph of Orson Welles performing magic act of sawing woman in half. (Welles is the central figure behind the box.) Welles gave nightly performances on Cahuenga Boulevard for World War II serviceman in 1943 as part of the *Mercury Wonder Show*. The original photo is in the Orson Welles Collection at the Lilly Library, Indiana University, Bloomington, Indiana.

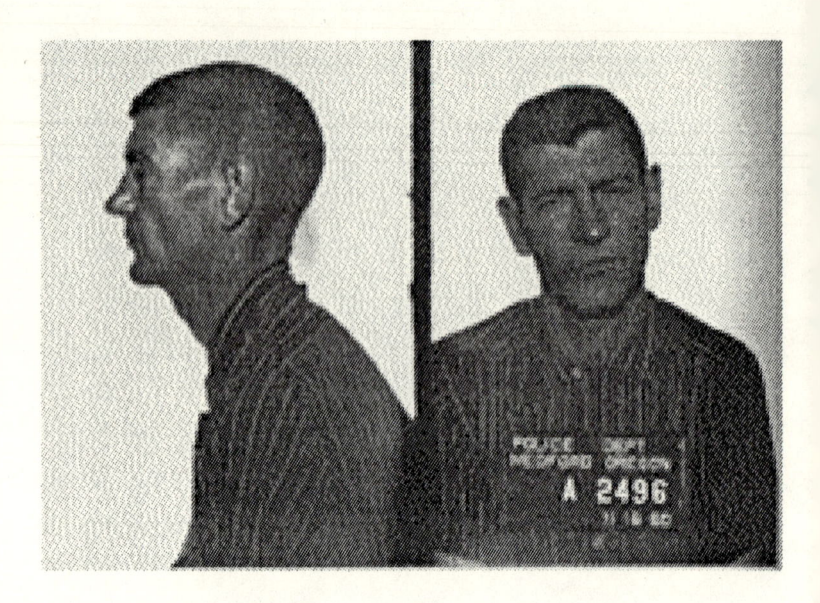

Jack Anderson Wilson aka Arnold Smith, who claimed "his friend" killed the Black Dahlia. *Photo: Courtesy of City of Medford Police Department (Oregon).*

Threatening pasted-up letter sent to Ron Kenner when he was collaborating with John Gilmore on a Black Dahlia manuscript. *Photo: Courtesy of Ron Kenner.*

APPENDIX C
TRANSCRIPT OF INQUEST
HELD ON THE BODY OF ELIZABETH SHORT
AT THE HALL OF JUSTICE. LOS ANGELES,
CALIFORNIA
JANUARY 22, 1947
At 10:30 A.M.

PHOEBE MAE SHORT, being duly sworn, testified as follows:
Q BY THE CORONER: Please state your name.
A Phoebe Mae Short.
Q Where do you reside?
A 115 Salem Street, Medford, Massachusetts.
Q Have you viewed the body of a deceased person in the mortuary here?
A I have.
Q Was that someone you knew in life?
A It was.
Q What was her name?
A Elizabeth Short.
Q Did she have a middle name?
A No middle name.
Q Was she related to you?
A My daughter.
Q Do you know her address?
A The address was in San Diego at the time.
Q That is the last address you had for her?
A That's right.
Q Do you recall what that was?
A 2750 Camino Padera Drive, Pacific Beach.
Q Did she have an occupation as far as you knew?
A As far as I know she was a waitress.
Q Where was she born?
A Hyde Park, Massachusetts.
Q What was her age?
A Twenty-two.
Q At the time of her death was she single, married,

    widowed , or divorced?
A Single.
Q And has never been married as far as you know?
A As far as I know she was not.
Q What is your information as to the date of her death?
A I was notified January 15.
Q That she died January 15?
A Yes.
Q Do you know where she died?
A She was murdered here in Los Angeles.
Q Is it your information that her body was found on a street out here in some part of Los Angeles?
A That's right.
Q Were you here at the time?
A No, I was not.
Q You were in Massachusetts?
A That's right
Q How long since you last had seen your daughter?
A In April, 1946.
Q Where did you see her then?
A At my own home in Massachusetts.
Q Did she remain with you for some time then, was she living there or just on a visit?
A She had come home from Florida in February and left in April the same year.
Q While she was at home did she tell you of any trouble or anyone that she feared or had any trouble with anyone or any enemies?
A No, she did not.
Q Or tell you of any love affairs?
A Yes, she was in love with Gordon Fickling at that time.
Q Have you since corresponded with her?
A I have.
Q And what address did you use for correspondence?
A Well, that one in Hollywood and this last one in San Diego.
Q Do you have the address in Hollywood?
A It is in my bag. That was the Chancelor Apartment in

Hollywood.

Q Did you have a later address in San Diego?

A The one that I mentioned.

Q Has she corresponded or been in communication with any of your other relatives?

A No, she just regularly wrote me once a week.

Q And those were the last addresses you had for her?

A That's right.

Q Are you giving to the officers every assistance you can towards determining who the perpetrator of this crime was?

A I am.

JESSE W HASKINS, being first duly sworn, testified as follows:

Q BY THE CORONER; Please state your name.

A Jesse W. Haskins.

Q What is your occupation?

A Detective Lieutenant, Police Department, Los Angeles attached to University Detective Bureau.

Q Mr. Haskins, were you called to the scene of the finding of the body of the deceased person, Elizabeth Short, over whom we are holding the inquest?

A I was.

Q When did you receive that call?

A Approximately 11:05 the morning of the 15th of January.

Q And what time did you arrive at the scene?

A At 11:18.

Q And where did you go in response to the call?

A Went on Norton Street between Coliseum and 39 Street.

Q Where did you find the body of the victim in this case?

A Found the body on the west side of Norton. From Coliseum to 39 on the property line is 1200 feet, it's all vacant property. There is a fire plug in the center of that which would be 600 feet from Coliseum or 600 feet from 39 the other way. The body was 54 feet north of the fire plug toward Coliseum.

Q   What is in that block, any houses or buildings?
A   The nearest houses face on Claybourne and there is a back wall that comes up to the property line of Norton.
Q   On the east side of Norton?
A   Yes, and they are clear across the property lines of the houses that face east on Norton.
Q   How wide is Norton Street?
A   Sixty feet wide, and 120 feet east of the property line to the walls of the houses that face on Claybourne.
Q   The body was found on the west side of Norton?
A   Yes, and from that point it is 585 feet to Crenshaw, all vacant property.
Q   Is that grown up with weeds?
A   Weeds and grass and rose clippings and such.
Q   Tell the Jury more definitely where you found the body, please?
A   The location of the body when we arrived there was as I said, 54 feet north of this fire plug which was directly in the center of the 1200 foot space. The sidewalk is in on this street and the curbs in and also the indentations for the driveway are in and paved. The driveway measures five foot from the curb in the sidewalk. The sidewalk is five foot wide. The body was lying with the head towards the north, the feet towards the south, the left leg was five inches west of the sidewalk. The legs were spread out and the body was severed in two. The body was lying face up and the severed part was jogged over about 10 inches, the upper half of the body from the lower half.
Q   Were there weeds at this location or grass?
A   Just grass at this location.
Q   High enough to hide the body?
A   The body would not be hidden at all from the street on Norton. It could have been hidden from the other direction, Crenshaw, because there are some tall weeds between there and where the body was found.
Q   Is this a sidewalk or is it a much traveled location?
A   It is possible there is a great deal of travel on the street

for cutting across to the two streets otherwise there is no reason for anybody to walk across there.

Q Did the body appear to have been dead for some time?

A From my observation it looked fresh.

Q Would you say death had occurred after midnight of the 15th or prior to midnight or would you be able to form any opinion?

A My opinion would be that it would be since midnight of the 15th.

Q Did you find any blood or tracks or anything of that nature at the scene?

A [Dropped line of words]... body was found to the street there was a tire track right up against the curbing and there was what appeared to be a possible bloody heel mark in this tire mark; and on the curbing which is very low there was one spot of blood; and there was an empty paper cement sack lying in the driveway and it also had a spot of blood on it.

Q Any other container or sack or cloth that the body might have been transported in?

A There was not.

Q From your examination of the body would you be able to form any opinion as to whether the crime had been committed at this scene or brought there from some other location?

A It had been brought there from some other location.

Q Was there any clot of blood on the body or did it appear to have been washed?

A The body was clean and appeared to have been washed.

Q Do you know who reported the finding of the body?

A All I know is how our Communication Division was notified of it and we were unable to locate the party. It was a woman's voice which called the Communication Division at approximately 10 minutes before we received the call from them; and their statement at this time was that there was a nude body on the west side of Norton about half way from Coliseum to 39th and the flies were bothering it and it needed attention and the

call necessarily was put over the air as a 390 down.
Q Is there anything else you can tell the Jury with regard to the facts surrounding the finding of the body or what you found at the location?
A No, I don't recall of anything else that would help the Jury.
Q Do you have the name of any witnesses who have been [line dropped] ...cently
A I do not. Only from investigation of other officers.
Q Did you have the name of one, Robert Manley?
A I have.
Q Is he here this morning?
A He is.
Q I'll call him later that's all then, thank you.

ROBERT MANLEY, being first duly sworn, testified as follows:
Q BY THE CORONER; Please state your name.
A Robert Manley.
Q Where do you live?
A 8010 Mountain View.
Q Your occupation?
A Salesman.
Q That is Mountain View in South Gate?
A That's right, sir.
Q Were you acquainted with the deceased in this case, Elizabeth Short?
A Yes, sir.
Q How long had you known her; approximately how long?
A Approximately, a month.
Q When did you see her, meet her the last time.
A I saw Miss Short January 9th, which was the last time.
Q Where was that?
A I left Miss Short at the Biltmore Hotel at 6:30 P.M., January 9, 1947.
Q Where had you picked her up from?
A I had driven her to Los Angeles from San Diego.
Q Had you met her in San Diego and brought her to Los

Angeles?
A Yes, sir.
Q Had she asked you to bring her to Los Angeles?
A Yes.
Q Did she say why she wanted to come to Los Angeles?
A She said she didn't like San Diego.
Q Did she say what she was going to do when she got here or where she was going?
A She said she was going to meet her sister in Los Angeles and was going to spend a couple of days up in Berkeley with her sister and then go to Boston which was her home.
Q And you left her at the Biltmore Hotel?
A That's correct.
Q Did she give you any address where she was expected to stay here?
A No, sir.
Q And that was the last time you saw her?
A That was the last time.
Q And that was January 9th?
A Yes, sir.
Q At what time?
A 6:30.
Q And you haven't seen or heard from her since?
A No, sir.
Q Is there anything else you can tell the Jury for the benefit of the officers that might aid in determining the perpetrator of this crime?
A No, sir.
Q You have given them every assistance you can, have you?
A Yes, sir.

H. L. HANSEN, being first duly sworn, testified as follows:
Q BY THE CORONER; Please state your name.
A H. L. Hansen.
Q And your occupation?
A Police Officer, City of Los Angeles, attached to the

Homicide Division.
Q Mr. Hansen, have you made a follow-up investigation of the deceased, Elizabeth Short?
A Yes, we have.
Q Have you been able to determine as to any possible identification of the death of the person who may have committed this crime?
A As to now, we have no definite information as to who perpetrated it.
Q And you are following all clues you receive?
A Every effort to locate the criminal is being made.
Q Is there anything else that you can say that might assist the Jury in arriving at a verdict?
A I think it has been pretty well covered.

FREDERICK D. NEWBARR, being first duly sworn, testified as follows:
Q BY THE CORONER; Please state your name.
A Frederick D. Newbarr.
Q What is your occupation?
A Physician and Surgeon.
Q And you are the autopsy surgeon for the coroner?
A Yes, sir, chief autopsy surgeon, Los Angeles County.
Q Did you perform an autopsy on the body of Elizabeth Short over whom we are holding the present inquest?
A Yes, sir.
Q When did you perform the autopsy?
A January 16, 1947 at 10:30 A.M.
Q From your examination of the body would you be able to form any opinion as to the date of the death as to whether it was on the 15th or prior to the 15th?
A It was my opinion that the appearance of the body was such that the death occurred not more than 24 hours previous to the 15th, probably less.
Q So that the death would have occurred either on the 14th or 15th?
A Yes, sir.
Q Will you please state to the Jury either briefly or in full

as you like, the result of your autopsy findings, please?

A The immediate cause of the death was hemorrhage and shock due to concussion of the brain and lacerations of the face. The body is that of a female about 15 to 20 years of age, measuring 5'5" in height and weighing 115 pounds. There are multiple lacerations in the midforehead, in the right forehead, and at the top of the head in the midline. There are multiple tiny abrasions, linear in shape on the right face and forehead. There are two small lacerations, 1/4" each in length, on each side of the nose near the bridge. There is a deep laceration in the face 3" long which extends laterally from the right corner of the mouth. The surrounding tissues are ecchymotic and bluish purple in color. There is a deep laceration 2&1/2" long extending laterally from the left corner of the mouth. The surrounding tissues are bluish purple in color. There are five linear lacerations in the right upper lip which extend into the soft tissues for a distance of 1/8". The teeth are in a state of advanced decay. The two upper central incisors are loose and one lower incisor is loose. The rest of the teeth [words illegible]... areas of subarachoid hemorrhage on the right side and small hemorrhagic areas in the corpus callosum. No fracture of the skull is visible. There is a depressed ridge on both sides and in the anterior portion of the neck. It is light brown in color. There is an abrasion irregular in outline in the skin of the neck in the anterior midline. There are two linear abrasions in the left anterior neck. It is light brown in color. There are two depressed ridges in the posterior neck, pale brown in color. The lower ridge has an abrasion in the skin at each extremity. The pharynx&larnyx are intact. There is no evidence of trauma to the hyoid bone, thyroid or cricoid cartilages or tracheal rings. There is a small area of ecchymosis in the soft tissues of the right neck at the level of the upper tracheal rings. There is no obstruction in the laryngotracheal passage. There is an irregular laceration with superficial loss in the skin of the right breast. The tissue loss is more or less square in outline and measures 3 & 1/4" transversely and 2 & 1/2" longitudinally; Extending toward the midline from this irregular laceration are several superficial lacerations in the skin. There is an elliptical opening in the skin located 3/4" to the left of the left nipple. The opening measures 2 & 3/4" in a transverse direction and 1 & 1/4" in a longitudinal direction in its midportion. The margins of these wounds show no appreciable discoloration.

Q Doctor, I don't believe it will be necessary for you to read all this. It is rather long and I don't think we need to read all of it here. The essential findings with regard to cause of death have already been expressed; and that is the concussion of the brain and the lacerations of the face. The portion of your findings with regard to the chest, would you read that on the second page there, the organs of the chest, were they in a normal [two lines dropped]...

A ... left lung is pink in color and well aerated. The right lung is somewhat adherant due to fairly firm pleural adhesions. The lung is pink in color and well aerated. There is calcified thickening of the 9th rib on the right side in the scapular line. The heart shows no gross pathology.

Q Then the next paragraph with regard to the severing of the body?

A The trunk is completely severed by an incision which is almost straight through the abdomen severing the intestine at the duodenum and through the soft tissues of the abdomen passing through the intervertebral disk between the 2nd and 3rd lumbar vertebra. There is very little ecchymosis along the tract of the incision. There is a gaping laceration 4 & 1/2" which extends longitudinally from the umbilicus to the suprapubic area. On both sides of this laceration there are multiple superficial lacerations. There are multiple criss cross lacerations in the suprapubic area which extend through the skin and soft tissues. No ecchymosis is seen.

Q Was there evidence of any sexual assault? You might read the last paragraph, and I believe that covers it, on the next page.

A The stomach was filled with greenish brown granular material, mostly feces and other particles which could not be identified. All smears for spermatazoa are negative.

Q Is there anything else which would contribute to the medical cause of death?

A No, sir, I don't think so.

Q Your finding is that the real cause of death was hemorrhage and shock due to blows to the head?

A Blows on the head and face.

VERDICT OF CORONER'S JURY
STATE OF CALIFORNIA, County of Los Angeles
In the Matter of the Inquisition upon the body of
Elizabeth Short, Deceased,

Before BEN H. BROWN, Coroner.

We, the Jurors, summoned to appear before the Coroner of Los Angeles County at room 102, Hall of Justice, Los Angeles County, California, on the 22nd day of January A.D. 1947, to inquire into the cause of the death of Elizabeth Short, having been duly sworn according to law, and having made such inquisition and hearing the testimony adduced, upon our oaths, each and all do say that we find that the deceased was named Elizabeth Short, a female, single, native of Mass., aged about 22 years, and that she came to her death found on the 15th day of January, 1947 at Norton St. Between 39th and Coliseum Drive, Los Angeles, Los Angeles County, California, and that this death was caused by hemorrhage and shock due to concussion of the brain and lacerations of face; and from the testimony introduced we find said injuries to have been inflicted on the deceased by some person or persons unknown at this time to this jury and at some location unknown to this jury; and we find this to be a homicide and recommend that every effort be made to apprehend the perpetrator or perpetrators responsible therefor, all of which we duly certify by this inquisition in writing, by us signed this 22nd day of January, 1947.

Choteau W. Paul, Foreman
Paul I. Todd R. W. Rose
Robert Kessler Fred Weller
H. W. LaChat H. E. Brier
S. R. Moore F. D. Tucker

APPENDIX D
THE MAJOR SUSPECTS

Robert Manley
Prime Suspect of Detective Harry Hansen.

Suspect's age at time of murder: 24

Occupation: Traveling salesman.

Whereabouts at time of murder: At home (8010 Mountain View Street in South Gate) with wife and Mr. and Mrs. Don Holmes.

Physical and mental condition: 6' tall, 175 pounds, red hair. Assumed in good physical condition. Section 8 discharge from army (mentally unfit for the service). No criminal record.

History of violence: None recorded, no criminal record.

Stress factors at time of murder: Having difficulties adjusting to the responsibilities of marriage and newborn baby.

Link to the victim: Last known person to be with Elizabeth Short. Claimed to have left victim at the Biltmore Hotel in Los Angeles on January 9, 1947, six days before victim's body was found.

Link to the signature and MO of perpetrator: None recorded.

Link to the South Norton Avenue site: None recorded.

Behavior after the murder: Periodic confinement to mental hospitals. In the 1970s threatened individual with an ax when individual asked how suspect was connected to the murder. Suspect diagnosed as a paranoid schizophrenic in 1954.

Additional comments: In January 1947, after an intense third degree and two polygraph exams, suspect was released by police. Truth serum was administered voluntarily to suspect in August 1954 at Brentwood Hospital. A police source said the results indicated that Manley "knows nothing of the crime."

Mark Hansen
Suspect of Los Angeles Police and Various Reporters

Suspect's age at time of murder: 55

Occupation: Owner of the Florentine Gardens nightclub, Roseland dance hall, and Marcel Theater; in the 1930s owned theaters with Charles Skouras; applied for Deputy Sheriff Commission in 1943.

Whereabouts at time of murder: Los Angeles

Physical and mental condition: 5'9" tall, 175 pounds. No physical and mental conditions recorded.

History of violence: None recorded, no criminal record.

Stress factors at time of murder: Long-term separation from wife but continued with joint real estate deals; womanizer; problems with disenchanted women.

Link to the victim: Aspiring actresses often stayed in his large home located behind the Florentine Gardens. The victim was a guest in suspect's home periodically between August 1946 and October 1946.

Link to the signature and MO of perpetrator: An old, brown address book belonging to Mark Hansen was included in packet mailed by the killer.

Link to the South Norton Avenue site: Unknown.

Behavior after the murder: On July 17, 1949, suspect was shot by one of his former dancers, Lola Titus. During Titus investigation photos of victim were found in suspect's house by police. (Not revealed whether photos were of the victim alive or of the victim dead.)

Additional comments: Jean Spangler, a bit player and former Florentine Gardens dancer who closely resembled the victim, disappeared in the Fall of 1949. FBI ran checks on suspect in 1948-1949. Suspect's fingerprints did not match fingerprints on letter sent by killer. Suspect died June 1964 of natural causes.

The "Cleveland Butcher"
Suspect of Lawrence P. Scherb

Suspect's age at time of murder: Unknown.
Occupation: Unknown.
Whereabouts at time of murder: Unknown.
Physical and mental condition: Unknown.
History of violence: Serial killer operating in the Kingsbury Run area of Cleveland from 1935 through 1938; twelve victims attributed to suspect, an additional seven or eight victims are questionable.
Stress factors at time of murder: Unknown.
Link to the victim: Unknown.
Link to the signature and MO of perpetrator: Suspect sent communications to the Cleveland police. Dissection varied. Some of suspect's victims were bisected at the waist, washed, and drained of blood. All victims were killed quickly and then decapitated—an important departure from the signature of the Black Dahlia killer.
Link to the South Norton Avenue site: March of 1947, Cleveland Det. Peter M. Merylo contacted Los Angeles police and raised the possibility that the Cleveland murders might be linked to the Black Dahlia murder. Det. Merylo forwarded a copy of a 1938 letter received by Cleveland Chief of Police Matowitz. Letter was postmarked Los Angeles, California and dated December 21, 1938. Text of the letter: "Moved to California for the winter Head minus features will be buried in gully on Century Blvd between Western & Crenshaw."
Behavior after the murder: Unknown.
Additional comments: May 3, 1940, two dismembered males and one dismembered female severed at the waist, were found in the Lake Erie rail yards; heads missing. Murders probably occurred in Youngstown, Ohio around December 1939. Possible victims of the Cleveland Butcher.

Jack Anderson Wilson
Suspect of John Gilmore

Suspect's age at time of murder: 27
Occupation: Sign hanger; cook.
Whereabouts at time of murder: Assumed in Los Angeles.
Physical and mental condition: Alcoholic, walked with a limp which may have been caused by a service-related injury.
History of violence: Criminal record prior to murder indicates one arrest in 1943 for suspicion of draft dodging. Suspect served in the army from January 12, 1944 to March 15, 1945.
Stress factors at time of murder: Claimed to have been participant in the Mocambo robbery of January 6, 1947 and to be hiding out the week of the murder.
Link to the victim: Claimed to have known victim.
Link to the signature and MO of perpetrator: Claimed that his friend confessed the murder to him. Suspect gave John Gilmore a description of how the murder and bisection took place, as told by his friend. (Information is consistent with the partial autopsy report.)
Link to the South Norton Avenue site: Suspect compared site (as seen on map) to female genital area. 1945 Los Angeles map roughly parallels markings that the killer carved into victim's body after death.
Behavior after the murder: Left for San Francisco a few days after murder. Four-page rap sheet indicates over 50 arrests for drunkenness, a few begging and mooching, a couple for assault and battery, a dozen theft and burglary, and one "crime against nature" (a Tennessee arrest for having sex with another man in a park).
Additional comments: The suspect's "secret" information about the condition of the body that theoretically only the killer would know, was also known to a few of the reporters that covered the case. Suspect died in fire February 4, 1982.

Orson Welles
Suspect of Mary Pacios

Suspect's age at time of murder: 32
Occupation: Radio/film actor, director, writer, set designer, artist.
Whereabouts at time of murder: In Los Angeles filming *The Lady From Shanghai* at Columbia Studios. The film was shut down January 14th, the day of the murder.
Physical and mental condition: 6'2" tall, 195 pounds. Rejected by army because of flat feet. Known alcohol and drug abuser—Benzedrine, Dexedrine, proloids and cocaine. Brief hospitalizations at sanitariums for "nervous breakdowns."
History of violence: Violent incidents extend to childhood when he cut his nanny's dress to shreds with a scissors. While portraying Brutus in the play *Julius Caesar,* suspect stabbed the actor playing Caesar with a real knife, penetrating deeply into the chest and severing an artery. (Actor survived but was incapacitated for months.) Suspect has well-documented history of violent rages both off and on the stage and history of "becoming" the role he played. Suspect paid off woman accusing him of rape.
Stress factors at time of murder: Suspect's wife, Rita Hayworth, was divorcing suspect (ending his presidential aspirations), his latest stage production was a flop, IRS and bill collectors were after suspect, and Harry Cohn, the head of Columbia Studios, was badgering suspect about the film that was in production.
Link to the victim: Fall of 1946 suspect frequented the Florentine Gardens and Brittingham's, a restaurant near Columbia Studios, as did the victim. Waitresses at Brittingham's heard rumors that the victim was going out with someone at Columbia Studios.
Link to the signature and MO of perpetrator: Suspect possessed knowledge of anatomy and had access to medical equipment; suspect's mentor and guardian was Dr. Maurice Bernstein, an orthopedic surgeon. A crazy house set for the film *Lady From Shanghai*, that was designed and worked on by

suspect three months before the Black Dahlia murder had many of the same signature elements as the Black Dahlia murder—dolls and figures cut in half, mutilations depicted in the same areas as the mutilations that were later inflicted on the victim's body, dismembered mannequin legs hanging down from the ceiling, anatomical murals, and clown heads with wide smiles similar to the smile that was cut into victim's face. The footage containing the set was cut out of the film under direct orders of Harry Cohn.

Link to the South Norton Avenue site: The victim's bisected body was posed in a vacant lot close to where the Ringling Bros. Circus had set up their tents in 1939 and 1941. In 1943, Suspect organized "The Mercury Wonder Show" to entertain servicemen. Under a circus tent set up on Cahuenga Boulevard in Hollywood, suspect performed a magic act nightly—the highlight was cutting a woman in half.

Behavior after the murder: Shooting on film became erratic the days following murder. Filming suspended for a month on January 23, 1947. Suspect applied for his passport on January 24, 1947, the same day the killer called a Los Angeles newspaper and said he was mailing a packet with the "Dahlia's belongings." A few months later suspect inquired about enrolling at a mortuary school. Suspect next directed and played the lead role in *Macbeth,* Shakespeare's masterpiece about murder and guilt for Republic Pictures. Suspect left for Europe before the editing of *Macbeth* was completed. Republic, wanting suspect to return to complete editing and dubbing, begged, pleaded, and threatened suspect who stayed away from Hollywood for close to ten years. During suspect's hiatus in Europe, suspect became grossly overweight. Suspect's drug and alcohol abuse and his violent behavior on and off stage continued. His career plummeted.

Additional comments: Suspect delivered the eulogy at the funeral of Darryl Zanuck (who had assisted in suspect's departure to Europe). Suspect ended his tribute by saying: "If I did something really outrageous, that if I committed some abominable crime, which I believe is in most of us to do under the right circumstances, that if I were guilty of something unspeakable, and if all the police in the world were after me, there was one man, and only one man I could come to, and that was Darryl. He would not have made me a speech about the good of the industry, the good of the studio. He would not have been mealy-mouthed or put me aside. He would have hid me under the bed. Very simply he was a friend." Suspect died October 10, 1985 of a heart attack.

Dr. Walter Alonzo Bayley
Suspect of Larry Harnisch

Suspect's age at time of murder: 67
Occupation: Surgeon.
Whereabouts at time of murder: Assumed in Los Angeles.
Physical and mental condition: Early stages of Alzheimer's, history of encephalomalacia, cerebral and coronary arteriosclerosis, and myocardial infarction (heart attacks).
History of violence: Unknown.
Stress factors at time of murder: By 1946 suspect had resigned his positions as Chief of Staff at the Los Angeles County Hospital and Associate Professor of Surgery at the University of Southern California. There is a high probability his resignation was due to his deteriorating physical and mental conditions. November of 1946, two months before the Black Dahlia murder, suspect separated from his wife and filed for divorce.
Link to the victim: On February 26, 1945, suspect's adopted daughter, Barbara Lindgren, was a witness to the marriage of victim's sister, Virginia Short, to Adrian West at a Presbyterian church in Inglewood, California, near Los Angeles.
Link to the signature and MO of perpetrator: As a surgeon, suspect would have knowledge of human anatomy. Suspect shared medical offices with Dr. Alexandra Partyka, at 1020 6th Avenue, six blocks from the Biltmore Hotel where the victim was last seen alive.
Link to the South Norton Avenue site: Until two months before the murder, suspect lived with wife and adopted daughter at 3959 South Norton Avenue, one block from the crime scene.
Behavior after the murder: Suspect was hospitalized with a heart attack on November 12, 1947. He was confined for fifty-two days and died on January 4, 1948 from bronchopneumonia. On December 22, 1947, a few weeks before his death, suspect drew up a new will disinheriting his wife and leaving his medical equipment and half his estate to his medical partner, Dr. Alexandra Partyka.

Additional comments: After his death, suspect's wife, Ruth A. Bayley and Dr. Alexandra Partyka fought over the estate, each wanting to be appointed administrator. Dr. Partyka, a former student of Dr. Bayley, had become his medical partner when Bayley was sixty-two years old and possibly showing the first signs of Alzheimer's disease. Mrs. Bayley accused Dr. Partyka of exerting undue influence over Dr. Bayley and taking him on extended trips to keep him away from his family. Mrs. Bayley accused Dr. Partyka of using "unnatural flattery and feminine wiles" to control Dr. Bayley. Mrs. Bayley further accused Dr. Partyka of blackmailing Dr. Bayley by threatening to reveal secrets about his medical practice that would ruin him. (In the 1940s, when abortions were illegal, doctors who had a high percentage of female patients were suspected of performing abortions. A doctor would lose his license to practice medicine and serve time in jail if proven to have performed the illegal operation.) The extent of Dr. Bayley's mental and physical incapacities at the time of the murder would be a major factor in determing if he is a viable suspect. Although some Alzheimer's patients may become violent, the violence is usually a reaction to frustration, a lashing out. It is not the sadistic, methodical, ritualistic, premeditated violence such as that perpetrated on the Black Dahlia victim.

APPENDIX E
SELECTED ANNOTATED BIBLIOGRAPHY
Compiled by Kyle J. Wood and Mary Pacios

Anthologies and Books: The Black Dahlia Murder

American Weekly: My Favorite True Mystery. New York, Coward-McCann, 1954. A collection of true-crime stories from the world's foremost crime writers. "Death of the Black Dahlia" by Craig Rice. Ed. Ernest V. Heyn. (238-242)

Anger, Kenneth. *Hollywood Babylon II.* New York, Penguin Books, 1984. The first book to publish Elizabeth Short's graphic death scene photos. (126-133)

Austin, John. *Hollywood's Unsolved Mysteries.* New York, Ace Star Publ., 1970. (17-27)

Crimes & Punishment. New York, Marshall Cavendish, 1986. An eight-volume crime anthology set. Includes an in-depth profile on the Black Dahlia case in Volume 5. Ed. Angus Hall. (721-728)

Crimes and Punishment: A Pictorial Encyclopedia of Aberrant Behavior - Volume 16. Phoebus, 1973. Anthology. Ed. Jackson Morley. (115-122)

Cyriax, Oliver. *Crime: An Encyclopedia.* Vermont, Trafalgar Square, 1996. Brief section on false confessions to the Black Dahlia murder. (122-123)

Douglas, John/Ann Burgess/Robert Ressler. *Sexual Homicide: Patterns and Motives*, New York, Free Press, 1996. A study of brutal sex crimes and why they are carried out. (54-56)

Dunne, John Gregory. *True Confessions.* New York, E. F. Dutton, 1977. Popular novel, loosely based on circumstances surrounding the Black Dahlia case combined with elements of the Brenda Allen prostitution scandal of 1949. (341p)

Ellroy, James. *The Black Dahlia.* New York, Mysterious Press, 1987. Best-selling crime novel, mixes real facts with fiction. (358p)

Ellroy, James. *My Dark Places.* New York, Knopf, 1996. Non-fiction account of the unsolved murder of Ellroy's own mother, and how Jack Webb's 1958 book, *The Badge*, fueled Ellroy's obsession with Elizabeth Short. (101-106)

Everitt, David. *Human Monsters*. Chicago, Contemporary Books, 1993. Anthology of brutal killers and unsolved mysteries. (132-134)

Fowler, Will. *Reporters*. Malibu, California, Roundtable Publishing, 1991. Reporter Will Fowler worked for the *Los Angeles Examiner* at the time of the Black Dahlia murder. Book includes graphic photos with a full chapter on the case. (71-93)

Freed, Donald and Raymond P. Briggs. *Killing Time: Who Murdered Nicole Brown Simpson and Ronald Goldman*? New York, MacMillan, 1996. The book contains two pages on the "Black Dahlia" case. Police corruption, coverups, and payoffs are put forth as reasons Elizabeth Short's killer was never brought to trial. (222-223)

Gilmore, John. *SEVERED: The True Story of the Black Dahlia Murder*. Los Angeles, California, Amok Press, 1998. Details the case and names an alleged killer. Book includes graphic photos. (237p)

Gribble, Leonard. *They Had A Way With Women*. Roy Publ., 1967. (67-80)

Harnisch, Larry. *Stairway to Heaven*. A work-in-progress by the *Los Angeles Times* reporter who wrote a feature newspaper article on the 50th anniversary of the Black Dahlia murder. Publication date to be announced.

Harvey, Diana & Jackson. *Dead Before Their Time*. New York, Friedman-Fairfax Publishers, 1996. Anthology of celebrities and other notables who died in the prime of life. (44-45)

Henderson, Bruce/Sam Summerlin. *The Super Sleuths*. New York, MacMillan, 1976. Written by two former members of the Associated Press. The book contains a full chapter on the case and profiles the efforts of LAPD's lead Black Dahlia detective, Harry Hansen. (75-98)

Infamous Murders. Verdict Press, 1974. Anthology. (149-156)

Katz, Ephraim. *The Film Encyclopedia* 2nd Ed. New York, Harper Perrenial, 1994. Lives up to its stated intention as "a primary source of information on world cinema for movie fans and film professionals alike." (1,408p)

Keppel, Robert D. with William J. Birnes. *The Riverman: Ted Bundy and I Hunt for the Green River Killer.* New York, Pocket Books 1995. Brief mention of the Black Dahlia case and Pierce Brooks, pioneer Los Angeles detective. (136)

Lamparski, Richard. *Lamparski's Hidden Hollywood.* New York, Simon & Schuster, 1981. Anthology of infamous Hollywood haunts and local historic sites. Brief section on the Black Dahlia case. (128p)

Marriner, Brian. *On Death's Bloody Trail: Murder and the Art of Forensic Science.* New York, St. Martin, 1991. First published in Great Britain as *Forensic Clues to Murder.* Brief mention of the Black Dahlia murder. (248)

Morton, James. *The Who's Who of Unsolved Murders.* London, Kyle Cathie, Ltd., 1995. Anthology. Brief chapter on the Black Dahlia case. (230-232)

Nash, Jay Robert. *Encyclopedia of World Crime.* Wilmette, Illinois, Crimebooks, 1989. A four-page profile of the case. (388-391)

Nickel, Steven. *TORSO.* Winston-Salem, North Carolina, J. F. Blair, 1989. The story of crimefighter Eliot Ness and the hunt for Cleveland's infamous "Torso Slayer." Brief mention of the Black Dahlia. (187-190)

Pacios, Mary. *Childhood Shadows: The Hidden Story of the Black Dahlia Murder.* Bloomington, Indiana, 1st Books Library, 1999. Personal account by a hometown friend who sets out forty years later to discover the truth about the murder with startling results. (314p)

Rice, Craig. *Still Unsolved.* New York, Carol Publishing, 1990. Anthology of unsolved crimes, with a brief chapter on the Black Dahlia murder. (40-44)

Richardson, James Hugh. *For the Life of Me.* New York, Putnam, 1954. Autobiography by the legendary city editor of the *Los Angeles Examiner*, the only known person to have spoken to the Black Dahlia's killer. Book includes a full chapter on the case. (295-312)

Rogers, Agnes. *Women Are Here to Stay.* New York, Harper and Brothers, 1949. Elizabeth Short, the Black Dahlia murder victim, is included in the chapter, "Is There a Criminal Type?"—with the likes of Bonnie Parker (of Bonnie and Clyde fame) and ax-murderer Winnie Ruth Judd among others.

Rowan, David. *Famous American Crimes*. London, Muller, 1957. Anthology. (11-27)

Schessler, Ken. *This is Hollywood*. Redlands, California, Ken Schessler Publishing, 1993. Los Angeles travel guide to unusual places, including Elizabeth Short's Hollywood apartment building and alleged murder site. (7 and 67)

Sifakis, Carl. *Encyclopedia of American Crime, Facts on File*. New York, Smithmark Publishers, 1982. Includes an overview of the case in three paragraphs. Copies of the thesis may be found in the History section of the Los Angeles Public Library. (802p)

Sjoquist, Capt. Arthur W. *From Posses to Professionals: The History of The Los Angeles Police Department*. A bound thesis presented to the faculty of the School of Political Science, California State University, Los Angeles. Contains three pages on the case. Available at the Reference Desk of the Sociology Section in the Los Angeles Public Library. (256-258)

Smith, Leon. *Famous Hollywood Locations*. Jefferson, North Carolina, McFarland, 1993. Brief description of the case, accompanied by photos of the Biltmore Hotel and Norton Ave. crime site. (37-39).

Sterling, Hank. *Ten Perfect Crimes*. New York, Stravon, 1954. Contains a full chapter on the case. (37-51)

Underwood, Agness Sullivan. *Newspaperwoman*. New York, Harper & Brothers, 1949. Reporter for the *Los Angeles Herald Express* at the time of the murder. Brief mention of the case and of her jailhouse interview with prime Black Dahlia suspect, Robert Manley. (6-10)

Unsolved Crimes. Time/LIFE Books, Alexandria, Virginia, 1993. A True Crime series. Includes a large one-page profile of the case entitled "Death of the Dahlia." (92-93)

Webb, Jack. *The Badge*. New Jersey, Prentice-Hall, 1958. Written by the star of "Dragnet," this non-fiction account details life inside the Los Angeles Police Department, with fourteen pages devoted to the Black Dahlia case. (22-35)

Wilson, Colin. *A Criminal History of Mankind*. London, Grafton Books, 1984. An anthology overview of murder and mayhem.

Wolf, Marvin J./Katherine Mader. *Fallen Angels, Chronicles of LA Crime and Mystery*. New York, Ballantine Books, 1986. Los Angeles crimes and unsolved mysteries. Includes five pages on the Black Dahlia case, with map and directions to the crime scene. (174-178)

Anthologies and Books: Related Topics

Baxter, Anne. *Intermission*. New York, G. P. Putnam's Sons, 1976. Biography of the actress with anecdotes about Hollywood personalities. (384p)

Bazin, André. *Orson Welles, A Critical View*. New York, Harper and Row, 1978. (138p)

Beja, Morris, Editor. *Perspectives on Orson Welles*. New York, G. K. Hall & Co., 1995. A collection of reviews, interviews and essays about the man and his work. (342p)

Brady, Frank. *Citizen Welles: A Biography of Orson Welles*. New York, Doubleday (An Anchor Book), 1989. (655p)

Christopher, Milbourne. *The Illustrated History of Magic*. New York, Thomas V. Crowell Company, 1973. (434p)

The Citizen Kane Book. Reprint. Originally published: 1st ed. Boston, Little Brown, 1971. First Limelight Edition, New York, 1984. A study of the film classic containing the infamous essay *"Raising Kane"* by Pauline Kael, the shooting script of *Citizen Kane* by Herman J. Mankiewicz and Orson Welles with notes by Gary Carey, the cutting continuity of the completed film, and the extensive film credits of Herman J. Mankiewicz. (440p)

Cleckley, Hervey Milton. *Mask of Sanity*, 4th ed. St. Louis, C.V. Mosley Co., 1964. An analysis of the psychopathic (sociopathic) personality.

De Carlo, Yvonne w/Doug Warren. *Yvonne: An Autobiography*. New York, St. Martin's Press, 1987. Life of the glamorous actress of the 1940s whose career began at the Florentine Gardens and who is best known for her TV portrayal of Lily Munster. (288p)

De River, Joseph Paul. *The Sexual Criminal*. Springfield, Illinois, Charles C. Thomas, 1949. Written by LAPD's foremost criminal psychiatrist. No mention of the Black Dahlia case. However, book provides interesting insight into why similar-type passion killings are committed. Includes graphic photos. (267p)

Douglas, John and Mark Olshaker. *Mind Hunter: Inside the FBI's Elite Serial Crime Unit*. New York, Pocket Books, 1995. An inside look at the pioneering, and often uncannily accurate art and science of profiling developed by the FBI Behavioral Science and Investigative Support Units at the FBI Academy in Quantico. (384p)

Dunne, John Gregory. *The Studio*. New York, Vintage Books, 1968. A revealing portrait of the inner workings of Twentieth Century Fox, based on the year that Dunne was granted free access to the studio by Richard Zanuck. (253p)

Eells, George. *Hedda and Louella*, New York, Putnam, 1972. Biographies of the two powerful Hollywood gossip columnists. (360p)

Friedrich, Otto. *City of Nets*. New York, Harper & Row, Publishers, 1986. Wealth of historical background material revealing the convoluted undercurrents of Hollywood in the 1940s. (495p)

Goode, Erich. *Deviant Behavior*. 3rd ed. Englewood Cliffs, New Jersey, Prentice Hall, 1990. Analysis of various theories and forms of deviant behavior. (470p)

Granlund, Nils Thor. *Blondes, Brunettes and Bullets*. New York, McKay, 1957. Biography of the Florentine Gardens Impresario. (300p)

Herman, Jan. *A Talent for Trouble: The Life of Hollywood's Most Acclaimed Director. William Wyler*. New York, G. P. Putnam's Sons, 1995. (528p)

Higham, Charles. *The Films of Orson Welles*. Berkeley, University of California Press, 1970. (210p)

Higham, Charles. *Orson Welles: The Rise and Fall of an*

American Genius. New York, St. Martin's Press, 1985. Unauthorized biography. (416p)

Houseman, John. *Run-through, A Memoir*. New York, Simon and Schuster, 1972. Inside look at theater and movie production with a revealing portrait of Orson Welles in the 1930s and 1940s. (507p)

Keppel, Robert D. with William J. Birnes. *Signature Killers*. New York, Pocket Books 1997. An informative and insightful exploration of serial killers and the calling cards they leave behind. Real cases examined. (354p)

Larkin, Rochelle. *Hail, Columbia*. New York, Arlington House Publishers, 1975. History of the humble studio on "poverty row" in Gower Gulch that became a Hollywood force to reckon with under the guidance of Harry Cohn. (445p)

Leaming, Barbara. *Orson Welles, A Biography*. New York, Viking, 1985. Authorized biography. Based on interviews with Welles and others. (562p)

Lunde, Donald T. *Murder and Madness*. San Francisco, The Portable Stanford Series, San Francisco Book Co, 1976. (141p)

Martinez, Al. *Jigsaw John*. New York, Avon Books, New York 1976. Biography of LAPD's famous detective. Basis for TV series. (219p)

McBride, Joseph. *Orson Welles*. New York, Da Capo Press, 1996. Considered a landmark study of Welles by critics and biographers. New edition after being out of print for 20 years. (243p)

Money, Dr. John. *LOVEMAPS, Clinical Concepts of Sexual and Erotic Health and Pathology, Paraphilia*. Buffalo, New York, Prometheus Books, ND. Written by the director of the Psychohormonal Research Unit at Johns Hopkins University School of Medicine. (331p)

Naremore, James. *The Magic World of Orson Welles*. Dallas, First Southern Methodist University Edition, 1989. Sociological and psychological implications of Orson Welles' work. (309p)

Saito, Shirley. *Aggie: A Biography of the Los Angeles Newspaper-woman*. Master of Arts Thesis in Mass

Communications, California State University at Northridge, 1987. Copies available in the Urban Archives at California State University, Northridge.

Seaburg, Carl and Alan Seaburg. *Medford on the Mystic*. Medford, Massachusetts, Medford Historical Society, 1980. History of Medford with photographs. (174p)

Stoker, Charles, *Thicker 'n Thieves*. Sidereal Co., 1951. Inside story of the Brenda Allen Scandal in the 1940s and the connection to Los Angeles police corruption. (415p)

Thomas, Bob. *King Cohn, The Life and Times of Harry Cohn*. New York, Putnam, 1967. Biography of the head of Columbia Studios. (381p)

Welles, Orson and Peter Bogdanovich. *This Is Orson Welles*. Autobiography, edited by Johnathan Rosenbaum. New York, Harper Perennial, 1993. (521p)

Wood, Brett. *Orson Welles: A Bio-bibliography*. New York, Greenwood Press, 1990. Most comprehensive bibliography on Orson Welles to date. (364p)

Films and Videos

The Battle Over Citizen Kane. A documentary depicting the lives of two American icons, William Randolph Hearst, and Orson Welles—each considered a genius in his own field. Culminates in the fight over release of the film *Citizen Kane*, the movie based on Hearst's life which starred Welles who also directed. "The American Experience," PBS 1998. (50:00)

The Black Dahlia: 50th Anniversary. News segment with Fox reporter Tony Valdez. This two-part local special has rare interview footage with Elizabeth Short's mother and sister, LAPD detective Harry Hansen, authors Mary Pacios and James Ellroy. FOX Television, KTTV Channel 11 Los Angeles, 15 & 16 January 1997. (14:28)

The Blue Dahlia. Detective thriller, starring Alan Ladd and Veronica Lake. This film is believed to be the original source for Elizabeth Short's "Black Dahlia" nickname—bestowed upon her by her friends. Paramount 1946. (96:00)

CHRONICLE: Crime Without Punishment. Local New England news magazine. Brief profile of the case and the placing of a monument to Black Dahlia victim Elizabeth Short in her hometown of Medford, Massachusetts. WCVB-TV Boston, 1 December 1993. (03:50)

Death Scenes. Video documentary of graphic police file photos from the golden age of Hollywood. Includes brief segment on the Black Dahlia murder. Wavelength Video 1989. (86:00)

A Double Life. Crime drama. George Cukor directed Ronald Colman in the academy award performance as an actor who confuses reality with his role of Othello. Ad for movie proclaimed: "Behind the cloak of his greatness, he nurtured a hidden madness, which, when fanned by the flames of genius, turned his greatest triumph into his greatest sin!" Bit actress in opening scene bears uncanny resemblance to Black Dahlia victim Elizabeth Short. Universal International 1947. (120:00)

Entertainment Tonight. Featured segment on newly uncovered evidence pointing to a new suspect in the Black Dahlia murder. Interviews with authors Mary Pacios and John Gilmore and former *Los Angeles Examiner* reporter Will Fowler. Paramount - ET #2456, 11 February 1991. (03:48)

Historic L.A. Two-part news special, hosted by Dr. George Fischbeck. Interviews with LAPD detective John St. John, author Mary Pacios, and former *Los Angeles Examiner* reporter Will Fowler. KABC-TV, Los Angeles, May 1990. (06:58)

Hollywood's Mysteries and Scandals. "The Black Dahlia Murder." Biography of Elizabeth Short. Interviews with Detective Brian Carr, the homicide detective who now has case, reporters Will Fowler, Larry Harnisch, and Tony Valdez, authors John Gilmore and Mary Pacios, police psychologist, Kris Mohandie, and filmmaker, Kyle J. Wood. E! Channel, 15 June 1998. (22:00)

Hunter. "The Black Dahlia." Popular 1980s TV police drama series, starring Fred Dryer and Stephanie Kramer. Guest Star: Lawrence Tierney. Stephen J. Cannell Productions.

NBC, 12 January 1988. (50:00)

Inside Edition. Nightly syndicated news magazine. Featured segment surrounding unsubstantiated claims by a woman who believes her father committed the murder. Interviews with LAPD detective John St. John and the niece of Elizabeth Short, Valerie Reynolds. KINGWORLD, 16 August 1991. (06:24)

The Lady From Shanghai. Released in 1948 after Columbia Studios cut out bizarre crazy house scenes. Directed by Orson Welles. Stars Rita Hayworth, Orson Welles, and Everett Sloane. Cinematography by Charles Lawton, Jr. The famous hall of mirrors scene climaxes the bizarre murder mystery about an Irish adventurer and evil seductress. Columbia Studios, 1946. (87:00)

Medford Girl: The Black Dahlia Murder. Video documentary focusing on the life and death chronology of the Black Dahlia victim, Elizabeth Short. Rockinghorse/Kyle J. Wood, 1993. (35:00)

Orson Welles: What went wrong? Video documentary with interviews of Orson Welles' daughter Beatrice and others. Raises questions: Was there a Rosebud in Orson Welles' life? A missing piece to the puzzle? Robert Guenette Productions, Inc., 1992. (57:00)

Street Wise. "Elizabeth Short, The Black Dahlia Murder Victim." Carol Queen interview of author Mary Pacios. San Francisco Public Access Cable, November 1997. (30:00)

Sunset Boulevard. Director Billy Wilder's acclaimed drama, starring William Holden and Gloria Swanson. A brief remark to Holden's character by actor Jack Webb during a party scene demonstrates how deeply the "Black Dahlia" case had worked it's way into the public consciousness—and Hollywood's. Paramount, 1950. (110:00)

True Confessions. Big-budgeted, feature film version of John Gregory Dunne's best-selling 1977 novel by the same title. The film stars Robert DeNiro and Robert Duval as brothers pitted against one another over a dark secret hidden in their past. MGM, 1981. (108:00)

Unsolved Mysteries. Popular TV series hosted by Robert Stack.

Examined writer Lawrence P. Scherb's claim that the Cleveland "Torso Slayer" and the "Black Dahlia" killer were one and the same. NBC, 7 December 1992. (12:52)

Who is the Black Dahlia? Made-for-TV movie, starring Lucy Arnaz in the title role. Retired LAPD detective Harry Hansen served as technical advisor on the project. Hansen liked original script but was unhappy with final version. NBC-TV, 1 March 1975. (100:00)

Web Sites

The Black Dahlia.
  http://www.bethshort.com This site, the oldest and most comprehensive Black Dahlia web site, went on line February 21, 1997. Features a discussion board and links to other sites, including the Los Angeles Public Library Black Dahlia photo collection. Pamela Hazelton, Web Meister, makes periodic updates and emails a monthly electronic newsletter. (Visited August 4, 1999)

Crime Library
  http://www.crimelibrary.com Web site of Dark Horse Multimedia, Inc. Features 64 of the world's most infamous murder cases including Lizzie Borden, Leopold and Loeb, Sacco and Vanzetti, Dr. Josef Mengele, and the Lindbergh kidnapping. The Black Dahlia murder section is written by Marilyn Beardsley and is based on the Gilmore book. Graphic photos. (Visited August 4, 1999)

The Los Angeles Public Library Virtual Gallery
  http://catalog.lapl.org/gallery.html A "Black Dahlia" search at the library's home page will bring up 84 annotated photographs related to the case. (Visited August 9, 1999)

The Medford Girl
  http://home.earthlink/~welkerlots Web Meister Kyle J. Wood, the documentary filmmaker who was instrumental in the placement of the memorial to Elizabeth Short in her home town, gives a factual overview of the Black Dahlia murder. Also includes sections on other Hollywood tragedies: Carole Lombard, Karyn Kupcinet, Jean Spangler,

etc. Went on line May 1999. (Visited August 4, 1999)
Stairway to Heaven.
http://www.geocities.com/Hollywood/movie/6936   On line July 29, 1999, the 75th anniversary of Elizabeth Short's birthday. Web Meister Larry Harnisch puts forth his theory about the murder and names a new suspect. Site includes background information that dispels some of the myths surrounding the crime. (Visited August 4, 1999)

Periodicals

Banks, Louis. "I Killed Her." *Life* 24 March 1947. Deals with the sudden rash of false confessions to the Black Dahlia murder.

Clark, George. "The Black Dahlia Murders." *True Detective* October 1948. Not only was this the first in-depth article on the case, it is also partially responsible for a massive and unnecessary LAPD "wild goose" chase, initiated by a man who read the story and thought he knew who the killer was.

Dougherty, Steve. "James Ellroy's Grisly New Novel—The Black Dahlia." *People* 14 December 1987.

"Hard-Pressed, Grim-Faced." *Time* 10 February 1947. Brief paragraph about the Los Angeles rivalry between various local newspapers covering the Dahlia story.

Mathews, Peter. "The Black Dahlia Murder Case." *Master Detective* March 1980. An extensive eleven page profile of the murder.

"Murder Suspect Forgiven By Wife." *Life* 3 February 1947. Has a brief paragraph on the case, along with a full page photo of Black Dahlia suspect, Robert "Red" Manley and his wife, Harriett.

Scherb, Lawrence P. "Black Dahlia Gate." *Los Angeles* June 1992. Discusses a possible link between Cleveland's infamous "Torso Slayer" and the "Black Dahlia" murderer.

Wheeler, Bonnie. "The Incredible Mr. Pinker" *Confidential Detective* March 1945. Early profile of LAPD's noted crime investigator, Ray Pinker—two years before he would find himself at the center of the "Black Dahlia" murder mystery.

Young, Stanley. "Obsession." *Los Angeles* September 1987. James Ellroy's secret agony over the unsolved murder of his own mother and how it influenced his new novel, *The Black Dahlia*.

Newspaper Articles

"78,000 Population Predicted for Camp Cooke Area in 1943." *Santa Barbara News-Press* December 1941.

"An Artist Foils A Slayer." *Washington News* 17 January 1947.

"Another 'Dahlia Killer' Pops Up." *Washington Times-Herald* 29 March 1948. Re: Charles E. Lynch.

Babcock, John. "The Black Dahlia—Friend Searches for Truth." *Los Angeles Herald Examiner* April 1988. Re: Mary Pacios.

"Best Suspect Yet Held in Slaying of 'Black Dahlia'." *Washington News* 11 January 1949. Re: Leslie Dillon.

"Black Dahlia Case Plagues Detective." *Los Angeles Times* 22 November 1951. Re: Harry Hansen.

"Black Dahlia Suspect Gets Truth Tests." *Los Angeles Times* 16 August 1954. Re: Robert Manley.

"Black Dahlia's Handbag and Shoe Identified in Los Angeles Dump." *Los Angeles Herald Express* 25 January 1947.

"'Black Dahlia' Murder Site Found in L.A." *Washington Times-Herald* 13 September 1949.

"'Black Dahlia' Suspect to Face Lie Detector." *Washington News* 20 January 1947. Re: Robert Manley.

"British Actress To Be Quizzed In Torso Murder Case." *Alameda Star Times* 18 January 1947. Re: Ann Todd.

"Charge Bayley Held 'Prisoner'." *Los Angeles Examiner* 21 January 1948. Re: Dr. Walter Bayley.

"City Asks FBI Aid in Solving 'Dahlia' Case." *Los Angeles Examiner* 19 February 1947.

"Clue to Bit Player's Disappearance Sought in Her Hollywood Datebook—'Black Dahlia' Case Reopened." *St. Louis Post Dispatch* 14 October 1949. Re: Jean Spangler.

"Cops Doubt Dahlia 'Slayer's' Addled Confession." *Washington News* 29 January 1947. Re: Daniel S. Vorhees.

"Cops Seeking Female Sadist." *Washington News* 21 January

1947.

Crystal, Chris. "Black Dahlia Murder: Information After 35 Years." *Carson City Nevada Appeal* 24 January 1982. Re: John Gilmore.

"Dahlia in Love—Slain Girl's Letters Found Unmailed." *Los Angeles Herald Express* 20 January 1947. Re: Joseph Gordon Fickling.

"Dahlia Killer Mails Contents of Missing Purse to Examiner." *Los Angeles Examiner* 25 January 1947.

"Dahlia Killing Story Checked." *Washington News* 6 January 1956. Re: Ralph Von Hiltz.

"'Dahlia' Murder Suspect Freed After 2nd Lie Detector Test." *New York Daily Mirror* 21 January 1947. Re: Robert Manley.

"Dahlia Probers at Pismo Beach." *Santa Barbara News-Press* 25 January 1947. Re: Camp Cooke.

"'Dahlia Slayer ' Skips Date, Note Expresses Fear." *Washington Times-Herald* 30 January 1947.

"'Dahlia' Suspect Held in St. Louis." *New York Daily Mirror* 19 March 1947. Re: Melvin Bailey.

"Dahlia Suspect Names Second." *Washington Times-Herald* 11 January 1949. Re: Leslie Dillon and Jeff Connors.

"Dahlia Suspect Veiled by Army; Story in Doubt." *Washington Times-Herald* 10 February 1947. Re: Corpl. Joseph Dumais.

"'Dahlia' Suspect's Alibi Attacked." *Washington Times-Herald* 12 January 1949. Re: Jeff Connors.

"Ex-wife Supports Suspect's Alibi in 'Dahlia' Murder Case." *Washington Times-Herald* 13 January 1949. Re: Jeff Connors.

"Examiner Scores Third Break in Case—Locates Luggage." *Los Angeles Examiner* 20 January 1947.

"Father of Slain Model Will Not Aid In Killer Search." *Santa Barbara News-Press* 18 January 1947.

"Father, Long Thought Dead, Located in California." *Boston Globe* 18 January 1947.

"FBI Identifies Girl Mutilated by Butcher Slayer." *Washington Times-Herald* 16 January 1947.

"Fingerprints on Letter Sent by 'Dahlia' Killer." *Los Angeles Herald Express.* 25 January 1947. Re: Packet sent by killer.

George, Lynell. "L.A.'s Fatal Attraction." *Los Angeles Times* 17 April 1995. Re: John Gilmore.

"Girl Torture-Slaying Victim Identified by Examiner, FBI." *Los Angeles Examiner* 17 January 1947.

"Gives Up, Says 'Can't Stand It Any Longer'." *Washington Times-Herald* 29 January 1947. Re: Daniel S. Vorhees.

Harney, Scott. "Setting the Black Dahlia Record Straight." *Medford Transcript* 11 December 1991. Re: Mary Pacios.

Harney, Scott. "The Tragic Life and Death of the Black Dahlia." *Medford Transcript* 24 July 1991. Re: Mary Pacios.

Harnisch, Larry. "Dahlia Slaying, a Tantalizing Mystery 50 Years Later." *Los Angeles Times* 6 January 1997.

"Hunt for Killer Hits Dead End in San Diego." *San Diego Union* 18 January 1947.

"James Held On Morals Count." *The Arizona Daily Star* 19 November 1944. Re: Arraignment of Arthur C. James Jr.

Johnson, Bob. "The Black Dahlia, 18-Year-Old Mystery." *Los Angeles Times* 11 January 1965.

Kaufman, Hayley. "Her Story is History: The Placing of a Plaque Where Murder Victim Elizabeth Short Once Lived Has Stirred Controversy." *Medford Citizen* 2 September 1993.

"Life Story of 'Werewolf' Victim, Trail Leads to Beach." *Los Angeles Herald Express* 17 January 1947.

"Los Angeles Bellhop Held in 'Black Dahlia' Slaying." [Washington] *Evening Star* 11 January 1949. Re: Leslie Dillon.

"Major Matt Gordon, Jr., Reported As Killed." *Pueblo Chieftain* 22 August 1945.

"Man Arrested In Check Case." *The Arizona Daily Star* 15 November 1944. Re: Arrest of Arthur C. James Jr.

"Medford Girl Slain on Coast." *Boston Daily Record* 17 January 1947.

Morrison, Patt. "Postscript: Black Dahlia Murder Mystery Deepens With Passage of Time." *Los Angeles Times* 15 January 1979.

"Murdered Girl Reminded Medford Woman of Deanna Durbin." *Boston Daily Globe* 17 January 1947.

"Names Vicki As Dahlia Case Alibi." *New York Daily Mirror* 13 January 1949. Re: Jeff Connors.

Nightingale, Suzan. "Black Dahlia: Author Claims to Have Found 1947 Murderer." *L.A. Herald Examiner* 17 January 1982. Re: John Gilmore.

"Orson Welles: Appreciating Darryl Zanuck." *Los Angeles Herald Examiner.* 13 January 1980. Full text of Welles' eulogy for Darryl Zanuck.

Payne, Libbie. "Medford Honors the Black Dahlia." *Boston Globe* 19 August 1993.

"Police Asked to Locate Cleo A. Short, Disappeared Saturday." *Medford Mercury* 15 October 1930. Re: victim's father.

"Police Quiz Salesman in Girl's Slaying." *Washington Post* 20 January 1947.

"Police Seek Mad Pervert in Girl's Death." *Washington Post* 18 January 1947.

"Push Hunt for 'Vain Red-Head' in Murder of 'Black Dahlia'." *New York Daily Mirror* 20 January 1947. Re: Robert Manley and Glen Thorpe.

"'Red' Released in 'Black Dahlia' Horror-Murder." *Washington Times-Herald* 20 January 1947. Re: Robert Manley.

"'Red' Seized in Butchery of Black Dahlia." *Washington Times-Herald* 20 January 1947. Re: Robert Manley.

"Salesman Claims Alibi In Mutilation Murder of Girl in Los Angeles." *Washington Star* 21 January 1947. Re: Robert Manley

"Second Brutal Murder in L.A. Spurs 'Dahlia' Probe." *Burbank Daily Review* 10 February 1947.

"Soldier Who Dated 'Black Dahlia' Held." *Washington Star* 6 February 1947. Re: Corpl. Joseph Dumais.

"Torture-Slaying Victim Feared Sadist Suitor." *Washington News* 17 January 1947.

"Two More Women Found Murdered in L.A." *Burbank Daily Review* 11 March 1947.

"Welles About Zanuck: Most Of All A Friend." *Variety* January 1979. Re: Edited version of Welles' eulogy for Darryl

Zanuck.
"Widow Says Doctor Intimidated on Will." *Los Angeles Examiner* 19 January 1948. Re: Dr. Walter A. Bayley
"Youth Grilled as 'Werewolf' Suspect." *Los Angeles Herald Express* 16 January 1947.

Research Archives

Academy of Motion Picture Arts and Sciences, Margaret Herrick Library, 333 La Cienaga Blvd., Beverly Hills, CA 90211
The American Film Institute, Louis B. Mayer Library, 2021 N. Western Avenue, Los Angeles, CA 90027
American Museum of Magic, 107 East Michigan, Marshall, MI 49068
Bancroft Library, Special Collections, University of California, Berkeley, CA 94720
Bettmann Archives, United Press International (UPI), 1400 "I" Street NW, Suite 800, Washington, DC 20005
California Section, California State Library, PO Box 942837, Sacramento, CA 94237-0001
California State Archives, 1020 "O" Street, Room 130, Sacramento, CA 95814
Department of Special Collections, A1713 Charles E. Young Research Library, Box 95175, University of California, Los Angeles, CA 90095-1575
Labor Archives and Research Center, San Francisco State University, 480 Winston Drive, San Francisco, CA 94132
Lilly Library, Film/Radio/TV Related Collections, Indiana University, Bloomington, IN 47405-3301
Los Angeles City Records Center & Archives, 555 Ramirez Street, Space 320, Los Angeles, Ca 90012
Los Angeles Public Library, 630 West 5th Street, Los Angeles, CA 90013
Medford Historical Society, 10 Governor's Avenue, Medford, MA 02155
Museum of Modern Art, Film/Stills Archives, 11 West 53rd Street, New York, NY 10019

Producers Library Service, 1035 Cole Avenue, Hollywood, CA 90038

Sutro Library, 481 Winston Drive, San Francisco, CA 94132

United States Department of Justice, Federal Bureau of Investigation, Freedom of Information-Privacy Acts Section, Office of Public and Congressional Affairs, 935 Pennsylvania Ave. NW, Washington, DC 20535-0001

University of Southern California, University Library Special Collections, University Park, Los Angeles, CA 90089-0182

Urban Archives, University Library, California State University, 18111 Nordhoff Street, Northridge, CA 91330-8329

Wide World Photo, Associated Press (AP), 50 Rockefeller Plaza, New York, NY 10020

About the Author

Mary Adeline Pacios, born and raised in Medford, Massachusetts, was a neighbor and friend of murder victim Elizabeth Short for ten years. Pacios' personal connection to Elizabeth Short has enabled her to focus with remarkable insight into the life, as well as the sensational death, of one of the most publicized and puzzled-over victims of the 20th century.

Pacios, an accomplished artist and writer with a special interest in urban affairs and history, has written and edited essays, reports, and technical papers dealing with environmental issues, social change, contemporary printmaking, African art, and German Expressionism. For a U.S. edition, Ms. Pacios "translated" *The Complete Manual of Relief Printing* (Dorling Kindersley, 1988) from British English to American English. She also edited the hilarious autobiography of underground filmmakers George and Mike Kuchar, *Reflections From a Cinematic Cesspool* for Zanja Press.

A frequent lecturer on college campuses, Pacios is a prize winning painter and printmaker with an extensive international exhibition record. Her work, frequently displayed in the United States, Europe, and Asia, is included in both prestigious public and private art collections. As an artist, she brings to this reconsideration of an infamous crime an unusual aptitude for detailed appraisal.